Understanding Language through Humor

Students often struggle to understand linguistic concepts through examples of language data provided in class or in texts. Presented with ambiguous information, students frequently respond that they don't "get it." The solution is to find an example of humor that relies on the targeted ambiguity. Once they laugh at the joke, they've tacitly understood the concept, and then it's only a matter of explaining why they found it funny. Utilizing cartoons and jokes illustrating linguistic concepts, this book makes it easy to understand these concepts, while keeping the reader's attention and interest. Organized like a course textbook in linguistics, it covers all the major topics in a typical linguistics survey course, including communication systems, phonetics and phonology, morphemes, words, phrases, sentences, language use, discourses, child language acquisition, and language variation, while avoiding technical terminology.

STANLEY DUBINSKY is Professor of Linguistics at the University of South Carolina. His primary areas of research are syntax, semantics, and linguistic theory.

CHRIS HOLCOMB is an associate professor of English at the University of South Carolina. His primary research interests include histories of rhetoric, humor, discourse analysis, and prose style.

Understanding Language through Humor

STANLEY DUBINSKY AND
CHRIS HOLCOMB

CAMBRIDGE
UNIVERSITY PRESS

CAMBRIDGE UNIVERSITY PRESS

Cambridge, New York, Melbourne, Madrid, Cape Town,
Singapore, São Paulo, Delhi, Mexico City

Cambridge University Press
The Edinburgh Building, Cambridge CB2 8RU, UK

Published in the United States of America by Cambridge University Press, New York

www.cambridge.org
Information on this title: www.cambridge.org/9780521713887

First published 2011
3rd printing 2012

Printed in the United Kingdom at the University Press, Cambridge

A catalogue record for this publication is available from the British Library

Library of Congress Cataloguing in Publication data
Dubinsky, Stanley, 1952–
Understanding language through humor / Stanley Dubinsky and Chris Holcomb.
    p.   cm.
Includes index.
ISBN 978-0-521-88627-7 (hardback)
1. Linguistics.   2. Wit and humor.   I. Holcomb, Chris.   II. Title.
P120.D83   2011
410.2′07 – dc23   2011023032

ISBN 978-0-521-88627-7 Hardback
ISBN 978-0-521-71388-7 Paperback

This book is dedicated to two special language users, Isaac and Elijah, whose language learning inspired so much of what is contained herein.

Contents

Acknowledgements

We would like to thank some of the many people who have been instrumental in making this book possible: the legions of undergraduate students, who have endured the "testing" of language humor in Stan's Introduction to Linguistics classes; Helen Barton, whose foray into South Carolina led to the conversation that started it all, and whose support and encouragement have been essential throughout; Hannah Peace, who worked tirelessly to copy and catalog Stan's voluminous file of language humor cartoons; and Sarah Green, who made sure that we had all the pieces in place, so that the book could actually be produced.

Stan would also extend special thanks for help extended to him by: Jing Li, Lan Zhang, and Tan Ye (for help in translating Chinese menus); Brad Warthen (for help in making sense of cartoon syndicate licensing costs); Caroline Heycock (for getting us a photo of men in kilts when we were in dire need of it); and Melanie Bretey (who was able to find me a source for a photo of a yellow stop sign when no one else could).

Chris, for his part, would like to acknowledge the English Department at University of South Carolina for awarding him a Research Professorship which helped him move portions of this book to completion. He would also like to thank two colleagues in particular, Federica K. Clementi and Elaine Chun, for pointing him to materials (both scholarly and humorous) that were incorporated into this book. Federica deserves special thanks for introducing him to the humor of Larry David, who continues to be a source of enjoyment.

1   Introduction

Former Hooters waitress settles toy Yoda suit

PANAMA CITY, Fla. (AP) – A former waitress has settled her lawsuit against Hooters, the restaurant that gave her a toy Yoda doll instead of the Toyota she thought she had won. Jodee Berry, 27, won a beer sales contest last May at the Panama City Beach Hooters. She believed she had won a new Toyota and happily was escorted to the restaurant's parking lot in a blindfold. But when the blindfold was removed, she found she had won a new toy Yoda – the little green character from the *Star Wars* movies. David Noll, her attorney, said Wednesday that he could not disclose the settlement's details, although he said Berry can now go to a local car dealership and "pick out whatever type of Toyota she wants."[1]

If you appreciate the pun behind the practical joke that led to this lawsuit, then you've understood, at least on some level, the linguistic features upon which it hinges. First of all, the company name *Toyota* and the two-word phrase *toy Yoda* both have stress on the second syllable "yo." In addition to that, the *t* sound in *Toyota* is produced sounding much like a *d* when it occurs between two vowels (such as *o* and *a*). The result is that both sound nearly identical when pronounced in normal, conversational, rapid speech. This is not just a fact about these two expressions. Try saying *Latter Day Saints* (as in *Church of the Latter Day Saints*) rapidly, and convince yourself that you didn't say *Ladder Day Saints*. The fact that *Toyota* and *toy Yoda* sound alike but refer to two very different things makes them homonyms. This, combined with the fact that they could each plausibly be prizes, is what fueled the joke that led to the lawsuit.

This example and our interpretation of it illustrate this book's central motif. Our goal is not to explain humor per se, although we occasionally comment on its nature and function. Rather, we use humor here as a vehicle for introducing linguistic concepts and the various subfields in which they play a part.

Students who don't have a formal background in linguistics often struggle to understand linguistic concepts when presented with examples of language data designed to illustrate them. Faced with ambiguous bits of data, such as

> The doctor interviewed the patient on pain medication.

which can either mean that the doctor was on pain medication or that the patient was, students frequently respond that they don't "get it."

The solution is to find a bit of humor that relies on the targeted ambiguity, in this case the fact that a modifier at the end of a sentence can sometimes describe either the sentential subject or its object. An example of humor illustrating this particular ambiguity is found in a *Wizard of Id* strip from several years ago

SPOOK [the prisoner]:   Have you ever eaten squid fried?
TURNKEY [the guard]: Yes.
SPOOK: How was it?
TURNKEY: Better than when I was sober.

Here, the adjective *fried*, just like the prepositional phrase *on pain medication*, can be understood to modify either the subject or the object. In Spook's question to Turnkey, he means for it to modify *squid*. Turnkey's answer takes *fried* as a synonym for *drunk*, and uses it to describe the sentential subject (that is, himself).

One cannot understand and laugh at the joke in the *Wizard of Id* strip without understanding and processing the ambiguity. The joke forces this, and laughing at the joke means that you "got it." Once someone has laughed at the joke, they've at least tacitly understood the concept, and then it's only a matter of explaining (as we've done here) why it's funny and what linguistic principles are leveraged by the joke. Utilizing cartoons and jokes to illustrate these principles, the present book makes it relatively easy to understand them, while keeping the reader's attention and interest. Organized like a course textbook in linguistics, this book covers (without the reader's realizing it) all the major topics in a typical linguistics survey course, and largely avoids technical terminology. The goal is to educate the reader about linguistic concepts without it feeling like a course book.

Note that this book is about linguistics and not humor. Although humor is featured prominently here and through the book, this volume is about understanding language (through humor), not understanding humor (through the vehicle of language). That said, we often assume a particular perspective on humor and its nature and effects. More specifically, in our interpretations of jokes, cartoons, and comedic bits, we often assume that laughter springs from incongruity (or from similar notions such as ambiguity or contradiction): in other words, a joke (or cartoon or comedic bit) typically combines two or more incongruous meanings into a single sound, word, expression, or situation. Recall the *Toyota/toy Yoda* prank. It fuses two very different meanings into a single sequence of sounds. Or recall the word *fried* from the *Wizard of Id* strip. It also combines two, incongruous, meanings into a single word. We don't argue the merits of using incongruity to discuss humor (other than to note here that it's used widely among scholars who do study humor), but we often rely on it as we reveal linguistic concepts at work in the comedic material we feature throughout this book.

If you've read this far, we might assume that you are thinking about reading the rest of this book. Before you do, we would like to briefly let you know what you should expect to find in each of the chapters that follow. As we've already noted, this book will introduce the reader to the various subfields of linguistic inquiry, and accordingly, in constructing it, we have arranged the content to mirror that of a typical textbook for a survey of linguistics courses. Keep in mind though, that this is not a textbook per se. So, if you already own one of those, keep it.

Chapter 2 presents the basic components of communication systems, surveying animal communication, and showing how human language is very distinct and specially endowed. Chapter 3 takes a close look at the sounds of human language, discussing both phonetics (their properties as sounds per se, as well as how these sounds are produced) and phonology (how language sounds are perceived and mentally represented by those using them). Chapter 4 moves on to contend with morphemes (the smallest meaningful bits of language) and words (which are sometimes individual morphemes and are sometimes combinations of them). In this chapter, we survey how these meaningful bits are assembled into words, and how they come to have the meanings they do. In Chapter 5, we step back a bit and examine the nature of phrases (that is, groups of words) and sentences (groups of words that represent complete thoughts or propositions). This chapter focuses on the internal structure of these phrases, and on how this structure can affect meaning (independently of the meaning of the individual component words). Chapter 6 steps away from language as an autonomous entity, and enters into the realm of language use. It focuses on sentences in context, discussing such concepts as deixis (that is, how language points or refers to things), indirect speech (how sentences meaning one thing are often used to convey something else), performatives (sentences that accomplish the act that they name), and principles of conversational cooperation (which underlie all linguistic discourse and which are used to leverage sarcasm, irony, and all sorts of creative language use). Building on the observations about contextually dependent meaning in Chapter 6, Chapter 7 examines sentences combined with other sentences to form discourses (longer structured texts), and then explains how those discourses function in their various contexts. Chapter 8 takes up the case of children acquiring language, how they do it, how they do it as effortlessly as they do, and how their errors reveal the inner workings of the acquisition process. Just as Chapters 6 and 7 work as a pair, so do the next two. Chapter 9 explores language variation across regional, social, cultural, and professional groups, treating variant forms at the levels of pronunciation, word choice, syntax, and language use. Chapter 10 takes matters a step further and examines how the meanings behind these formal variations differ and how, because of these differences, they can lead to cross-cultural miscommunication. With Chapter 11, we place language in perhaps its broadest context and consider how language varieties, distinct languages, and certain expressions are policed through informal and formal means. This chapter is also the one place in this book where the nature of humor and its functions shares the spotlight with linguistic concepts (our otherwise primary focus). In other words, this chapter suggests that because humor secures its effects through incongruity, ambiguity, and contradiction, it often allows speakers to circumvent any prescriptions and laws meant to regulate language in use. The final chapter is a short epilogue in which we recap some of the high points of the book, provide suggestions for further study and reading, and point to additional sources and resources that are readily available.

One might at this point be wondering who this book is written for. The short answer to this question is, you (the reader). We really think that this book will be of great utility to a broad range of readers, from those who are not yet really sure what "linguistics" are, to those who are secure in their knowledge of what linguistics is and who have studied it for some time. If this is your first exposure to linguistics, you may have picked up the book because you're interested in language generally. This book will serve nicely to introduce you to the major moving parts of language, without your having to go take a course on the subject. If you are already enrolled in such a course, then this book is probably assigned to supplement the main text that you'll be using. In that case, you should know that many of the topics in your textbook will be covered here, in a nontechnical fashion and in a way that should make them more understandable. If nothing else, you will at least be more entertained by our presentation of these concepts than you will by that in the course book. If you are a student or teacher of linguistics and already quite familiar with the conceptual material in this book, then we think that you will have a great appreciation for the manner in which the topics are presented. The presentations in the following chapters will hopefully provide you with some readily understandable material that you might use to explain these concepts to your students, your friends, or your family. Finally, if you are a linguistics major or a professional linguist, you might consider giving this book as a gift to everyone who ever asks you: "What are linguistics, anyway?"

2 Talking to Garfield

Human and animal communication

"Phyllis, step over here for a minute."

This cartoon panel, from *The Neighborhood* by Jerry Van Amerongen (1988),[1] is funny because it is so wrong in so many ways that it is hard to enumerate them all. Fourteen dogs conspire to spell out the message "Hi" on an elderly man's lawn. Presumably, they're "playing with his head." So, outside of manipulation by aliens, what would be necessary for this to happen? Well first off, this gang of dogs would have to know that a standard salutation among English speakers is a word pronounced [hai] (they would also have to know that the residents of the home in question are English speakers). They would further need to know that the graphic representation of this salutation consists of two letters "H" and "i" (notice that these dogs also appear to know capitalization conventions!). Beyond this, they would have to have some way of communicating amongst themselves in order to arrange themselves into the proper configuration to spell out the letters. Finally, one must presume that these creatures have also developed a level of communicative competence to at least desire to send a "greeting," and perhaps also to completely rattle the elderly couple living in the house. This last bit requires, beyond having knowledge of meaning, pronunciation, and graphic form, that this canine club have somehow mastered the social conventions of human language use and the subtleties of indirect communication and humor.

5

We know that this isn't right. Animals communicate, that much we're sure of. But they don't have what we would call "language" per se. Humor on this topic abounds. Gary Larson, of *The Far Side* fame, had a field day with this in the 1980s. One cartoon shows Professor Schwartzman "donning his new canine decoder" (a helmet with a bizarre array of signal reception hardware). The barking of neighborhood dogs, as he walks down the street, is now "translated" as:

> "Hey! Hey! Hey! Hey!" and "Hey! Hey!" and "Heyyyyyyy!"

Another Larson cartoon riffs on what dogs understand. In it, under the caption "What we say to dogs," a dog owner is saying:

> "Okay, Ginger! I've had it! You stay out of the garbage!
> Understand, Ginger? Stay out of the garbage, or else!"

Under the caption "What they hear," the dog is observed to be hearing:

> "blah blah Ginger blah blah blah blah blah blah blah Ginger blah blah blah blah blah . . . "

The Larson cartoon isn't far off the mark here. We know, intuitively, that dogs (and other pets) do understand some of the words we use. As the cartoon suggests, they understand their names. They may also understand some commands, such as *sit*, *stay*, and *beg*, along with other words like *food* and *out*. That said, the likelihood that a dog would make anything of *I've had it*, *or else*, and *okay* is pretty remote.

Of course, alongside what we're sure of is a whole lot that we don't exactly know. For instance, researchers are pretty sure (though not 100% certain) that dolphins don't have the equivalent of what we would call human language. But, then again, dolphin communication is indeed quite sophisticated, and is likely on the edge of where animal communication comes very close to human language.[2] Larson, for his part, had a field day with this notion in a cartoon showing animal researchers recording and trying to decipher dolphin messages. In it, one researcher is listening to the dolphins with a headset and another is transcribing onto a blackboard. The transcriber has noted thirteen instances of "kay pas-uh," eight occurrences of "aw blah es spanyol," and five occasions of "bwayno dee-us." The one listening with the headset says:

> "Matthews . . . we're getting another one of those strange 'aw blah es span yol' sounds."

Larson's point, which is well taken, is that dolphins might be communicating amongst themselves, or even to us, in language-like ways, and we would have a hard time knowing it.

In this chapter, before we get anywhere near the "nuts and bolts" of human language per se, we will need to have a close look at what we mean by communication and the ways in which communication systems vary. In this way, we can

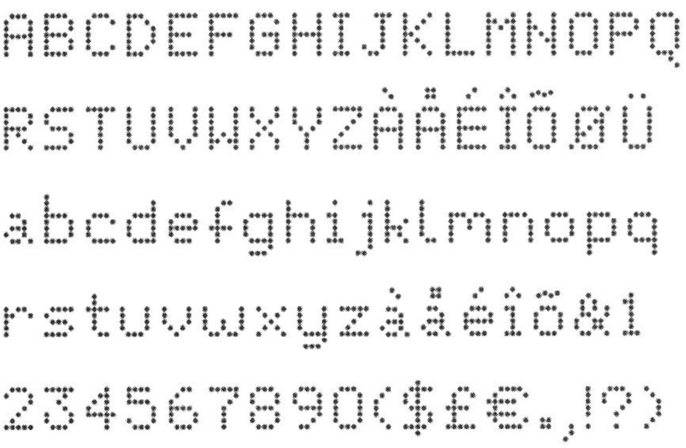

ABCDEFGHIJKLMNOPQ

RSTUVWXYZÀÄÆÉÍÕØÜ

abcdefghijklmnopq

rstuvwxyzàäæéíõøü

234567890($£€.,!?)

Figure 2.1 *Dot matrix printer output.*

better understand what it is that humans do (and that other creatures don't) that makes human language, our primary form of communication, so special.

So, how do we distinguish *language* from *communication*? To begin to talk about this, one must understand that all forms of language involve communication, but not all communication involves language. At its core, communication is the sending and receiving of messages . . . but there are many examples of message exchange that don't even involve sentient beings. The traffic light turns red and communicates to oncoming drivers that they must stop (or risk paying higher rates on their car insurance). The microwave beeps and communicates to us that the popcorn is done (but not that it's going to taste good). It is even possible for two non-sentient things to communicate. Back in the 1970s and 1980s, when dot matrix printers ruled and produced such aesthetically "pleasing" output as shown in Figure 2.1, the computers they were attached to typically generated output much faster than the printers' tiny memory could handle. To prevent the printer from losing track of the characters it was supposed to print, it was set up to communicate with the computer. The messages were two in number, and quite simple: 'Pause' (stop sending for a moment, I'm full) and 'Continue' (OK, go on). While neither machine could be said to have understood these messages, they nonetheless were programmed to behave as though they did.

If we look at the concept of *communication* more closely, we can see that communicated messages have certain properties and (importantly) that these properties can vary. First, messages can travel down different pathways and take different forms. We normally think of human language communication as involving sound, and sound is certainly a primary medium in this. However, if I produce the letters *H* and *i* to form *Hi* (much as the dogs have done in the cartoon panel above), then I have changed the medium of the message from sound-based to visual. And even when we think we're utilizing sound, it often isn't sound all the way across. I speak the word *Hi* into my cell phone. The sound waves are converted into electrical impulses and then into digitized microwave signals, received on the other end as microwaves, converted to electrical current, and then back into sound. In addition to writing, human communication can be visual in other ways as well, as is the case with American (and other forms of) Sign Language. Some common visual gestures (used by hearing speakers as well) include the OK sign . . . which means "OK" to us (but can be mistaken for "butthole" in Brazil . . . so be careful!):

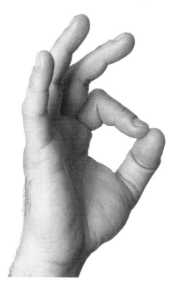

Messages can take many mediums, including chemical "scent." Many creatures, insects being foremost among them, release chemicals in order to send particular messages (the technical name for these is *pheromones*). Ants mark their trails with them to help guide other members of the colony to a food source. Dogs (presumably ones who cannot spell) and cats are well known for marking their territory with the scent of their urine. And many moths and butterflies release a "sex" pheromone for the purpose of attracting a mate, a chemical scent that can be detected by a potential mate from several miles away.

Of course, not all chemical scents have a meaning or message. We may understand from the smell of the month-old cottage cheese in our refrigerator that it's not fit to eat, but that isn't the cheese's way of telling us so. No, for something to actually count as communication, the signal needs to have a fixed, or at least generally regular, meaning. We expect, for instance, that someone's flashing the OK sign (except perhaps in Brazil) indicates approval. If your friend Roger started using it to let you know that he was mad at you (in place of the more commonly accepted "one finger salute"), you would be annoyed . . . not only because you came to learn that he didn't really mean *OK*, but also because he wasn't using the signal consistently. Likewise, an ant's laying down a scent trail to let her teammates know "NOT to go down this path" would just mess everything up. Imagine a 25,000 ant traffic jam on the trail.

Along with a consistent meaning, communicated signals need to have some purpose. It might be (and most commonly is) the transmission of information – the "red" traffic light telling the drivers to "Stop!," the bank clerk telling the person at the head of the line ("Next!") to approach the window. But it need not involve information to be purposeful, as when someone I recognize (but don't know well) passes me on my way down the block and says "How'r'yadoin'?" They are not, I am certain, asking me to share information regarding my current economic, spiritual, or emotional state. Rather, the purpose of this communication is to acknowledge me as a fellow traveler on the same street, and give me a verbal pat-on-the-head, so to speak. My response "Fine, thanks, and you?" is no more informative, and has the same general purpose.

The three properties that we've spoken about so far are necessary for anything to even be considered communication. That is, all communicated messages are sent through some medium, have a meaning, and serve some purpose. So, thinking linguistic thoughts cannot count as communication (unless your friends are telepathic). And sticking your head out the window and screaming "aaaaaahhh!!!" at the top of your lungs doesn't count as a message, even though it's carried through the medium of sound and might have some purpose (such as letting off steam), for the simple reason that *aaaaaahhh* has no fixed or regular meaning. Finally, if you walk up to a complete stranger and say the word *monkey* for no apparent reason, we would not consider you to have communicated (even though the word *monkey* itself has a regular and stable meaning), since your message has no arguable purpose.

There are also properties of communicated messages that can be considered optional. That is, some forms of communication have the properties and some don't. Take, for instance, the notion of *interchangeability* (or mutuality). In some kinds of communication, the message sender and message receiver can easily trade places. This is certainly true of most human communication. I say some words to you for some purpose, a communicated message, and you reply with some words of your own, another communicated message. We are each able to use the same stock of words (provided we're speaking the same language), so our communication system is interchangeable (we each can use it interchangeably).

This isn't always the case. Take the case of the dot matrix printer and the computer mentioned above. The printer has a simple pair of messages that it communicates to the computer, in order to manage the flow of information to it: *Pause* (stop sending for a moment, I'm full) and *Continue* (OK, go on). This is not an interchangeable system. The type of information sent by the computer to the printer (i.e. commands to print letters) is not the same type of information sent in the opposite direction (i.e. instructions to start and stop).

There is no way to know without close examination whether a given system is or is not interchangeable. For instance, if the worker ant laying down a chemical trail to guide her compatriots might on another occasion be the one reading the chemical messages set down by her colony-mates, then the system is indeed interchangeable. On the other hand, if the sex pheromones particular to a creature are only emitted by one sex (as is the case with moths and butterflies, where the female uses a chemical scent to attract males), then the communication is not interchangeable.

Communication systems also vary according to whether they are inborn or learned. Obviously, the messages communicated by machines (such as computer printers and microwaves) are part of their design (they are built into the system). For instance, your microwave is not designed to learn how you prefer it to signal that it's finished the popcorn (although it could be). Human language, though, is obviously a learned form of communication, and whether it is also partly inborn is a vexed question that has occupied linguists for some time. There are adamant proponents for both the negative and positive conclusion (N.B. the authors of the present book would be among the latter). Some forms of communication are clearly and necessarily inborn, such as the chemical pheromone communication systems mentioned above. There's really no way for an ant to learn how to produce the right chemical to mark its trail, or for the female gypsy moth to be taught which scent will attract her mate. They either come into the world with the chemical scent-making capacity built in, or they don't.

With other species, though, there is some variability. It has been shown that some bird species, such as the zebra finch, do in fact develop their song through exposure to adults, albeit with some help from nature. When finches are raised in isolation, without any exposure to the mating songs of other finches, they produce a song that is similar to that of their own species (suggesting that they're born with some capacity for this) but they do it pretty badly (suggesting that they need to hear and learn from other finches to really get it right).

Recent research into the behavior of other bird species, such as the cowbird, has also shown that inheritance combines with learning to insure that communication is passed along. The cowbird is what is called a "brood parasite," which means that the female lays its eggs in the nest of another species and allows the female owner of that nest to raise its young (now you know what to call human parents who abandon their children to be reared by other adults). Given that young cowbirds will not have much contact with adults of their own species early on, it has long been assumed that they would need to have some genetically hard-wired knowledge of their own species' mating songs, in order to insure that they don't learn the wrong mating song and doom their own species to extinction.

However, recent research by Meridith West and Andrew King at Indiana University[3] has shown that the circumstances of "brood parasites" are more complex and that their environment plays at least as strong a role as their genes in helping them to get their song right. West and King discovered that males are fairly indiscriminate and will sing to and chase the tails of whatever birds they're raised with, including (with no hope of success) canaries. What they also discovered is that females provide the males with the cues (i.e. the flirtatious gestures) necessary to coax them into singing their mating song correctly. That is, the females knew what they wanted to hear better than the males knew what they wanted to sing, and the females were sophisticated enough to get them (the males) to do it.

Also quite amazing in West and King's findings was the fact that females actually inherit their song preferences from their mothers. In the case of a cross-bred female (whose mother was a Texas cowbird and whose father was a North Carolina cowbird), the preference was clearly for a Texas-style mating song even though she could not have learned this from her mother (who wasn't present to teach it to her). So in the case of the cowbird, the producer of the communicated message (the male) needs to be instructed in it by his targeted audience (the females), and it is the audience (the female) that has inborn knowledge of what needs to be sung.

Another variable we find in communication systems has to do with the relationship between the meaning of the message and its form. Does the form of what is used to express the message somehow give hints to its meaning? This common sign in public buildings does so:

The meaning of this message, that a stairway is nearby, is obvious from the form (which is a side-view of the basic shape of a stairway). If the sign were arbitrarily used to indicate a fire exit or a restroom, you would think that the building's designers were consciously trying to confuse people. Likewise, this sign for a women's restroom is also self-explanatory, despite the likelihood that most of those using it won't be wearing dresses or skirts.[4]

And it would still be usable in Scotland for a women's restroom sign, even during the July 2009 Gathering of Scottish clans in Edinburgh.[5]

Figure 2.2

The point is not that the form of the sign is a true and accurate *picture* of its meaning, but that it is just indicative of its meaning. When a sign does this, we would say that the form is "iconic" relative to the meaning.

Now, just as some signs do give out hints as to their meaning, many do not. When there is no obvious connection between form and meaning, then the link is "arbitrary." Take, for instance, the roadside meaning of a red octagon.

We recognize this as a "stop" sign, regardless of what letters are written on it. So, if you're driving along and approach a corner with one of the signs in Figure 2.3, you will stop, irrespective of whether you can read Spanish, Chinese, Arabic, or Algonquin.[6]

Figure 2.3 *Stop signs from around the world.*

Now, what is clear about this is that there is nothing about the color red or an octagonal shape that carries an inherent meaning "stop." In fact, in the early part of the last century US stop signs were typically yellow. The octagonal shape was determined in 1922, but the red color didn't become standard until the mid-1950s. The image below is that of a black and yellow enamaled stop sign from the 1940s (used in Chicago and made by Lyle Signs Inc., Minneapolis, MN).[7]

Now just as the connection between the form of a road sign and its meaning can be arbitrary or not, so it is with almost any form of communication, including spoken human language. The sound of some words is "iconic" relative to their meaning, while the sound of others (the vast majority) is "arbitrary." Take, for instance, the word for a house pet of the "feline persuasion," *cat*, and the word for the sound that this creature typically makes, *meow*. There is nothing special about the sounds [k], [æ], or [t] or in combining them in this particular order [kæt] that would lead anyone to prefer them in selecting a name for the species *felis catus*. In fact, these three sounds can be combined (arbitrarily) in a variety of ways to form several different, unrelated English words, such as: *act* [ækt], *tack*, [tæk], and *tact* [tækt]. If we look at the word for this animal in other languages, we find that they differ widely from one language to the next: *macja* (Albanian), *mao* (Chinese), *kočka* (Czech), *kissa* (Finnish), *hatool* (Hebrew), *kicing* (Indonesian), *neko* (Japanese), *pisică* (Romanian), *gato* (Spanish), *kedi* (Turkish), *con mèo* (Vietnamese). On the other hand, many unrelated languages do use the same word (one that sounds like [mee-ow]) to indicate the sound that the creature makes. These include French, Spanish, Hebrew, Chinese, Japanese, and Greek. The reason for this similarity across languages is obvious. They all mimic the actual sound that the animal makes and, in doing so, create words that are "iconic" rather than "arbitrary." In contrast, the words we use to name things in the world, with very few exceptions, are typically arbitrary sequences of sounds that don't exhibit any direct connection between their sound and their meaning.

Another aspect of communication systems worth talking about has to do with whether pieces of a message can be broken down into smaller bits of meaning. To see what this means, consider two equally good ways that you might use to get someone to cross the room and come over to where you're standing. You might use a familiar hand gesture involving a curved index finger,

or you might simply say "come here!" The spoken message consists of two words *come* and *here* plus the implied *you*. That is, there are three bits of meaning in this message and they are (to a degree) independent of one another. This is obvious from the fact that we can swap one of them out to change the meaning of the message. Replace *come* with *stand*, and we get "stand here!" . . . a different message entirely. We could then replace *here* with *there* to get another message, "stand there!" And we could even replace the implied *you* with an overt *let's* [i.e. let us] to get "let's stand there!"

In contrast, the hand gesture doesn't break apart into any meaningful components. The extended index finger doesn't have a meaning separate from the curled-back three fingers or the thumb. The orientation of the hand (facing upwards) doesn't represent any separable piece of the message. One can, of course, swap the index finger for another (of ill-repute) to change the message entirely (and perhaps start a fight in the process). But notice that, in this case, the entire message changes, not just one piece of it.

It is the ability to piece together complex (or simple) messages through the use of many independent, meaningful bits that allows human communication (i.e. language) to have the richness that it does. Imagine how many things we could say if each message required its own separate and un-analyzable hand gesture.[8] Not many.

A brief comparison of human language to animal communication is helpful here. The vocalizations of vervet monkeys have been extensively studied, and they have been found to utilize four distinct types of alarm calls in order to warn others of impending danger.[9] One type of call (a loud bark) is used when a leopard is spotted. Leopards are quite fond of vervets (for lunch), and the troop responds to this call by climbing high up into trees that are outside of its range. Another call (sort of a double cough) is used to alert the troop to an aerial predator, such as an eagle. The response to this warning is to run into low bushes, so as to be hidden from the air. The third call (something that is called, and sounds like, a chutter) is a response to snakes. This alarm causes the troop to look for the snake, and to mob it when they find it. There is, lastly, a call that they use for mammalian ground predators who don't (unlike leopards) have a special preference for vervets. This alarm is a quiet but very high pitched call that causes the troop to become very vigilant and move toward trees.[10]

While these monkeys use a fairly sophisticated system for communication, the calls they use for the various types of alarms cannot be broken down into component parts. The "leopard alarm" might mean something like "Watch out, a leopard!" or "Run, climb a tree!" or "Danger on the ground!" The "eagle alarm" might mean something like "Watch out! An eagle!" or "Quick, hide in a bush!" or "Look out for something in the sky!" However one might characterize the message in these alarms, it's clear that there is no part of the message that can be separated out to mean "danger" or "run" or "climb" or "hide" or "leopard" or "eagle." This being the case, we can assume that vervets (unlike people) cannot readily use their system of alarms to construct new ones. There is simply no way for a vervet to signal "Watch out for that creature coming out of the lake!" or "Run! Guy with a gun!" or "Danger! A creature that we've never seen before who looks hungry and is likely to eat one of us!" In this regard, human communication, having the property of being decomposable into bits of meaning, can be counted upon to do a better job at communicating about novel dangers (as well as many other things).

Another important property of communication, one that appears restricted to human language, is ability to transmit messages about things and circumstances that are not physically or temporally present. When we survey various non-human communication systems we can see right away that the messages sent are all about here and now. The dot matrix printers relays the messages 'Pause' (now) and 'Continue' (now). There would be no point in having it tell the computer that it wanted it to *pause* a minute ago, or that it is ok to *continue*, provided someone else refills the paper tray. Birds' mating and territorial songs, vervet monkeys' alarm calls, and ants' pheromone trail markings are all and only about current situations. No bird can communicate "I **would have wanted** to mate with you, **were you a faster flyer**." Vervet monkeys can't reminisce about alarm calls from last week. And ants won't lay down a trail that they anticipate **will** lead to food tomorrow.

Human communication (i.e. language), on the other hand, is often, if not most often, about this. We regularly use language to transmit messages about what we did, what we're about to do, and what we would or would not do if circumstances were different. Consider the famous nursery rhyme about the three "wise" men of Gotham:

> Three Wise Men of Gotham
> Went to sea in a bowl.
> If the bowl had been stronger
> My tale had been longer.

The point of the poem is to let us know that the three were fools, and that they didn't stay afloat for long. In a world where it's true that the bowl is strong, it's also true that the poem is long. Ours is not that world. Messages like this, which describe the world as it might be (but isn't) and which suggest further how things would turn out in such a world, are called counterfactuals. We use them all the time,

> "If I had more money, Lulu would probably go out with me."
> "I could get an A on this test, if I only had five more hours to work on it."
> "This coffee wouldn't taste so bad, if the white stuff in the sugar bowl hadn't turned out to be salt."

Communicating about the world as it was, will be, or could be is a property unique to human (language) communication.

One final property to discuss is the degree to which a communication system is open-ended or productive. In the universe of animal communication, there is a fairly wide difference regarding the number of messages that different species have at their disposal. Some have only a few, while others have a few dozen. In experimental environments, some primate species and other mammals (such as sea lions) have been trained to recognize, respond to, and sometimes use, many dozens of signs ... and to use combinations of these in various ways to form or understand hundreds of distinct messages. For instance, Ron Schusterman (a researcher at the University of California, Santa Cruz)[11] and his research team spent years training sea lions to recognize and respond to a variety of signed gestures. Sea lions were trained to distinguish signs for the adjectives 'large', 'small', 'black' and 'white', for various objects ([toy] car, ring, cube, ball, football, pipe, etc.), and for certain actions (e.g. swim-over, swim-under, touch-with-flipper, touch-with-mouth, fetch, etc.). They could accurately follow commands such as "swim over the large black football" in a pool loaded with an assortment of different floating objects. The sea lions' ability to respond to sequences of as many as seven signs resulted in their potentially having the ability to decode some 7,000 distinct messages.[12]

Now, even with 7,000 possible messages (which sounds like a lot), sea lion communication doesn't hold a candle to human language communication in terms of its open-endedness or productivity. If you can only say (or understand) 7,000 sentence-like messages, you can certainly do quite a bit, but your ability to communicate on a human level would be pretty mediocre. If 500 or so messages are dedicated to getting what you want at eateries (e.g. *Supersize me!*; *I'd like fries with that.*; *Waiter, there's a fly in my soup!*; etc.) and 1,000 messages are needed to deal with direct marketing phone calls (e.g. *No, I'm not interested!*; *There's no one here by that name.*; *Can you call back next year?*; etc.), that only leaves about 5,500 messages to handle all of Shakespeare and anything Rush Limbaugh might have to say (the latter being presumably less of a problem).

So how many distinct messages is a speaker of a human language capable of? Well, if one considers that the vocabulary of the average college graduate might be somewhere around 65,000 to 75,000 words,[13] and that these words may combine into multiword sentences of variable length, we can conclude the human language is a communication system capable of a practically infinite number of possible messages. We are constantly hearing sentences we've never heard before and producing sentences that we've never spoken before, and this goes on for most of our lives. That isn't to say that we don't often repeat ourselves. That isn't to say that we don't often repeat ourselves. But the fact is that we most often don't. Consider, for instance, the fact that most of the sentences in this book are, and will be, sentences that you the reader have never heard or read before. Repeat this for just about every book you've read, and will read, and you get the idea of the limitlessness of it all.

It's not just because we have so many words either. Human language has the limitless capacity that it does at least in part because we are able to embed expressions inside other expressions which are embedded inside yet other expressions that are themselves embedded inside expressions. Consider the "Hallmark Vortex" imagined by Dan Piraro and shown in Figure 2.4.[14]

According to this cartoon, the thank you card that I send in response to a thank you card that I received in response to a thank you card that I sent in response to a thank you card is called a "thank you for the thank you for the thank you for the thank you card." While it may be hard to follow, it can certainly be (very carefully) unraveled and understood. And one doesn't even have to have

Figure 2.4 *The Hallmark vortex.*

very complex expressions to illustrate this either. A joke that is funnier than a joke which was funnier than the joke which I consider "very funny" could be called a "very, very, very, very funny joke." There is no limit to the number of *very*'s that I might add, and thus no limit to the number of such expressions I can produce using the word *very*.

Animal communication lacks this embedding capacity, even when animals are taught to use symbols to communicate in relatively sophisticated ways. For example, in the 1970s, Herbert Terrace conducted communication experiments with a chimpanzee he named Nim Chimpsky (cf. Noam Chomsky).[15] Having taught Nim to manipulate some 125 differently shaped and colored plastic chips (each being equivalent to a word) to make expressions, he was found to be capable of numerous complex expressions. But Nim's expressions rarely went beyond two or three symbols (chips) and his longest utterance (plastic chip-wise) was,

> "give orange me give eat orange me eat orange give me eat orange give me you"

Clearly, length aside, there is absolutely no grammar here. No embedding of the sort that would result in a human child's saying something like,

> "You should give me the orange, so that I can eat the orange"

It is grammar, which provides the capacity for embedding, which in turn allows a speaker of human language to produce an expression like,

> "Your mother's sister's cousin Matilda's drunkard of a husband is passed out in the driveway"

and have you understand what is meant.

Having looked in some detail at the nature of communication systems generally, we can now compare animal and human communication, to get a sense of how human language is special and how it differs. One system that has been extensively studied is that of forager bees. Forager bees (like many other varieties) have a specialized group of worker bees called "scouts." These bees go out looking for food sources, and then report their location back to the hive. Since the main goal of the hive is to collect enough food (i.e. calories) to get through the winter and since flying around spends calories, it would be pretty wasteful if every worker bee went out on their own looking for food. The method of sending out scouts is quite efficient, but comes with one requirement. The scouts have to have some way of telling the rest of the hive what they've found and where to go get it.

Essentially, what needs to be communicated about the food source is (1) whether it's any good, (2) where it is relative to the hive, and (3) how far away it is. The first part is pretty straightforward. All the scout needs to do there is to bring back samples and pass them around . . . and this is indeed what they do.

The second part requires some actual communication. The scout must tell everyone in what direction to go. They don't have GPS, or maps, or words for landmarks like trees and streams. But they can orient themselves relative to something everyone can see, the sun (of course, this won't work on rainy days, but who wants to go out in that sort of weather anyway?). The way they do this is by doing a little "dance" (see Figure 2.5) in which the wiggle (technically the "waggle") part of the dance shows the hive the direction of the food source relative to the sun.

Now, one must understand that the "dance floor" inside the hive is vertical (like a wall), and the scouts use "down" (the direction of gravity) as symbolic of "away from the sun." So, if the wiggle is 30 degrees to the left of perpendicular, then the other worker bees know that they must leave the hive and fly in a direction 30 degrees to the left of the sun. We can see pretty clearly here that this particular aspect of the communication system is what we called "iconic" earlier . . . that is, the form of the dance (like the stairway sign in the public building) has a pretty direct relationship to the meaning it is trying to convey.

Scouts have a different way of communicating distance. This bit is communicated through the rate of repetition. The faster the scout dances (that is, the more times per minute she repeats the dance) the closer the food source is. Slower means farther away. This is also somewhat iconic, since:

> Faster = it took me less time to get back to the hive
> Slower = it took me longer to get back to the hive

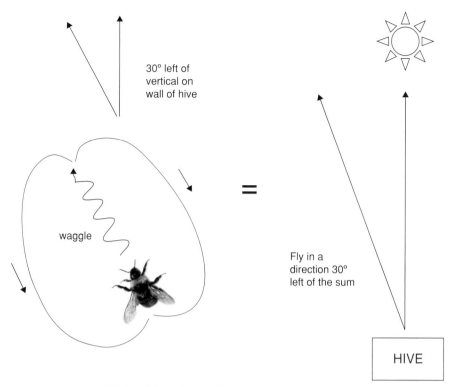

30° left of
vertical on
wall of hive

waggle

=

Fly in a
direction 30°
left of the sum

HIVE

Figure 2.5 *The "dance" of the bees.*

Forager bee communication appears to be true communication, but how can one really know? That is, how do we know that the "dances" that the scout bees do express something that we would call "meaning" (the location of food) and are used for a "purpose" (to let the others in the hive know about it). Maybe the scout bees are just nervous or excited. Maybe the other bees can just sniff out where the food is, and the dance doesn't really tell them anything.

Experiments with forager bee behavior have shown otherwise. Namely, that the scouts are communicating information and that the other bees receive this information and act accordingly. In one experiment, scouts were sent out of the hive and the rest of the bees were removed from the hive before they returned. Coming back to an "empty house," one imagines that they were confused and lonely. But they didn't wander around the hive for a long time calling out the names of their friends (presumably either because they don't have "friends" or because their friends don't have names). They also didn't dance. Now, if the dance was just a reaction to finding food, then they would have done it anyway. But the fact that they didn't do it with no one else in the hive suggests that it is done for the purpose of communicating.

In another experiment, scouts' wings were taped to their backs and they were made to walk (rather than fly) back to the hive. One imagines that they were really pissed off about having to walk, after all the money they spent on a "wing job."

That being beside the point, when they did get back, they nevertheless danced to let everyone know where the food was, and the frequency of their dance directly communicated the amount of time that it took them to walk back (and didn't match the flying distance to the food source, since they hadn't flown back). So, though we know that they don't have little chronometers, it is pretty clear that they are measuring their travel time and directly communicating that to their hive mates.

Other experiments have tested whether the other bees actually got the message. We know right off that they sampled the food brought back by the scout, so that's not at issue. And observers noted that the worker bees all flew off in the correct direction, indicating that the directional dance worked. But what about distance? A couple of experiments tested this. In one, experimenters placed food-scent cards along the flight path, hoping to trick the worker bees into "pulling over" early (to prove that they might just be sniffing their way along the path until they get to a food source). But, by and large, the worker bees overflew the cards, and went all the way to the actual food source, indicating that they had been paying attention to the scout's message. Other observations confirmed this, as the worker bees generally ate just enough before going out to get them out to the food source and back. That is, they "knew" before leaving, how far they would need to fly and prepared accordingly.

So, we know that the bees have a true communication system. It has a medium (movement), and communicates information (location of food) for a purpose (helping others to retrieve the food). We also know that the major pieces of the system (direction and distance) are iconic, rather than arbitrary. Notice also that the communication system doesn't involve two-way (i.e. interchangeable) communication. Scouts report information to the other workers about what they've found, but there's no communication of consequence going the other way. Workers have no way to ask specific questions related to the messages, such as:

> "What did you find out there?"
> "So how far is it?"
> "Which way do we turn when we leave the hive?"
> "Did you have a good flight?"

We even know that it doesn't involve learning on the part of the scouts – they are born with the ability to communicate their messages. We know this because of other experiments that have been done. It happens that there are two related varieties of forager bees, an Austrian variety living north of the Alps and an Italian variety living to the south of the mountains. The two varieties can be told apart by their markings (and no, the Austrian bees do not have lederhosen). In addition, their communication systems are slightly different. The Austrian bees dance more quickly than the Italian bees to communicate a particular distance. If you place an Austrian scout in an Italian hive and allow it to dance the distance of a food source in its own "dialect," the Italian bees will be looking for food closer to the hive than the Austrian bee intended. The reverse happens if you place an Italian scout in an Austrian hive (that, and the Italian scout asks for chianti instead of hefewiezen). In experiments where the two varieties were cross-bred, it turned out that those offspring that sported Austrian markings danced an Austrian "dialect" and those offspring with Italian markings danced like Italians.

Looking further along at what bee communication does not have (and consequently how it is not like human language), one first lights upon the fact that the bee direction/distance message cannot be broken into component parts. There's no way to separate (as there would be in human language) the direction part of the message from the distance part. A scout bee has no way to say "it's 90 degrees to the right of the sun, but you're going to have to guess how far." It's further the case that, unlike human language, the scout bee's messages are all and only about here and now. It cannot communicate anything about the location of a food source from yesterday. It can't even communicate about where it found food a couple of hours ago, since the sun moves in the sky and the message at 2 p.m. won't mean the same thing at 4 p.m. It can't (and won't) communicate where it wishes there were food, or where would be a good place to find food.

Of course, the productivity of bee communication is also limited and distinct from human language. There's no communication from scout bees about anything other than the quality, direction, and distance of a food source. That is, a scout can't communicate the direction and distance of anything else, such as a competing hive. She can't provide information about whether the food source is close to the ground, or high off it. She can't tell her hive mates how enjoyable the trip back was, or how nice the weather's been for flying. And as we noted above, she can't even tell everyone that her flight was "canceled" and that she had to "walk back."

It's clear from all this that the forager bees really do communicate in complex and sophisticated ways. It's also clear that their communication is only similar to that of humans in our overactive imaginations. Our propensity for overestimating what other creatures are capable of where communication is concerned is legend. So much so, that we can often laugh at ourselves about it. Consider this bit of humor:

> Each evening bird lover Tom stood in his backyard, hooting like an owl and, one night, an owl finally called back to him. For a year, the man and his feathered friend hooted back and forth. He even kept a log of their "conversations." Just as he thought he was on the verge of a breakthrough in interspecies communication, his wife had a chat with her next-door neighbor. "My husband spends his nights calling out to owls," she said. "That's odd," the neighbor replied. "So does mine."[16]

Or this one:

> A man is at the zoo and asks the keeper, "Have you got any talking parrots?" "No," says the keeper, "but we've got a woodpecker that knows Morse code."[17]

We want to believe that animals communicate just like we do, and those beliefs help populate joke books, fables, fairy tales, movies, and all sorts of stories that get passed around from pet lover to pet lover. It isn't uncommon for pet owners, like Judy Brookes (featured in a *Scientific American* article "Fact or fiction: Dogs can talk"), to believe that her dog Maya is actually trying to say "I love you," when she says "Ahh rooo uuu." People have been deluded into thinking that animals are actually talking, or at least trying to talk, since at least the beginning of the last century.[18] Our (and especially pet owners') desire to anthropomorphize our pets leads more than a few pet lovers and owners to interpret their pet's responses in this way (whether it's believing that they are trying to produce language or that they are able to understand it). The fact is that animals such as Maya haven't got a clue what they're doing, only that whatever it is, it gets them treats. It should be clear from what we've seen in this chapter that human language is on a completely distinct communicative plain from the sort of messaging that other creatures are capable of.

Before closing out this discussion, there is one other issue that we need to address: some common misuses of the word *language* to describe things that humans do, which are not in fact really language at all. Among those things needing weeding are *the language of flowers*, *the language of love*, and *the language of music*. Generally speaking, you can be assured that anything called "the language of X" where X is something other than human language is not really language. People commonly refer to the way we might communicate through any medium as the "language" of that medium. So, if your mom makes a "mean" lasagna and her making the lasagna communicates how much she loves and cares for you, somebody is going to write about this and call it the "language of food." Of course, there's simply no way that we can assign a semantic meaning of "I love and care for you" to the preparation and serving of lasagna. If we did so, then it should and would always have that meaning. But while your mom serving you lasagna might communicate this message from her to you, be assured that she doesn't want it to mean the same thing when she has to serve her alcoholic brother-in-law, Anthony. No, in order for some system of communication to be a "language" of anything, or even a system of communication, its messages must have consistent and stable semantic meanings.

For example, there's a fellow in North Carolina named Dr. Gary Chapman who writes books about marital communication.[19] One of Dr. Chapman's books is titled *The Five Love Languages*. The five "languages" that he refers to are: words of affirmation, quality time, receiving gifts, acts of service, and physical touch. Now, as important as these five elements might be in building marital communication, they are not "languages." If anything they are means through which couples might convey messages and feelings to each other. They are mediums of communication rather than systems of communication or "language."

While it is certainly possible to communicate through the medium of physical touch for instance, we do not have in most cases an established communication system involving touch (with the exception of a few ritualized gestures such as shaking hands). Take hugging for example. Hugging can and usually does communicate something. But what it communicates will vary according to the participants. Hugging one's children and hugging one's spouse are supposed to communicate somewhat different messages. And I can assure you that a very different message is going out when Jimmy has to hug his Great Aunt Bella, who he can't stand.

Speaking of what some refer to as the "language of music" is a bit more complicated. It has recently been shown (unsurprisingly) that music is capable of communicating emotions. In a recent study, Thomas Fritz and his research team found that there is a universal ability to recognize three basic emotions expressed through Western music (happiness, sadness, and fear).[20] What is rather remarkable is that these messages come through even to people who have never before heard Western music. Now, the ability of a musical passage to elicit a nebulous emotional response is rather different from the ability to communicate a message. Music that communicates happiness cannot be said to have transmitted the message "I (the composer) am happy" or "You (the listener) should be happy" or "Happiness is a good thing to feel." And even if one were to consider "happiness," "sadness," and "fear" to be (on their own) messages transmitted by particular musical passages, to go on from there and suggest that music is some sort of communicative system would be absurd (and would lose sight of the fact that music is infinitely more than a system of transmitting messages). Given that music does not even rise to the level of "system of communication," calling it "language" is hyperbolic nonsense.

Among all the "language of X" expressions out there, there is one, *the language of flowers*, which comes close to qualifying as a communication system (although not as a language). As noted by Beverly Seaton, the language of flowers was (in Victorian times) "a vocabulary list, matching flowers with meanings, [but] differing from book to book."[21] In this system, the presentation or display of certain flowers would communicate (coded) meanings. The specific meaning conveyed by a particular flower might differ from book to book, and from country to country. A white rose could signify "silence" or "celibacy" or "virtue." A yellow rose variously translated as "devotion" or "jealousy" or "infidelity." Of course, the red rose with its meaning of "love" and "beauty" has remained rather constant. So to the extent that different species of flowers could be assigned meanings that correspond to different feelings and to the extent that these were used to send messages in circumstances when open communication was not possible, the "language of flowers" is a viable, albeit restricted, communication system. Nevertheless, a "language" it is not.

As the reader proceeds through this book, it will be helpful to remember what constitutes true language, and the ways in which human language is a specially endowed form of communication that has no peer among the myriad types of communication that are possible.

3   Did I hear that right?

The sounds of language

    by johnny hart

This B.C. cartoon[1] illustrates an important fact about human language, namely that it is, in the first instance, a communicative behavior whose primary medium is sound (ignoring for the moment the visual and gestural basis of sign languages). It is for this reason that we have placed this chapter ahead of all the remaining chapters of this book.

Written language is secondary to spoken language and is derivative of it. It is the primacy of spoken language which enables and contributes to the vast store of sound-based jokes, puns, and other linguistic diversions that we have at our disposal. Certainly, were it not for the disparity between speech sounds and spelling (which is particularly great in English), the joke about welcoming one's Aunt Teeter to an ant colony would not be so easily put. In this chapter, we will first discuss the difference between language sounds and the letters (i.e. symbols) used to represent these sounds, noting that this gap is not one to be easily remedied given the demands of literacy. We will then focus on language sounds themselves, and on the difference between phonetics (the physical realization and properties of these sounds) and phonology (which concerns how these sounds are mentally represented in the mind of a speaker or hearer). Finally, we will go through a brief catalog of the kinds of linguistic diversions (puns, spoonerisms) that arise out of sound–spelling discrepancies and out of the interaction between phonetics and phonology.

Letters and sounds

A delightfully insightful episode of Art and Chip Sansom's *The Born Loser*, from several years ago, has Hurricane Hattie O'Hara being asked by her teacher how to spell the word *coconut*. She dutifully recites "k-o-k-o-n-u-t," to which her teacher answers, "That is incorrect!" Hurricane Hattie responds quite reasonably, asking, "Well, if k-o-k-o-n-u-t doesn't spell *coconut*, what does it spell?"

As the Sansom comic strip makes so very clear, there is a disconnect between our pronunciation of sounds and the letters (or symbols) we use to represent them. In the particular case above, we have a letter "c" which is sometimes used in English to represent the same sound as "k" and sometimes used to represent the same sound as "s." So, as far as pronunciation is concerned, "k-o-k-o-n-u-t" and "c-o-c-o-n-u-t" do indeed spell out the same sequence of sounds for a speaker of English. All, the same *kokonut* is not an accepted written word in the English language.

There are many other idiosyncrasies that make English spelling appear rather arbitrary and illogical (even though a good number of them make some sense from an historical perspective). Take, for instance, the way that the first vowel sound in *strip* is affected by the addition of an "e" at the end of the word *stripe*. The letter "i" winds up representing the sound [i] as in *din* when the "e" is absent, and [ai] when the "e" is added, as in *dine*. A corollary of this pattern is the fact that one "p" in the word *striper* has the preceding vowel pronounced [ai], while the imposition of "pp" gives the [i] in *stripper*.[2] Only the latter gets to work as an exotic dancer. A 1992 panel of Dan Piraro's *Bizarro* cartoon takes advantage of this spelling oddity. In it, the plate glass window of a store front prominently displays "Ed's Dinner." Inside the store is a guy in his undershirt sitting alone at a table, looking up from his supper at two men standing in the doorway. One of the men says to the other, "See? I told you it's not just a misspelling!"

And it's not just the case that odd combinations of letters yield unexpected sounds in English. It is also a fact that the same letters and combinations of letters yield quite different sounds when used in different words. This fact is particularly vexing to any non-native speaker of English who has ever tried to learn the language. Try explaining to a learner of English why the vowel sounds in the words *pull* and *wool* are the same but are spelled with "u" and "oo," respectively. And why it is that the "oo" in *fool* represents a different sound from the "oo" in *wool*, but the same sound as the "u" in *rule*. The frustration engendered in such spelling arbitrariness was best caricatured in 1894 in this poem titled "O-U-G-H" by Charles Battell Loomis, which depicts a French speaker's frustration with the spelling conventions of the English language (read this poem with the best French accent you can muster):

I'm taught p-l-o-u-g-h
S'all be pronouncé "plow."
"Zat's easy w'en you know," I say,
"Mon Anglais, I'll get through!"
My teacher say zat in zat case,
O-u-g-h is "oo."
And zen I laugh and say to him,
"Zees Anglais make me cough."
He say "Not 'coo' but in zat word,
O-u-g-h is 'off.'"
"Oh, Sacre bleu! Such varied sounds
Of words make me hiccough!"
He say, "Again mon frien' ees wrong;
O-u-g-h is 'up'
In hiccough." Zen I cry, "No more,
You make my t'roat feel rough."
"Non, non!" he cry, "You are not right;
O-u-g-h is 'uff.'"
I say, "I try to spik your words,
I cannot spik zem though."
"In time you'll learn, but now you're wrong!
O-u-g-h is 'owe.'"
"I'll try no more, I s'all go mad,
I'll drown me in ze lough!"
"But ere you drown yourself," said he,
"O-u-g-h is 'ock.'"
He taught no more, I held him fast
And killed him wiz a rough.

In explaining how English spelling differs so radically from English pronunciation, it is important to note that spelling conventions are extremely resistant to change, much more so than pronunciations. One can demonstrate this by looking at English words that end in "ight" such as *night*, *light*, and *bright*. The spelling of these words is faithful to their pronunciations in Old English, an historical ancestor of Modern English not much heard for some 800–900 years. In Old English, the letter "i" was pronounced [ee] and the "gh" represented the sound [h], such that *night* would have been pronounced something like [neeht] up until the fifteenth century, and its spelling would thus have very closely mirrored its pronunciation. This Old English ["strong h"] sound represented by "gh" is very close to, and historically related to, the German ["strong h"] sound in *nacht* 'night'. The spelling of these words thus trails the changes in their pronunciation by a good five hundred years.

Alongside the standard "ight" spellings, we find that some of these words also show up with "new and modern" spellings, often used to pitch products, such as *nite* and *lite* in *Nite Lite* (a brand of rechargeable hunting lights) and *lite* in *Bud Lite* and *Miller Lite* (beer). People often take such spellings to be bold and avant-garde (at least the ad agencies seem to). In this "lite," it is sobering to realize that the nouveau spelling of *lite* actually represents a spelling convention held over from Middle English (that is, fourteenth-century English) where the "i" was still pronounced as [ee] and the final "e" was optionally pronounced, as in [leeteh] or [leet]. So, "avant garde" in spelling terms means something like "only 300–500 years out of date." If we were to adopt a truly avant-garde (or at least au courant) spelling for these words, we would want to spell them as *layt*, *nayt*, and *brayt*.

So why don't we? The best explanation for the resistance to change shown by spelling conventions is that literacy and the preservation of written records depend upon it. Spelling reform of any significance would likely render incomprehensible much of what has been written in English over the past few centuries. A short but convincing essay on this topic was penned by Mark Twain (or some say, by one M. S. Shields in a letter to the *Economist*):

> *A Plan for the Improvement of English Spelling*
>
> For example, in Year 1 that useless letter *c* would be dropped to be replased either by *k* or *s*, and likewise *x* would no longer be part of the alphabet. The only kase in which *c* would be retained would be the *ch* formation, which will be dealt with later.
>
> Year 2 might reform *w* spelling, so that *which* and *one* would take the same konsonant, wile Year 3 might well abolish *y* replasing it with *i* and Iear 4 might fiks the *g/j* anomali wonse and for all.
>
> Jenerally, then, the improvement would kontinue iear bai iear with Iear 5 doing awai with useless double konsonants, and Iears 6–12 or so modifaiing vowlz and the rimeining voist and unvoist konsonants.
>
> Bai Iear 15 or sou, it wud fainali bi posibl tu meik ius ov thi ridandant letez *c*, *y* and *x* – bai now jast a memori in the maindz ov ould doderez – tu riplais *ch*, *sh*, and *th* rispektivli.
>
> Fainali, xen, aafte sam 20 iers ov orxogrefkl riform, wi wud hev a lojikl, kohirnt speling in ius xrewawt xe Ingliy-spiking werld.

Consider the last sentence in this piece, and the likely result of "xe orxogrefkl riform ov Ingliy." Such a radical change, if accomplished in twenty years or even forty, would make it all but impossible for anyone schooled in the "nu orxogrefi" to read anything printed in the last century. So, we are stuck with the spelling system that we have and will, for the foreseeable future, run the risk of having the French students in our English classes want to kill us "wiz a rough."

Having noted the difficulties of the English spelling system and the discrepancies between letters and sounds, we can see more clearly why one cannot really use the standard orthographical system of letters to speak about or describe sounds. We find that some letters such as "x" represent two sounds: [ks]. Conversely, there are plenty of two-letter combinations, such as "sh" and "ch," that each represent a single sound. It is further the case, as we have seen, that some letters and letter combinations are unstable. The letters "th" have one sound in

THE INTERNATIONAL PHONETIC ALPHABET (2005)

CONSONANTS (PULMONIC)

	LABIAL		CORONAL				DORSAL			RADICAL		LARYNGEAL
	Bilabial	Labio-dental	Dental	Alveolar	Palato-alveolar	Retroflex	Palatal	Velar	Uvular	Pharyngeal	Epi-glottal	Glottal
Nasal	m	ɱ		n		ɳ	ɲ	ŋ	N			
Plosive	p b	ƥ ɓ̃		t d		ʈ ɖ	c ɟ	k g	q ɢ		ʡ	ʔ
Fricative	ɸ β	f v	θ ð	s z	ʃ ʒ	ʂ ʐ	ç ʝ	x ɣ	χ ʁ	ħ ʕ	ʜ ʢ	h ɦ
Approximant		ʋ		ɹ		ɻ	j	ɰ				
Trill	ʙ			r					ʀ		я	
Tap, Flap		ⱱ		ɾ		ɽ						
Lateral fricative				ɬ ɮ		ꞎ	𝼅	𝼄				
Lateral approximant				l		ɭ	ʎ	L				
Lateral flap				ɺ		𝼈						

Where symbols appear in pairs, the one to the right represents a modally voiced consonant, except for murmured ɦ. Shaded areas denote articulations judged to be impossible. Light grey letters are unofficial extensions of the IPA.

CONSONANTS (NON-PULMONIC)

Anterior click releases (require posterior stops)	Voiced implosives	Ejectives
⊙ Bilabial fricated	ɓ Bilabial	' Examples:
ǀ Laminal alveolar fricated ("dental")	ɗ Dental or alveolar	p' Bilabial
ǃ Apical (post)alveolar abrupt ("retroflex")	ʄ Palatal	t' Dental or alveolar
ǂ Laminal postalveolar abrupt ("palatal")	ɠ Velar	k' Velar
ǁ Lateral alveolar fricated ("lateral")	ʛ Uvular	s' Alveolar fricative

CONSONANTS (CO-ARTICULATED)

ʍ	Voiceless labialized velar approximant
w	Voiced labialized velar approximant
ɥ	Voiced labialized palatal approximant
ɕ	Voiceless palatalized postalveolar (alveolo-palatal) fricative
ʑ	Voiced palatalized postalveolar (alveolo-palatal) fricative
ɧ	Simultaneous x and ʃ (disputed)
k͡p t͡s	Affricates and double articulations may be joined by a tie bar

VOWELS

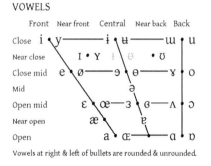

Front   Near front   Central   Near back   Back

Close   i y   ɨ ʉ   ɯ u
Near close   ɪ Y   ɪ ʊ   ʊ
Close mid   e ø   ɘ ɵ   ɤ o
Mid   ə
Open mid   ɛ œ   ɜ ɞ   ʌ ɔ
Near open   æ   ɐ
Open   a ɶ   ɑ ɒ

Vowels at right & left of bullets are rounded & unrounded.

SUPRASEGMENTALS

ˈ Primary stress	ˈˈ Extra stress
ˌ Secondary stress	[ˌfoʊnəˈtɪʃən]
eː Long	eˑ Half-long
e Short	ĕ Extra-short
. Syllable break	‿ Linking (no break)

INTONATION

ǀ Minor (foot) break	
ǁ Major (intonation) break	
↗ Global rise	↘ Global fall

TONE

Level tones		Contour-tone examples:	
e̋ ˥ Top		ě ˩˥ Rising
é ˦ High		ê ˥˩ Falling
ē ˧ Mid		e᷄ ˦˥ High rising
è ˨ Low		e᷅ ˩˨ Low rising
ȅ ˩ Bottom		e᷈ ˥˧ High falling
Tone terracing		e᷉ ˧˩ Low falling
ꜛ Upstep		e᷈ ˧˥˧ Peaking
ꜜ Downstep		ẽ ˥˧˥ Dipping

DIACRITICS

Diacritics may be placed above a symbol with a descender, as ŋ̊. Other IPA symbols may appear as diacritics to represent phonetic detail: tˢ (fricative release), bʱ (breathy voice), ˀa (glottal onset), ᵊ (epenthetic schwa), oʷ (diphthongization).

SYLLABICITY & RELEASES		PHONATION		PRIMARY ARTICULATION		SECONDARY ARTICULATION			
n̩ ɹ̩	Syllabic	n̥ d̥	Voiceless or Slack voice	t̪ b̪	Dental	tʷ dʷ	Labialized	ɔ̹ x̹	More rounded
e̯ ʊ̯	Non-syllabic	s̬ d̬	Modal voice or Stiff voice	t̺ d̺	Apical	tʲ dʲ	Palatalized	ɔ̜ xʷ̜	Less rounded
tʰ ʰt	(Pre)aspirated	n̤ a̤	Breathy voice	t̻ d̻	Laminal	tˠ dˠ	Velarized	ẽ z̃	Nasalized
dⁿ	Nasal release	n̰ a̰	Creaky voice	u̟ t̟	Advanced	tˤ dˤ	Pharyngealized	ɚ ɝ	Rhoticity
dˡ	Lateral release	n̪͆ a̪͆	Strident	i̠ t̠	Retracted	ɫ z	Velarized or pharyngealized	e̘ o̘	Advanced tongue root
t̚	No audible release	n̼ d̼	Linguolabial	ä j̈	Centralized	ṳ̈	Mid-centralized	e̙ o̙	Retracted tongue root
e̞ β̞	Lowered (β̞ is a bilabial approximant)			e̝ ɹ̝	Raised (ɹ̝ is a voiced alveolar non-sibilant fricative, r̝ a fricative trill)				

Figure 3.1 *The IPA chart.*

the word *thigh* and another in the word *thy*. The letter "a" has a different sound in each of the following words: *cap*, *car*, and *caper*. Conversely, the sound [oo] has a variety of spellings: "oo" in *fool*, "u" in *ruler*, "ough" in *through*, and "ew" in *threw*. And the sound [ee] can be represented by all of "ee" in *sleep*, "ea" in *treat*, "ie" in *retriever*, "ei" in *receiver*, "y" in *folly*, and "i" in *Traci*.

It is for this reason that, in representing language sounds, we must adopt a standard and predictable system. The International Phonetic Alphabet (IPA) is one such system, and passes the basic requirements in place for any such system: (i) each symbol represents one sound and each sound is represented by one symbol, and (ii) each symbol always represents the same sound and each sound is always represented by the same symbol. Figure 3.1 shows a chart of the IPA,[3] which we will refer to occasionally in the rest of this chapter, and throughout the book. In representing sounds, though, we will not necessarily adopt the symbols and descriptions from the table, as they are rather technical and would take the reader far beyond the scope of this little book. And to the extent that we do so, we will make certain that they are accompanied by some plain-language description.

Phonetics (actual sounds) and phonemics (the idea of those sounds)

It is pretty easy to distinguish between sounds that are not language sounds (e.g. the "beep beep" of a truck backing up or the sound of a woodpecker hammering on a tree) from those that are. There is the English word *meow*, which consists of language sounds, [m]-[i]-[ae]-[w], and the actual sound that a cat makes, which doesn't.

However, when we talk about the sounds involved in human language, there are a number of ways that they can be described and categorized. We can, for instance, talk about the movements made by our lips, tongue, jaw, etc. in order to **articulate** (that is, pronounce) the sounds in question. For example, the first sound in the word *meow* is [m] and is produced by closing one's lips together (in contrast with the [n] in *now*). The two-lip ("bilabial") effort to produce an [m] sound is also used in making the [b] sound in *bow-wow* and the [p] sound in *pow*. Try saying each of these three words without allowing your lips to touch each other. You can't!

We can also talk about the nature of the sounds themselves (i.e. their **acoustics**) in describing them. For example, the first sound [s] in *see* and the first sound [ʃ][4] in the word *she* are similar in that they both sound like "white noise" or the sound of steam escaping from a pipe. They are also different in that the sound made by [s] is at a higher pitch than that made by [ʃ]—if you pronounce them in alternation, you will notice that the [s] sound corresponds to a "smaller" leak in the pipe than does the [ʃ] sound. In both of these cases, we are describing (either articulatorily or acoustically) the actual sounds produced or a manner of producing them. This is (articulatory or acoustic) **phonetics**.

There is yet another way to talk about language sounds. We can deal with them in terms of how they are perceived. For instance, we perceive some language sounds as belonging to the language that we speak (e.g. English in this case). And while we identify other sounds as true human language sounds, we also know that they are not part of the sound system of our own language. Take the German word *nacht* 'night' that we mentioned earlier. The first sound of this word is [n] and the same as the English word *night*. The second sound [ɑ] is the same vowel sound that occurs in the English word *hot*, and of course the last sound is the familiar [t]. What about the sound spelled with "ch?" It's not the "ch" sound of *chair* or *church*. Rather it is a sound that we represent with [x] (first table, third row of the IPA chart) and which we described earlier as a "strong h" sound. If you can't produce it or imagine it, ask a German speaker or someone who has studied German to produce it for you. One thing is certain—it is not a sound that belongs to the English language (that is, it is not part of the English **phonemic** system).

Besides knowing what sounds belong to the phonemic system of the language we speak, we are also acutely aware of how they may be arranged. For example, the sounds [p] as in *pear*, [ɑ] as in *hall*, [l] as in *full*, and [t] as in *hot* could be arranged in that order [p]-[ɑ]-[l]-[t] to form the nonsense word *palt*. Now, we assure you that *palt* is not by itself an English word . . . although the combination of letters and sounds shows up in *paltry*. *Palt* itself is the name of a traditional Swedish dish (meat-filled dumplings), and we understand that it's quite good when served with butter and lingonberry preserves. However, *palt* is not an English word.

Yet, it could be. That is, now that you know what *palt* means for a Swede, you would have no problem borrowing the word into English and using it. It sounds like a reasonable English word. But what if you took those same English sounds and rearranged them in a different order [t]-[l]-[ɑ]-[p] to make the word *tlap*? Not only would you not have an English word, you wouldn't even have a possible English word. While the sound sequence [t]-[l] does occur in some English words, such as *bottle*, no English word can **begin** with these two sounds. That fact is part of what we know about our language, and is part of our "phonemic" knowledge.

Another critical part of our phonemic knowledge has to do with the knowledge that groups of mostly similar but slightly distinct sounds "go together" in our language. Take for instance the sound [t] in the word *stop*. You may not have ever noticed before, but it differs ever so slightly from the first sound of the word *top*. The latter is accompanied by a small burst of air, while the former doesn't have this. You can discover this for yourself by pronouncing both words, *stop–top*, in alternation, while holding your fingers about one inch from your lips. You should feel the burst of air on your fingers with *top* but not with *stop*. The sound at the beginning of *top* is a t-like sound that is represented in the IPA chart (bottom table, third row) with a "t" accompanied by a small "h": [tʰ]. Both [t] and [tʰ] "count" as the same sound /t/ in the English phonemic system (although there are other languages, such as Chinese, which would count these as two distinct sounds).

Let's consider one more example. Take the words *leaf* and *pull*. If you pronounce them in alternation, very carefully, you may notice that the first sound in *leaf* and the last sound in *pull* do not sound exactly the same and that you don't produce them in exactly the same way. For the first sound in the word *leaf*, the tip of your tongue is pressed up against the gum ridge right behind your front teeth. For the last sound in the word *pull*, your tongue still touches the gum ridge, but the back (or body) of your tongue is also raised into the back of your mouth. The l-sound in *leaf* is called "light l" and is represented in the IPA chart with the letter [l] (top chart, eighth row). The l-sound at the end of *pull* is called "dark l" and is represented by an "l" with a squiggle or bar through it: [ɫ] (bottom chart, fifth row). These two l-sounds are indeed different, yet they both count as /l/ for a speaker of English. That is, despite the differences in how they sound and how they are made, if you ask a speaker of English whether *leaf* begins with the same sound that *pull* ends with, the answer you will get will be "yes." Even though they may "count" as the same sound, English speakers are quite sensitive to where they are used. The [l] sound is reserved for the beginning of words and [ɫ] only occurs at the end. Try saying *leaf* using the [ɫ] of *pull* at the beginning. You now sound like a Russian speaker trying to say *leaf*. If you turn this around and use the [l] from *leaf* at the end of *pull*, you will likely sound a bit like an Indian or Pakistani speaker of English.

A 1990 *Calvin and Hobbes* strip by Bill Watterson presents a very straightforward application of phonemic knowledge in the rendering of dialogue. The strip has Calvin coming into the house with his dad, holding his nose and wincing in pain. His mom asks, "Goodness, what happened?! You were only out there a minute!" Calvin's dad says, "A grounder bounced up and hit Calvin in the nose." As Calvin's mom is trying to tend to him, saying "Hold your head back, honey. Here's some more tissues," Calvin screams:

> I'b bleedig! By ode dad id tryig to gill me! . . . I'b nod playig badeball eddy more! Nebber again! I hade it!

The strip continues with his cynical dad saying, "I guess we can forget having a millionaire baseball player support us in our old age."

Laying the dad's wry cynicism aside, the linguistically interesting part of this cartoon consists of how Watterson delivers the effect of a bloody nose on Calvin's speech. While Watterson's "spelling" special effects are not precise from a phonetic point of view, he does capture some bits accurately. Calvin says *I'b* in place of *I'm*; *bleedig* instead of *bleeding*; *by* instead of *my*; *tryig* instead of *trying*; *playig* instead of *playing*; and *eddy* instead of *any*. As anyone who has had a seriously stuffed up nose can tell, we need to have air passing through our nose in order to produce "nasal" sounds like [m] and [n]. Thus, Calvin's attempt to say *my* with a bloody nose comes out sounding like *by*, and *any* comes out sounding like *eddy*. It is our knowledge of the English sound system (our phonemic knowledge) which allows Watterson to depict what Calvin should sound like with a bloody nose, and which allows us to decipher his rendition of that.

All of the above constitutes phonemic knowledge. That is, knowing which sounds "belong" to the language you speak (and which don't), knowing the possible orderings of these sounds, knowing which groups of similar sounds "count" as the same sound in your language, and knowing where each variant of a sound group can be properly inserted. We use this knowledge to speak our own language, understand the rapid and sometimes poorly articulated speech of others, figure out who speaks our dialect and who is not a native speaker of our language, and also to make jokes, puns, and play sound-based games with our own language. It is often the gap between the "phonetic" and the "phonemic" which is utilized to leverage all these.

Traversing the phonetic–phonemic divide

It is simply a fact that what we actually hear, sound-wise, is not what we consider ourselves to have heard. Take for instance this well-known, and usually respected, Big Ten school: Ohio State University. It is more often than not referred to simply by its initials, OSU. Carefully pronounced, we would render this as [ow]-[ɛs]-[yu]. Notice, however, what happens when you say OSU very rapidly and very casually. Unless you are really being careful, you will likely replace the [s] sound with the [ʃ] ("sh") sound, as in [owɛʃyu]. Now, if you say it this way, no one who knows the name of the school will think that you said "Oh Esh You." And if you quiz them about it, they will swear that they heard you say OSU even though you in fact did pronounce it as "Oh Esh You." So, what has happened? Your phonetic rendition of [ɛs] did indeed come out [ɛʃ] in rapid speech, but you intended it (phonemically) to be /ɛs/, and that is what anyone listening will have heard. From the perspective of (phonetic) articulation, it is easier to pronounce a [ʃ] sound before [y] (the tongue being in a similar position for both, than it is to pronounce [s] followed by [y]. So, [owɛʃyu] is easier to produce than [owɛsyu]. At the same time, the person hearing you produce [owɛʃyu] uses their phonemic knowledge of English (as well as the conversational context in which the sound is produced) to decode the phonetic changes that you've made, and correctly interprets it as /owɛsyu/.

There are a host of such changes that are done in the production of speech and then undone in its comprehension. One instance of this is the tendency to delete sounds that are difficult to pronounce or that are unstressed. Accordingly, we tend to pronounce the three-syllable name *Barbara* with the middle unstressed syllable left out: [bɑr-brɑ]. In producing a word with altogether too many consonants in a row, such as *sixths*, we tend to leave at least one out. So, where *six* has [ks] at the end and *sixth* has [ksθ] at the end, *sixths* will often be pronounced without the [s] that follows the [k] and will end in [kθs] instead of [ksθs]. The deletion of the [d] sound in the word *hands* (a common occurrence; think of the expression *clap hands* [klæp hænz]) plays a lead role in a fairly silly 1992 cartoon by Gary Larson in *The Far Side*®. In it, a farmer enters his bedroom grinning lasciviously. His wife is in the bed, with four chickens sitting on top of her, and she says to him:

> This is it, Maurice! I've warned you to keep your hens off me!

It is the frequent deletion of the [d] sound in the rapid-speech production of the word *hands* that powers this joke.

Just as deletion of sounds plays a role in the pronunciation of words, so does insertion. There are certain instances when it is difficult to produce a word without adding an extra sound. For example, take the words *prints* and *prince*. They both are usually pronounced as though they have the sound [t] right before the final [s]. Yet only the first one contains a /t/ in the mind of the speaker (that is, a phonemic /t/). From this, we obtain the joke that won't die (said or sung while standing around the One Hour Photo counter): "Someday my prints will come."

The July 4, 2001 edition of Johnny Hart's *B.C.* had the character B.C. announcing that "Today is Independence Day." Clumsy Carp responds, asking:

> Jim Jeffords has a day?[5]

To which Peter replies:

> No – You're thinking of independent's day.

The insertion of another consonant between the nasal sounds [n] and [m] and a following [s] is quite common. Where [t] is inserted between [n] and [s], [p] gets introduced between [m] and [s]. Compare the words *dumpster* and *hamster*. The first does indeed have a /p/ sound in it, and is quite clearly pronounced with the sound [p]. The second doesn't have a /p/, but is often pronounced as though it does. The insertion of [p] between [m] and [s] is so natural that many people frequently misspell the word as "hampster." To get a sense of how frequent this is, we note that while a Google search for the correctly spelled word *hamster* yields over 17 million results, searching for the incorrectly spelled *hampster* yields a not-shabby 421,000 hits. What is happening in each of these cases is that the transition from pronouncing a nasal consonant like [m] or [n] to pronouncing a following [s] is a difficult one. The inserted [p] or [t] makes the word easier to produce. Of course, the reason that [p] is inserted after [m] and [t] after [n] is that the inserted consonant is produced, in each case, in the same way as the one that precedes it. Take [m] and [p], for instance. Both are produced by closing both lips (bi-labial). So, if you are looking for a consonant to insert after [m], [p] would be the easiest one to use. In the same way, [n] and [t] are similar. Try saying *nest* and *test*, paying close attention to where your tongue is at the beginning of each word. You should notice that the tip of your tongue is, in each case, pressed up against the gum ridge behind your front teeth. So, [p] is a natural candidate for insertion after [m] and [t] is a natural candidate following [n].

Insertions of the sort that we're talking about here are frequent and natural enough to change the words in our language and how we perceive and spell them. It was [t] insertion, for example, that changed the Middle English exhortation *For peace sake!* into the Modern English *For Pete's sake!* Sorry to disappoint, but there never was a "Pete" . . . despite the appearance of a 1993 Quigmans cartoon (by Jeff Thompson and Buddy Hickerson) depicting "God and Pete arm wrestle to decide for whose sake it really is." The intrusion of [p] after [m] has also gradually changed the original spelling of many names:

> Simson became Simpson. (There are 631 Simsons and 124,000 Simpsons in the US)

> Thomson became Thompson. (There are 21,000 Thomsons and 450,000 Thompsons in the US)

> Hamton became Hampton. (There are 70 Hamtons and 53,000 Hamptons in the US)[6]

Words together, words apart

Word boundaries are another place where a speaker's phonetic pronunciations can collide with their phonemic intentions. Try saying *some ice* and *some mice* quickly, without pausing between the words. You may find that it is hard to keep the [m] sound at the end of *some* from also becoming the first sound in the second word: [m]. Or vice versa . . . it might sound as though both expressions involve *ice*. There are ways in which you can make these two expressions sound different, without pausing between the words. This would involve moving quickly and lightly through the [m] sound for *some ice*, and pressing the lips together harder and more deliberately on the [m] sound in *some mice*. That said, it is very clear that the boundaries between words are places where ambiguity thrives.

Mike Peters, creator of *Mother Goose and Grimm*, excels at this sort of word-boundary humor. In a 2006 strip, Attila (the cat) asks Grimmy (the dog):

> Anything in the fridge?

Grimmy, standing on a chair with his head deep inside, answers:

> Same mold, same mold.

The strip capitalizes on the fact that it is often difficult to figure out whether nasal consonants like [m] or [n] belong at the end of one word or at the beginning of the next. So, *same old* and *same mold* are liable to sound nearly identical, unless a speaker makes a special effort to distinguish them.

Again, this tendency has yielded some interesting changes in our language. The familiar word *orange* was borrowed into English through French (*orange*) and Italian (*arancio*) from Arabic (*naranj*). The [n] sound at the beginning of the Arabic word was likely lost through confusion with the [n] of the indefinite article *an* (or in French *une*). So, the French *une norange* (or something like it) becomes *une orange*. This change can travel in the opposite direction as well. Consider the unlikely pair of words used to distinguish male and female goats, *billy* and *nannie*. The male is signified by a male name, *Billy*. And the other? It is likely the result of peeling the [n] sound off of the word *an* before the female name, *Annie*. So, *a billy goat and an annie goat* becomes *a billy goat and a nannie goat*. The goats can't tell the difference either.

Another place where word boundaries tend to get confounded is between words that end or begin with the sound [s]. Consider the following phrases:

> this sky   (first word ends in [s], second word begins with [s])
> the sky   (second word begins with [s])
> this guy   (first word ends in [s])

If you say these three phrases rapidly, in quick succession, it is hard to tell them apart. There are altogether too many opportunities for humor just with the examples above. The phrase *the sky* is often understood, misunderstood, or revised as *this guy*, turning the Chicken Little story on its head, by having her announce (as in numerous cartoons):

> "This guy is falling! This guy is falling!"

This Guy is Falling also appeared as the title of a 2000 indie romantic-comedy-adventure-action-disaster short movie by Gareth Smith.[7] The ubiquity of this type of misheard phrase/pun has extended so far as to lend itself to the name of a well-known website/archive for misheard song lyrics: www.kissthisguy.com. The domain name derives from a line in the lyrics of the 1967 Jimi Hendrix song *Purple Haze*. The first stanza is:

> Purple haze all in my brain
> Lately things just don't seem the same
> Actin' funny, but I don't know why
> Scuse me while I kiss the sky

It is the last line which is commonly misheard as "Scuse me while I kiss this guy." This mishearing was apparently so pervasive and well known to Hendrix himself that he actually performed it that way at several shows in Washington DC in 1968. The "Kiss This Guy" website has the story and a video of him singing it this way.[8]

So, how is it that a word ending in [s] immediately followed by a word beginning with [g] comes to sound identical to a word beginning with [sk]? That is, how do we confuse the [g] and the [k] so readily? To understand this, we need to go back to our earlier discussion of the difference between the /t/ sounds in the words *stop* and *top*. Recall that when /t/ is at the beginning of a word, not preceded by "s," it is accompanied by a small burst of air (aspiration). The /t/-sound pronounced without aspiration (in *stop*) is represented as [t], and the one with aspiration (in *top*) is represented as [t^h]. The very same difference is found with /k/-sounds. The sound following the [s] in *skein* has no aspiration (and is written as [k]) while the first sound in *cane* does have it (and is represented as [k^h]). Now, it is also true that the first sound in *gain* (the sound [g]) also does not have any aspiration. If you place your fingers an inch in front of your lips and recite these three words—*skein, cane, gain*—you will find aspiration only at the beginning of the second. Also notice that [k] and [g] are pronounced with the tongue in the same position, raised into the back of the mouth. So, it turns out that [k] preceded by [s] sounds a lot like [g], in that they both involve the same tongue position and neither have aspiration.

Word pastimes

Having gone over the nature of spelling and sound, and the gap between the idea of sound and its properties and production, we can now briefly review some entertaining types of word-play that are based, at least in part, on the sounds that make up words. We will discuss *spoonerisms*, *malapropisms*, and *mondegreens*.[9]

Spoonerisms

Spoonerisms are named for William Archibald Spooner, a nineteenth-century Oxford dean who was renowned for tips of the slung (that is, slips of the tongue). Spoonerisms involve the swapping of individual sounds or syllables between the words in a phrase. These can be accidental or intentional, and the result is often amusing. Like many who commit such slips of the tongue, Spooner was notorious for stumbling on his words in this way when he was excited or agitated. A spoonerism most often involves swapping the first sounds of two words in a phrase, as Spooner is reported to have done on trying to salute Queen Victoria with a toast:

> Three cheers for our **qu**eer old **d**ean!

Notice that the words need not be adjacent. On other occasions, other sounds (such as the vowel sounds) might be swapped, as when Spooner (officiating at a wedding) swapped an "i" a "u" and intoned:

> It is now k**i**sstomary to c**u**ss the bride.

The swapped elements of a spoonerism may involve more than single sounds, as when all the word-initial consonants of two words are switched, here [h] with [pl]:

> **pl**eating and **h**umming

Entire syllables may also be swapped, as with the spoonerized title of this fairy tale:

> Goldie **bear** and the three **lock**s[10]

The mechanism by which sounds switch places is called metathesis, and is a process that shows up in more than spoonerized slips of the tongue. The sounds [s] and [k] are frequent candidates for switching, as can be seen from the fact that the word *ask* [æsk] was formerly pronounced [æks], and now appears (in some dialects) to be turning back to [æks] again.

Using a spoonerism is a great way for a cartoonist to show that a character is nervous or excited, since that is when we are most likely to commit these errors. In a 2001 edition of *Zits*, teenage Jeremy's dentist father is introducing him to a colleague:

JEREMY'S DAD:	Jeremy, this is my roommate from dental school, Dr. Siddiqi.
JEREMY:	[shaking his hand] Nice to meet you.
JEREMY'S DAD:	... and this is his wife, Aliya...
JEREMY:	[shaking her hand] Nice to meet you.
JEREMY'S DAD:	... and their daughter, Amira. [Amira is pretty enough for the sky to open up and the angels to sing ... as shown in the panel.]
JEREMY:	[shaking her hand all too vigorously] Meese to nite you.
AMIRA:	You're hurting my arm!!

Jeremy's spoonerism helps us to know that he's nervous, excited, and smitten.

Malapropisms

Another related category of verbal slip-ups (also typically involving sound substitutions) are called malapropisms. These do not entail the metathesis (sound swaps) typical of spoonerisms, but do instead involve the replacement of one word (or more) with a similar sounding word. Typically, the best of these make nonsense or new sense out of a familiar phrase, such as when former president George W. Bush replaced the word *hostage* with *hostile* in this quote:

> "We cannot let terrorists and rogue nations hold this nation hostile or hold our allies hostile."

The term malapropism comes from the French *mal à propos* (where *mal* means 'bad' and *mal à propos* is the opposite of *à propos* 'appropriate'). Eighteenth-century playwright Richard Sheridan used this expression *mal à propos* to name a character, Mrs. Malaprop, in his play *The Rivals*. True to her name, the Mrs. Malaprop in the play was a fount of verbal slip-ups, such as:

> "He is the very pine-apple of politeness!" [pinnacle]

Sometimes malapropisms are born out of misunderstandings about, or ignorance of, word meanings. Children typically do this, replacing words that they don't understand (like *moss*) with others that are familiar. In a 2007 panel of Bill Keene's *Family Circus*, Dolly tells her little brother,

> Mrs. Clarke told our class, "A rolling stone gathers no moths."

We have experienced similar instances, where one of our children has come home from school reporting that some of the other kids have "head lights" [head lice]. The best of these involve a combination of phonological similarity and a new meaning that is funny, as in the following samples plucked from the Web:

> He's a wolf in cheap clothing. [sheep's]
> Michelangelo painted the Sixteenth Chapel. [Sistine]

Perhaps one of the more memorable (and intentional) of these is a 1992 panel by Andrew Lehman, showing a heavy-set man standing over a wok on a kitchen range, thinking "God, I'm sick of stir fry. Do I really want to cook healthy again?" The caption for the panel:

> "Caught between a wok and a lard place."

Mondegreens

Like malapropisms, mondegreens also involves linguistic, and often sound-based, slips. But where the first involve spoken errors, mondegreens are instances where something is misheard (and then misinterpreted). We examined one of these, Hendrix' "'Scuse me while I kiss this guy," in the section on word boundaries. It is, of course, hard sometimes to say whether something is a malapropism or a mondegreen without knowing how it came about.

Many mondegreens come about as a result of children mishearing (and reinterpreting) something that they cannot otherwise understand, such as:

> I pledge allegiance to the United States,
> And to the republic of Richard Stanz . . .

In fact the name for the phenomenon, mondegreen, is itself a mondegreen and was coined by Sylvia Wright. When she was a child, Wright was introduced to the Scottish ballad titled "The Bonny Earl of Murray," which contains the following lyrics:

> Ye highlands and ye lowlands
> Oh where hae you been?
> Thou hae slay the Earl of Murray
> and laid him on the green,

In place of the last line, Wright heard the equally plausible and slightly more tragic:

> And Lady Mondegreen

From this was born a name for misheard lyrics, and misheard practically anything else. As we noted before, the "Kiss This Guy" website is an archive and treasure trove of misheard song lyric mondegreens. And while some are silly and some appear to be fabrications, many are priceless. Anyone who remembers Credence Clearwater's song *Bad Moon Rising* and its lyric "There's a bad moon on the rise" will appreciate the misheard "There's a bathroom on the right." And "the girl with kaleidoscope eyes" from The Beatles' song *Lucy in the Sky with Diamonds* has become (for some individuals with even stranger imaginations):

> "The girl with colitis goes by."

There are many more, enough to make it worth a visit.

Having worked through some of the important aspects of language sounds, our next chapter will turn to an examination of the words and other bits of meaning that these sounds are used to represent.

4   Twisted words

Word structure and meaning

Lucy is trying to come up with a word.[1] She knows more or less what she wants to say, but she's not sure how to get that meaning into a form that would count as an acceptable English word. In this chapter, we will first try to understand Lucy's problem and try to explain why she is so unsure and guesses as she does. In the rest of the chapter, we will continue to look at various aspects of words. We will examine how they are formed, from compounding to idioms to the use of brand names. We will also explore how words come to have the meanings that they do.

Prefixes, suffixes ... affixes

The first and most common kind of word formation involves taking a word and adding some non-word bit to it. If the bit is added at the beginning, we call it a prefix. The *pre* part of *prefix* is a prefix. So is the *un* part of *unkind*. If it's added at the end, we call it a suffix. The *ed* part of *added* is a suffix, as is the *ing* part of *beginning*. There are even infixes, which are bits inserted right into the middle of a word. In the Philippine language Tagalog (pronounced tuh-GA-lug), the infinitive of a verb is formed by sticking *um* after the first consonant. So, the verb *sulat* (meaning 'write') becomes *sumulat* 'to write', and *basa* 'read' becomes *bumasa* 'to read'. English doesn't much go in for infixes, except in the case of expletives. We often observe the insertion of *fuckin* or *bloody* into the middle of a word to provide emphasis, as in *fan-fuckin-tastic* or *abso-bloody-lutely*.[2] Another, more recently noted kind of infixation in English is that attributed to the Homer Simpson and Ned Flanders characters in *The Simpsons*. These are known as *ma*-infixation (or "Homeric" infixation) in the first case and

40

diddly-infixation in the second.[3] Those who know the TV show will be familiar with Homer Simpson's *wonder-ma-ful* and *secre-ma-tary*. And while Homer might say that his daughter Lisa plays the *saxa-ma-phone*, he would not refer to it as a *sa-ma-xaphone* or say that something is *won-ma-derful*. Ned Flanders is known for saying things like *wel-diddly-elcome* and *or-diddly-order*. He does not ever say anything like *wel-diddly-come* or *or-diddly-der*. Unlike "Homeric" infixation, Ned's variety involves the repetition of sounds on each side of *diddly*, making it a little more complicated than a simple infix. Then again, Ned is a more "complicated" character than Homer, so perhaps that's not surprising.

For our purposes, though, we really don't need to "fix"-ate on the position of these additions (that is, whether they are pre-, suf-, or in-). We can, and will, just call them all affixes. The attempts that Lucy makes to create the right word in the cartoon strip above are all attempts at affixation, and we should acknowledge that Lucy's confusion in this task is not surprising, nor even insurprising or antisurprising. Why is this? Well, for one thing, several of her guesses at the negative counterpart of *obvious* are perfectly reasonable and logical. *Un-*, *in-*, *dis-*, *non-*, and *anti-* are all perfectly good English prefixes which can or usually mean *not*. Consider the following examples:

unreal	=	not real
insincere	=	not sincere
disbelieve	=	not believe
noncompliant	=	not compliant
antimatter	=	not matter; the opposite of matter

So at the very least, *unobvious*, *inobvious*, *disobvious*, *nonobvious*, and *antiobvious* all have the logical potential to mean 'not obvious'. So why don't they? Because determining which prefixes or suffixes in English go with which words is often quite arbitrary. Looking back at the examples above, we see that we cannot shift these perfectly good negative prefixes around and apply them to the other words in the list. *Antireal*, *unsincere*, *inbelieve*, and *discompliant* are all "non-words" of the English language. Only *non-matter* might stand as an exception (although it doesn't mean the same thing as *antimatter*).

We don't have to look very far to see other examples of this. For instance, the English suffix *-ment* can be added to a verb, such as *govern*, to form a noun *government* which means 'the act of governing or an institution that governs'. Similarly, the suffix *-tion* can be added to a verb, such as *educate*, to form a noun *education* which means 'the act of educating or the outcome of educating'. What is not possible, for no particularly logical reason, is to add *-ment* to *educate* or to add *-tion* to *govern*. Neither *educatement* nor *governtion* are words of the English language, although they are certainly "possible" words.

Affixes like *dis-* and *-ment* are what we call "derivational" affixes, in that we "derive" new words from them. Typically, they change the meaning and/or the part of speech of the word that they attach to. Derivational affixes are also "irregular." That is, they each combine only with an arbitrary subset of all the words that they potentially **could** combine with. We therefore arbitrarily have the words:

> disable, disappear, disrepair, disapprove
> advertisement, retirement, judgment, entitlement

and just as arbitrarily do not have the words:

> discapable, dismaterialize, dismend, disendorse
> publicizement, rehirement, arbitratement, distractment

Alongside the menagerie of derivational affixes, there is another quite different group called "inflectional" affixes. These don't form a new and different word when we attach them (in the sense that the plural of a noun or the past tense of a verb isn't a distinct word from its base). They are also much more "regular" than the derivational type. In English, these are always suffixes, and include -*ing* and -*ed* which attach to verbs, and plural -*s* or -*es* which attach to nouns. In contrast with the irregular derivational affix -*ment*, which only attaches to a small and unpredictable set of words, the verbal suffix -*ing* happily affixes itself to every verb of the language. The plural noun suffix -*s*/-*es* would readily attach to every noun of the language, except that some nouns are already appropriated by the "irregular" plural -*en* (*children*), while others "irregularly" don't have any plural form at all (*fish, sheep*).

So, what's the difference between the "derivational" and "inflectional" groups described above? Well, for one thing, the "inflectional" affixes are typically "grammatical." By this we simply mean that they have more to do with the insertion of words into sentences, than with the creation of new words. The verbal suffix -*ing* does a better job of illustrating this, as it is most often added to a verb in order to determine the tense of the entire sentence (using some form of the verb *be* as an accomplice in this). So,

> They buy books.

is "simple present" tense, while

> They are buying books.

which uses *are* and -*ing* together, is "present progressive" tense (explicitly describing an ongoing activity). It's a bit harder to understand the plural -*s* as having anything to do with "grammar" per se, but it is clear that adding it to a word does not really give us a new word. The sentence

> The boy bought the book.

and the sentence

> The boys bought the books.

both contain the same words in the sense that we do not consider *boy* and *boys* to be "different" words as much as the singular and plural form of the same word.

Now contrast this with our derivational affixes. These are, without question, "new word creators." Add the suffix *-able* to a transitive verb (such as *love*, *wash*, *fold*) and you'll get an adjective that means 'able to be whatever it is that the verb means'. Thus, *readable* means 'able to be read' and *foldable* means 'able to be folded'. There is also no word *faintable*, since *faint* is not transitive. Of course, there is no word combining the transitive verb *terminate* with *-able* (*terminatable*), although we have *terminable* which is an odd construction of the "rump" of *terminate*, *termin*, plus *-able*. But then, remember that these affixes are all irregular (at least to some small extent).

The prefix *re-*, added to an appropriate verb, means 'do whatever it was that the verb means . . . again'; *refold* is 'fold again', *rewash* is 'wash again', and so on. Of course, *re-eat* doesn't work since one can't eat something "again." And once again, the unpredictability of the class leads us not to be surprised that there is no word *repromise* ('promise again', in contrast with *reconvince*) . . . although there could be.

Coming back to Lucy, what is it that makes her response to Linus so amusing? First, there's the fact that she's a child (that is, a person who is still learning the language). We wouldn't expect an adult to be quite so confused, and Lucy's words coming from an adult wouldn't be credible (in that we wouldn't perceive the errors as naïve). Children, learning language, are quite often in the position of not knowing how the pieces fit together. So, Lucy's mistaken attempt to combine *in-* with *obvious* is totally believable. We find that children regularly make mistakes of this sort, and especially with the derivational affixes described earlier. Substituting *foots* or *feets* for the correct form *feet*, for example, is something that almost every child does at one stage or another. However, Lucy's experimentation with "irregular" word-creating prefixes is rather over the top, even for a child. Where children might frequently be expected to get the pieces of a word wrong, such as *yellowmade* for *lemonade* or *feetses* for *feet*, they usually stick with their mistake until they unlearn it. Lucy's response is funny because it is both believable in each of its parts (that is, each mistake is more or less credible for a child) and over-the-top as a whole (that is, no child would make so many wrong guesses). But then, Lucy is headstrong, as we all know, and her headstrong overabundant answer is both typical for her and funny.

Compound words

Affixation is not the only way to form new words, nor even the most productive way. Another way is to just stick two words together to form a new one. Put together *milk* and *man*, and you have the compound *milkman*. English has been forming "compound words" this way for at least 1,000 years, with some words like *sunbeam* going back that far. Of course, compounding is not simple addition...

> A: "What's that?"
> B: "A walnut."
> A: "What's it doing on the floor?"

Yes, a *sunbeam* is a beam of light emanating from the sun, and makes a good pair with *moonbeam* (of course, stars aren't bright enough to project *starbeams*). But once two words are compounded, they are free to wander far from their original meaning. That is to say, there's no way to accurately predict their relationship. The word *man*, in compounds such as *milkman*, has a wide range of meanings.

milkman	person who brings milk
fireman	person who helps put out fires
garbageman	person who takes away garbage
snowman	a snow sculpture in the shape of a person
hitman	a person hired to kill someone

The only thing that all these have in common is that they somehow involve the notion 'person' or 'man'. So, while a *milkman* delivers milk, you really don't want your *garbagemen* or *firemen* bringing garbage or fire. And while an 8½ by 14 inch pad of paper is a *legal pad*, that doesn't mean that an 8½ by 11 inch pad is illegal.

In addition to combining nouns, we can form words by compounding a noun with an adjective, as in *wine-red*, or an adjective with a noun, as in *red wine*. In every case, though the meaning of the compound typically derives in some manner from the original meaning of the compounded parts, it does not do so transparently. In noun + noun compounds, sometimes the first noun tells you what the second one is made of or with, as in *cheesecake* or *apple pie*. Sometimes you hope that it doesn't, as in *shepherd pie* (more commonly known as *shepherd's pie*) or *Girl-scout cookies*. Or you find out that it does, and wish you hadn't, as in *headcheese*. Of course, the relationship between the parts is quite arbitrary and unstable. The thing referred to by the noun + noun compound *cheesecake* is made from the first noun, but *snow tires* are not.

One fact worth noting about compounds (and about words formed from affixes, as we will see shortly) is that it is the right-hand side of the word that tells you what part of speech it belongs to. Accordingly, adjective + noun compounds such as *red wine* are nouns, and noun + adjective compounds such as *wine-red* are adjectives. This principle applies when nouns and verbs are compounded as well:

verb + noun = noun	*pick + pocket = pickpocket*
noun + verb = verb	*sky + dive = skydive*

This right-handedness of formed words also extends to affixes, the central principle being that only suffixes (and never prefixes) alter the part of speech of the words they attach to. So, an adjective with a prefix such as *un* + *real* is still an adjective, *unreal*. A noun with a prefix such as *anti* + *matter* is still a noun, *antimatter*. On the other hand, suffixes such as *-ment* turn verbs into nouns, e.g. *government*, *establishment*, and *confinement*. The suffix *-able* turns verbs into adjectives, as in *loveable*, *laughable*, and *predictable*.

Returning again, briefly, to compounds, one might ask: How do you know when you have a compound word (that is a new word made out of fused word-parts) and when you just have a series of autonomous words? The answer, it turns out, has little to do with spelling practice. Spelling a compound as a single word (*sunbeam*), inserting a hyphen (*wine-red*), or leaving a space (*apple pie*) varies arbitrarily from word to word, and is of less significance than one would imagine. It is true that *highchair* is a compound word (referring to a toddler feeding station), while *high chair* might simply be a chair with a seat that is inordinately elevated off the ground. You don't need a space bar or a typed text to tell the difference though. The toddler-entrapment-feeding-station is pronounced with an accent on the first part, <u>*high*chair</u>, while the chair with the high seat is pronounced with equal stress on both parts, <u>*high chair*</u>. The same is true for all compounds. A <u>*black bird*</u> could be a raven, a crow, or a blackbird, while <u>*blackbird*</u> refers to any one of thirty-one specific species of birds, none of which are crows or ravens, and some of which have grey wings or scarlet heads.

Clipping old words and growing new ones

Another quite productive way of getting new words involves something called clipping (that is, lopping off some major bit of them). You can clip off the end, so that *mathematics* becomes *math*, *chemistry* becomes *chem*, and *biology* becomes *bio*. You can take the clipped bit from *biology*, add it to *chemistry* as in *biochemistry*, and then clip that, *biochem*. Or you can clip off the beginning, getting *gator* from *alligator* or *phone* from *telephone*. Putting the clipped bits of a compound together can get *motel* out of *motor hotel* or *sci-fi* from *science fiction*. This is all pretty arbitrary, though, as we don't have *geo* (*geography*), *phys* (*physics*), or *hist* (*history*) classes.

One very productive way to get lots of yardage from these "clippings" involves generating series of words from the tail end of one. The word *alcoholic* is a good example. It involves the noun *alcohol* plus a suffix *-ic* that turns nouns into adjectives (e.g. *German* → *Germanic*, *mania* → *manic*, *cycle* → *cyclic*). So, *alcoholic* means something containing alcohol, *alcoholic drink*, and then by extension someone affected by alcoholism. The piece *-holic* means nothing by itself, but has come to mean 'someone with an addiction to or compulsion for . . . whatever word bit precedes it'. From this we get *shopaholic*, *chocoholic*, *carbaholic*, and *sexaholic*. The *-gate* from the Watergate Hotel scandal of the Nixon administration is the scandal term that keeps on giving, *contragate* (the 1980s Iran-contra scandal), *Kofi-gate* (the purported 1990s abuse of an oil-for-food program by former UN Secretary General Kofi Annan), and *troopergate* (surfacing three times in reference to scandal allegations in the Clinton administration in 1993, against New York governor Eliot Spitzer in 2007, and against Alaska governor Sarah Palin in 2008). From the *-tainment* of *entertainment*, we get entertainment-oriented journalism labeled as *infotainment*. Bill Griffith (creator of Zippy) imagines his protagonist finding progressively more banal diversion in *infotainment*, *confrontainment* (i.e. confrontational reality shows), and finally *laundrotainment* (i.e. watching the washing machine at the coin laundry).

Idioms

In common parlance, the word *idiom* is often used to refer to a manner of speaking that is natural to the speakers of a particular language, or to some smaller group of them as defined by profession, region, class, or ethnicity. Here, we will use the term "idiom" in a narrower sense. An "idiom" is a word-like expression, but not a word in the way described thus far above. That is, it doesn't involve the mechanics of combining whole words, clipped bits of words, or affixes into new words. But it is word-like in one sense: it is a fixed expression (a fixed and frozen string of words) whose single meaning is not directly calculable from the meaning of its parts.

Let's notice first of all how the expression is frozen. A child, Julie, complains to the teacher, "Amy made a face at me!" and the teacher understands what that means. If Amy makes a face at Julie again, Julie would say "Amy made a face at me, again," "Amy made that face at me, again," or "Amy is still making faces at me," but not "Amy made two faces at me." That is, the expression *make a face* (with its idiomatic meaning) necessarily involves the indefinite article *a* and the singular noun *face* or else the bare plural noun *faces*. If a speaker says *make two faces*, *make the face*, or *make many faces*, we do not interpret any of these as an instance of the idiom *make a face*. Neither can we replace the verb *make* with a synonym and retain the idiom. None of *create a face*, *construct a face*, or *compose a face* can have the idiomatic meaning of *make a face*.

Not only is the idiom "frozen" in terms of the very specific words which form it, but it's also fixed in regard to word order. That is, the pieces of an idiom cannot always be moved around in a sentence.

Frankenstein's monster gets into an argument at a bar and says:

"You want a piece of me? Huh? Huh? You want a piece of me?"

The humor arises out of the play between the literal meaning of *a piece of me* (Frankenstein's monster presumably has a lot of these) and the idiomatic challenge to fight: *You want a piece of me?* This idiom can't be passivized: *Is a piece of me wanted by you?* doesn't have the idiomatic meaning any more.

As Ray Jackendoff suggests, idioms are ultimately not that much different than other sorts of opaque and semi-opaque lexical compounds that we've already looked at.[4] *Take someone to the cleaners* involves relieving them of their money or possessions. You don't have to take them anywhere. And while *the cleaners* certainly does evoke the particular reference to a retail dry-cleaning establishment (as opposed to, say, a commercial carpet-cleaning company), no such establishment is involved in the actual meaning of the idiom. Similarly, while *crew cut* does involve (at least historically) reference to the sort of haircut sported by a member of a rowing crew, such a haircut certainly doesn't evoke membership in a rowing club.

Thus, both idioms and compounds can contain words whose literal meaning does not actually contribute directly to the meaning of the whole, but is only suggestive. Neither the idiom *butter him up* nor the compound *peanut butter* actually involve butter. Along the same lines, both idioms and compounds can contain parts that are not actual words, parts that don't mean anything at all by themselves. Neither *amok* in the idiom *running amok* nor *cran* in the compound *cranberry* have any meaning or use alone. Further, individual words that appear in a variety of idioms and compounds don't necessarily have a stable role. As we have seen earlier in the chapter, the word *man*, in compounds such as *milkman* and *snowman*, has a wide range of meanings relative to the noun that it follows (with only some vague notion of 'person-hood' being common to all of them). Likewise, the verb *eat* appears in a range of idioms that have nothing to do with actual eating (a fact that did not prevent Roz Chast from picturing, in a cartoon from the 1990s, a diner with *Your Words*, *Your Hat*, *Crow*, and *My Dust* on the menu).

Reduplication

One final kind of word formation process worth talking about is *reduplication* (a funny word in itself since it means 'copying a word or word part to make a new word' ... *duplication* might have been sufficient). It is used in many languages to express things such as verb tense and plurality.

Tagalog (a language of the northern Philippines) copies the first syllable of verbs to form the future tense:

Verb root	Future
tawag 'call'	*ta-tawag* 'will call'

Japanese and Chinese have some reduplications that form plurals:

Chinese
ren 'person'   *renren* 'everybody'
Japanese
toki 'time'   *tokidoki* 'from time to time'

English also duplicates words on a regular basis, although this is less recognized as anything standard or regular in the language. There are plenty of rhyming copies and partial copies (with changed vowels), such as *flip-flop*, *ship-shape*, *criss-cross*, *okey-dokey*, and *hanky-panky*. There is also reduplication to provide emphasis. So, when someone asks *Are you tired, or TIRED-tired?*, we understand them to mean 'are you tired or very tired?' This doubled occurrence of *tired* is contrastive with a word in the first part of the sentence, and the first copy needs to be stressed (i.e. louder). So, while you can say,

> I'll bring the tuna salad, and you bring the SALAD-salad.

You cannot say,

> I'll bring the tuna salad, and you bring the salad-SALAD.

That is, the first occurrence of *salad* contrasts with *tuna* and has to be louder than the second. Alongside this pattern, we also find that three (never two) copies of a word at the end of a sentence can mean *very* (or carry the intensifying meaning of *very*). So, instead of saying *You are very mean*, I might instead say:

> You are mean, mean, mean!

I would not, however, say

> **X** You are mean, mean![5]

to get that same meaning.

Another form of reduplication, originally particular to New York and now spread throughout American English, is the Yiddish-inspired *shm-* reduplication. *Shm-* reduplication is commonly known as "deprecative" reduplication because it deprecates or denigrates whatever it's applied to. Someone deriding my profession might say *Linguist-shminguist, I don't think he knows anything about language*. The most famous *shm-* person, of course, would be *Joe Shmo* (also known as *Joe Blow*). This name is a generic term for someone who is rather ordinary, and not special in any way (observe the deprecation or belittling effect of the *schm-* copy). And one well-worn joke using this device goes:

> A: I have to tell you, madam, that your son is suffering from an Oedipus complex.
> B: Oedipus, Schmoedipus! What does it matter so long as he loves his mother?

The device is rather productive for people who use it, and can be added to most any word. For words that begin with a vowel, *shm-* is simply added to the word, as in *apple-shmapple*. If the word begins with a consonant, then *shm-* often replaces the consonant, as in *fancy-shmancy*.[6]

Brands and generics

This discussion on word formation should not end without considering the creation of brand names from common words and its inverse, the creation of common words from brand names. Certainly, if I tell you that I just bought an Impala, you will not think I am in possession of an African antelope (the name *impala* comes from the Zulu language of South Africa). The Chevrolet model name, which has been around for over fifty years, is the more common use for the word *impala* than its African source. We don't have to look far to find other examples. In a recent panel of Dana Summers' *Bound and Gagged*, a couple of butterflies are hovering around a Caterpillar bulldozer as one remarks, "I can't wait to see what **that** turns into."

Of all the branding traditions one can think of, using common nouns to create car names is perhaps the most widespread. In addition to animal species, we find car models named after trees (*Chrysler Aspen*), natural disasters (*Chevrolet Avalanche*), chemical elements (*Chevrolet Cobalt*), professions (*Dodge Diplomat* and *Subaru Forester*), sports (*Volkswagen Golf*), criminal activities (*Chrysler Prowler*), and geographical regions (*Toyota Tundra*). Sometimes, model names are drawn from other languages (*Isuzu Amigo*, *amigo* being Spanish for 'friend'), places (*Chevrolet Colorado* and *Hyundai Tucson*), and peoples (*Volkswagen Touareg*, the *Touareg* being a nomadic Saharan tribe living in Algeria, Libya, Mali, and Niger).

Certainly, the choice of which nouns should be used for model names is a delicate art. It is hard to imagine a market for a *Chrysler Oak*, a *Chevrolet Mudslide*, a *Chevrolet Tin*, a *Dodge Bureaucrat*, a *Subaru Fisherman*, a *Volkswagen Ping-pong*, a *Chrysler Pickpocket*, a *Toyota Rainforest*, an *Isuzu Enemigo* (i.e. 'enemy'), a *Chevrolet Iowa*, a *Hyundai Pittsburgh*, or a *Volkswagen Serb*. Moreover, names that work in one language can be a disaster in another. The Buick LaCrosse had to be renamed when it was introduced into Canada, on account of the fact that *se crosser* is a colloquial French Canadian word meaning 'masturbate'. Apparently, the same problem occurred when Mitsubishi introduced its Pajero in Spanish-speaking countries, where *pajero* means 'masturbator'. Other similar marketing disasters included the Toyota Fiera in Puerto Rico (*fiera* meaning 'ugly old woman' there) and the Ford Pinto in Brazil (*pinto* in Brazilian Portuguese being a 'small penis').[7]

The inverse of turning common words into brand names is using brand names as common nouns. This process is called "genericization." Examples of this abound.

> Earlier, while walking along carrying my Frisbee and playing with my Hackey Sack, I slipped on some jell-o that Jack spilled on the linoleum floor. Luckily, I didn't cut myself and didn't need a band-aid. But I was afraid that my ankle would swell up, so I took some aspirin. After cleaning the jell-o off my hands and feet with a Kleenex, I had to find a Q-tip to dig the mess out of the Hackey Sack. I then turned off the crock-pot, and went out to let Jack (who was lying in the Jacuzzi) know what a slob he is.

Each underlined word in this paragraph either was, or still is, a brand name. If we were to remove the former and current brand names from the paragraph, it would read as follows:

Earlier, while walking along carrying my flying disk and playing with my foot bag, I slipped on some gelatin dessert that Jack spilled on the linoxyn-based floor covering. Luckily, I didn't cut myself and didn't need an adhesive bandage. But I was afraid that my ankle would swell up, so I took some acetylsalicylic acid. After cleaning the gelatin dessert off my hands and feet with a facial tissue, I had to find a cotton swab to dig the mess out of the foot bag. I then turned off the slow cooker, and went out to let Jack (who was lying in the hot tub) know what a slob he is.

It is clear from a comparison of the two paragraphs that we genericize lots of words. This is, in fact, an ongoing problem for the manufacturers of popular products. How do you have the most popular item on the store shelves, without losing control of its name?

Q-tips, currently manufactured by Unilever, were originally called *Baby Gays* and later renamed as *Q-Tips* (devised as a shortening for "Quality"-tips).[8] The name Q-tip is obviously so popular that almost no one refers to them any longer by their common noun designation "cotton swab." In fact, one might venture to guess that there are plenty of people who can identify a Q-tip, who could not tell you what *cotton swab* means. While this might help people recognize Q-Tips (the official brand) on the store shelves—a benefit to Unilever—it does not always play to Unilever's advantage, since someone going to a pharmacy to "pick up some Q-tips" is just as likely to come out, satisfied, with a package of store-brand cotton swabs.

It was this very problem that the led Xerox Corporation to insist on people using the term *photocopying* rather than *Xeroxing* to describe the process of making copies. This is probably a good thing, since *xerography* (the name given to a process originally called *electro-photography*) is slightly different from *photocopying*. As originally patented, xerography consisted of creating an electrostatic image directly on lightweight paper, and developing that image with toner and a heat process. The copiers that we are most familiar with (i.e. the ones that actually *photocopy*) develop the desired copy image onto a rotating drum, and then transfer the toner-image onto paper in a two-step process. The Xerox Corporation's goals, of course, were less about service to accuracy, and more about keeping its name from becoming a generic word in the English language and thereby losing or weakening their trademark protection.[9]

Sound-alikes, spell-alikes, and shades of meaning

Having spent quite a bit of space discussing how words are formed, we should not end this discussion without a foray into how words "mean," that is, how the meanings of words are arranged in our consciousness. One very important distinction, which propels a good deal of humor but which is sometimes not easy to sort out, is the difference between two or more words that happen to have the same sound, and one word which has acquired several meanings.

The first of these two types is often the most obvious, and goes by the name *homophone* (meaning 'same sound'). A good example of this is found in a 2001 *Fox Trot* panel, where Jason Fox and his friend Marcus have lined up seven carved pumpkins along a wall. They've carved into them in succession: the numeral "3," a decimal point, the numeral "1," the numeral "4," the numeral "1," the numeral "5," and the numeral "9." Jason tells his sister:

> We're calling it "pumpkin pi."

The play here is between the homophone pair *pie*, as in *pumpkin pie*, and *pi* (or π), the mathematical constant expressing the circumference of a circle divided by its diameter. Notice that while *pie/pi* sound the same, they are not spelled the same. Alongside *homophone*, we can speak of *homographs*. These, as the name suggests, are pairs of words that are spelled the same (that is, have the same **graphic** representation), even if they don't sound the same. A good example of this would be the word *tears*, which is pronounced differently depending on whether it's a verb:

> Whenever he makes a mistake, he **tears** another sheet of paper out of the notepad.

or a noun:

> Whenever he makes a mistake, he sheds a lot of **tears**.

In case a pair of words are both a *homophone* and a *homograph* (sound and are spelled the same), then we can call them *homonyms*. A good example of a full homonym pair are the words *bear* (a noun referring to the animal that we try to keep out of campgrounds) and *bear* (the verb meaning *to carry*).

Let's turn to the second category we mentioned above, that involving one word that has several meanings. The term for this is *polyseme* (where *poly* means 'many' and *seme* means 'meaning', as in *semantic*). Consider the adjective *loud*. We can easily use this word with two very different meanings,

> Turn down the volume please! The music's too **loud**.
> Please get a different tie! That one's too **loud**.

In the first instance *loud* means 'strongly audible; having great amplitude'. In the second case, the adjective means 'obtrusive or overly flashy'. Or consider this dialogue from a *Quigmans* cartoon that plays upon two possible meanings of the noun *reinforcement*:

> SERGEANT: Captain! I'm in trouble up here on hill 42! I need reinforcement!
> CAPTAIN: OK, Sarge ... well ... you're a good looking man ... always
>   well-groomed ... good sense of humor ... snappy dresser ... is
>   that enough?

In this exchange, the sergeant is clearly requesting 'fresh troops to assist in an armed engagement'. The captain offers instead some 'words that give strength or support'.

Now looking back at the pair *bear* [noun] and *bear* [verb], and at the adjective *loud* or the noun *reinforcement*, how are we to decide whether we're dealing with one word or two? For the most part, we have to rely on our intuition. Sometimes the two uses are clearly unrelated, as in the case of *bear*, in which it is impossible to imagine any reasonable link between its meaning as a noun (the animal) and its meaning as a verb ('to carry'). *Bear* is clearly a homonym. In contrast, the two uses of *reinforcement* in the *Quigmans* cartoon are transparently related. The word in both instances is used to mean 'strengthening' (in one case by virtue of military force and in the other case psychologically).

The case of *loud* is less obvious, although in the end is it clearly a polyseme. While the connection between sound and color is not direct, this adjective has acquired these related uses through the concept of 'intensity'. So a highly intense sound is one that is 'strongly audible' and highly intense colors are very bright and flashy. In this way, we can say with some confidence that we are dealing with two meanings of the adjective *loud*, rather than two distinct words that happen to have the same pronunciation and spelling.

So the requirement for having a pair of *homonyms* is that they be completely unrelated, while *polysemy* can be had through no more than a tenuous connection. In a 2006 *Bound and Gagged* panel, one winged resident of heaven finding a hole in his shoe, complains to another:

> Hey! I thought we had immortal soles!

Here, in addition to the fact that they're not homographs, *soul* ('the spirit or mind of a person') and *sole* ('the bottom part of a shoe') have no connection meaning-wise. Polysemy, in contrast, can be had rather cheaply. In another, more recent *Bound and Gagged* panel, one ant says to another:

> Sorry I'm late, I got lost on a cloverleaf.

In the same vein, in a *Mother Goose and Grimm* panel, Grimmy (the dog) and Attila (the cat) are making photocopies (not *Xeroxes*) of dinner rolls, and Grimmy remarks to Attila:

> I don't get it . . . what's so fun about copying your buns?

In both of these cases, the words in question have two, albeit highly unrelated, meanings. *Cloverleaf* refers to 'the leaf (or leaves) of a clover plant' as well as to a 'two-level highway interchange in which loop roads handle traffic needing to turn left'. *Buns* refer both to 'dinner rolls' and the 'fleshy part of the buttocks'. It is pretty apparent that clover plants have little to do meaning-wise with highway interchanges, and that baked goods have no natural connection to human bottoms. Nevertheless, the polysemy arises in both cases as a result of form. The highway *cloverleaf* is so-called because it has a shape similar to a (four-leaf) clover, and the fleshy parts of buttocks are called *buns* on account of their resemblance to the baked product.

Because the connection between polysemous meanings of words can be so tenuous, it should not be surprising that they can develop into full-fledged homonyms. That is, for some speakers, the multiple meanings may be unrelated because they're not conscious of the connection or because they have no awareness of one of the meanings at all. Take the word *crane*, for example, which means either 'the long-necked wading bird' or 'the construction equipment that lifts and transfers heavy objects'. It is plausible, if not certain, that many people who regularly see and refer to construction cranes have no knowledge of the species of bird that they are named for. So, for the person that encounters a marsh crane for the first time, having long known and used the word to refer to construction equipment, *crane* [the bird] and *crane* [the construction equipment] may very well count as homonyms.

Bushisms and Steven Colbertisms

It would be unfair to end this chapter without a brief discussion of ways in which people intentionally and unintentionally violate word formation principles, often with humorous effect. An iconic example of this is found among *Bushisms* (a term referring to various linguistic errors and other speaking faux pas that the former President George W. Bush was prone to making in public appearances). One of the first and most famous *Bushisms* occurred in November 2000, when the President is quoted as having said, "They misunderestimate me." The word *misunderestimate* involves the fabrication of a new word with a novel use of the affix *mis-*, and as such it reminds us of Lucy's confusion at the beginning of this chapter. Some other malformed "Bush" words include *vulcanize* in place of *Balkanize*, and *resignate* instead of *resonate*.

Another well-known example of this phenomenon involves a *faux-Bushism*, *strategery*, introduced in an October 2000 *Saturday Night Live* sketch by Will Ferrell (impersonating Bush). This term combines the word *strategy* and the common suffix *-ery*. The suffix *-ery* itself, as applied to some words such as *bribery*, *slavery*, and *bakery*, involves some connection (place, state, activity) to the word preceding the affix (e.g. the action of making a *bribe*, the state of being a *slave*, or the location where *baking* is done). So, *strategery* is the action of making *strategy* or perhaps the location where it happens. The recent history of *strategery* is rather interesting. A malformed word invented for the purpose of mocking George Bush, it was taken up by others in his administration who took to referring to his strategists as the *Strategery Group*, and ultimately appeared in the title of a book by Bill Sammon, *Strategery: How George W. Bush Is Defeating Terrorists*.

Malformed words are sometimes coined for effect, and sometimes created inadvertently by professionals attempting (usually unsuccessfully) to sound more authoritative than they have any right to be. One of the best recent examples of a word coined for effect is *truthiness*, which was coined by Steven Colbert in 2005 to refer to the truth that someone feels to be true or knows to be true in their gut (as opposed to objective truth). This word's effect was so great and its usage proliferated so rapidly that it was named *Word of the Year* in 2005 by the American Dialect Society. While commonly thought to be (and claimed to be) a new coinage, *truthiness* actually dates back to the early nineteenth century and is cited in the *Oxford English Dictionary* from a text by Joseph John Gurney, "Everyone who knows her is aware of her truthiness" (as pointed out by Benjamin Zimmer).[10] That fact notwithstanding, Gurney's use of *truthiness* was clearly less notable than Colbert's. So, if nothing else, we can give Colbert credit for **re**-inventing the word, and for introducing it for greater effect.

We close this discussion by noting the malformation of words by people who clearly should (and who pretend to) know better. There is no one source for this sort of thing, but we are used to seeing it practiced most widely and most ridiculously in the world of business-speak and bureaucrat-ese. Rather than offer live examples, a dialogue from a 2007 *Dilbert* cartoon between the Pointy-Haired Boss and Tina (the tech writer) should suffice:

> BOSS: Tina, I need you to edit this before I send it out.
> TINA: Sure. I could use a good laugh.
>   Let's start with the words that aren't words.
>   Incentment . . . robustify . . . flexitate . . . and leadershipping.
>   I'll take those out and see what's left. . . .
>   "If you're not onboard with quality excellence, you're underboard."
>   [laughs hysterically]
> BOSS: [walking away, thinking to himself]
>   Why do I even bother trying to moralify these people?

5   Fitting words together

Phrase structure and meaning

DILBERT © Scott Adams / Dist. by United Feature Syndicate, Inc.

The ambiguity that propels the humor of this Dilbert cartoon[1] resides in the five words *one and two billion readers*. But it does not depend, as in the previous chapter, on any one word having multiple meanings. *One* means '1', *and* means '&', *two* means '2', *billion* means '1,000,000,000', and the word *readers* means 'those who read'. Rather, something more is going on than simply stringing individual words together. That something is *syntax* or *sentence grammar*. In this chapter, we will look at how words combine to form phrases and sentences. We will look at groupings and subgroupings of words, at how some words in a sentence come to be associated with other words, at the ways in which a verb determines the roles of other words in a sentence, and at other factors that sometimes make a seemingly straightforward sentence ambiguous. At the outset, jumping off from the Dilbert cartoon, we will take a close look at ambiguities that arise from alternative grouping of words in a sentence (what are called *structural ambiguities*). The chapter then turns to humor that is connected with the peculiarities of verbs and verb phrases, namely that some verbs are transitive (take objects) all the time, some are never transitive, and some alternate. The fact that some verbs take objects optionally, *John met Sally* and *John and Sally met*, allows for humor as well as for a closer look at how verbs work. Following this, the chapter takes up the various ways in which pronouns are used and sometimes misunderstood. The chapter ends with a quick survey of how expressions of quantity (such as *all* and *some*) interact with each other and with negation (i.e. *not*) to create ambiguity and open the door to humor.

Structural ambiguity and the grouping of words in a sentence

Consider again the noun phrase *one and two billion readers* from the Dilbert cartoon at the beginning of the chapter (NB: the term 'noun phrase' here simply means a phrase whose central word is a noun). It means either:

> 1,000,000,000–2,000,000,000 readers

or:

> 1–2,000,000,000 readers

The second includes the number 3, while the first does not. This, and many other similar ambiguities we will look at, depends on the 'grouping' of words into phrases. In selling advertising in *Gullible World*, Dogbert would like Pointy-Haired Boss to understand what he's saying as:

> [[one and two] billion]

What he's covertly meaning, though, is:

> [one] and [two billion]

The principle of grouping-based ambiguities is made even clearer when we compare the grammatical grouping of words with the arithmetical grouping of numbers. Consider this numerical expression, which mirrors what we just saw in the Dilbert cartoon:

> 1 + 2 * 1,000,000,000 (one plus two times one-billion)

Without grouping these three numbers in some way, we can't determine how much is meant. We need, as we did with the words above, some kind of bracketing, so that we have either:

> [1 + 2] * 1,000,000,000 = 3,000,000,000

or:

> 1 + [2 * 1,000,000,000] = 2,000,000,001

Just as the answer to the arithmetical expression varies according to its bracketing, so does the meaning of the noun phrase above it.

Key in the grouping-dependent ambiguity shown above is the fact that *one* can stand alone as a number expression, or can modify *billion*. This pattern can occur any time that the word in front of the conjunction *and* or the conjunction *or* is potentially autonomous. Noun + noun compounds are especially vulnerable to this sort of ambiguity. Consider the phrase *garbage and fire men*, which can be understood to mean either 'garbage men and firemen' as in:

> The garbage and firemen all went out on strike.
> [garbage and fire] men

or 'firemen and garbage' as in:

> There was <u>garbage and firemen</u> blocking the sidewalk, on account of the first not being collected and the second milling around after the fire was put out.
>
> [garbage] and [fire men]

Snow and radial tires is ambiguous in the same way, meaning either 'radial tires and snow tires' as in:

> They had <u>snow and radial tires</u> both on sale and I couldn't decide which to buy.
>
> [snow and radial] tires

or 'radial tires and snow' as in:

> I would blame the accident on <u>snow and radial tires</u>. There was too much of the first, and the second were defective.
>
> [snow] and [radial tires]

Of course, if the word before the conjunction *and* cannot stand alone, then the ambiguity does not arise. Consider the expression yellow and purple ribbon. Since *yellow* cannot stand alone and **must** modify something, only one grouping is meaningful:

> [yellow and purple] ribbon   = 'ribbon that is both yellow and purple'
> [yellow] and [purple ribbon] = NOTHING
>   (since *yellow* can't refer to anything alone)

So, like any other kind of grammatical ambiguity (as we shall see), it all depends upon each grouping (or structure) having an actual meaning.

   In the Dilbert example, we saw a word (*one*) which could either serve as a modifier or stand alone. There are many more cases in which a single modifier is taken to modify only the word that follows it, or a pair of conjoined words. In an episode of the comic strip *Shoe*, a customer at Roz' diner asks the character Cosmo about the menu:

> CUSTOMER: Is the fish served here previously frozen or fresh?
> COSMO: Previously fresh.

Here, the humor rests on the fact that *previously* can modify *frozen* alone (which is how the customer intended it), or can modify both *frozen* and *fresh* (as Cosmo's answer makes clear). As before, the ambiguity is grouping-dependent. The customer's question intends this grouping:

> [previously frozen] or [fresh]

but Cosmo's answer assumes this one:

> previously [frozen or fresh]

Another arithmetic example can help make it clear. Without any information about grouping, the following numerical expression cannot be interpreted:

> 5 * 3 + 1   5 times 3 plus 1

We can either add 1 to the product of 5 times 3, as in:

> [5 * 3] + 1 = 16

or we can multiply the sum of 3 and 1 by 5, as in:

> 5 * [3 + 1] = 20

Note that, in the second case, 5 times the sum of 3 and 1 is the same as 5 times 3, plus 5 times 1:

> 5 * [3 + 1] = 20
> [5 * 3] + [5 * 1] = 20

This 'commutativity' of multiplication over addition, helps to illustrate how Cosmo goes from understanding *previously* [*frozen or fresh*] to saying [*previously fresh*].

> previously [frozen or fresh] =
> [previously frozen] or [previously fresh]

Adjectival modification here is like multiplication, in that modifying the conjunction (or 'sum') of *frozen or fresh* is equivalent to modifying each of them separately.

Our grouping-dependent ambiguities have all, thus far, involved the presence of a conjunction such as *and* or *or*. However, the sort of ambiguity that we're describing can readily occur in a phrase that has no conjunction at all. This is to say that lots of phrases can have alternative groupings of their constituent words, and have different interpretations thereby.

As we have already seen above, Jeff MacNelly's *Shoe* uses grouping ambiguity to great effect. In an episode from 2006, the cigar-smoking character Shoe is on a dinner date, where his companion says:

> Shoe, darling . . . I wish you'd give up smoking for me.

His reply:

> Who ever said I was smoking for you?

In another episode, Marge is at Roz' diner and tells her:

> I tried on that red dress in the window of Dingle's department store today!

Roz replies:

> Yeah, I heard . . . You know, Marge. They do have dressing rooms.

Both of these jokes rely on the same sort of grouping ambiguity. They each involve a prepositional phrase, *for me* in the first instance and *in the window of Dingle's department store* in the second, that is grouped either with the object of the verb or with the verb itself.

Let's look at the first of these more closely. The words in the phrase *give up smoking for me* can be grouped in the following two ways:

> [[give up smoking] for me]
> give up [[smoking] for me]

Using the first grouping, Shoe's date meant that she wants Shoe to 'give it [smoking] up for my sake'. Using the second grouping, Shoe perversely pretends that it was 'the practice of smoking for her' that she wished him to 'give up'. So, in the intended interpretation the prepositional phrase *for me* modifies the whole verb phrase *give up smoking*, and in the humorous interpretation it only modifies the object of that verb, *smoking*.

In the second case, we find the reverse. In the intended interpretation, the prepositional phrase *in the window of Dingle's department store* modifies the object *that red dress*, while in the humorous interpretation, it modifies the verb phrase *try on that red dress*. What Marge says she did was:

> try on [[that red dress] in the window of Dingle's department store]

Notice here that the prepositional phrase is added directly to, and is grouped with, the object noun phrase *that red dress*. Roz, in suggesting to Marge that she might have used a dressing room, takes the perverse interpretation that relies on this grouping:

> [[try on that red dress] in the window of Dingle's department store]

Notice in this second case that the prepositional phrase is added directly to, and is grouped with, the entire verb phrase *try on that red dress*.

Another kind of ambiguity worth noting relies on the variable 'association' of some words with others in the sentence, but cannot transparently be illustrated as 'grouping' in the way that we've used it up until now. Adjectives and prepositional phrases at the ends of sentences can variously be used to describe either the subject or the object of a sentence. Consider these two cases in which the subject *John* is described by the adjective *half-naked* and the prepositional phrase *in a kilt*, respectively (the associated words are underlined for clarity).

> At the game, <u>John</u> sang the national anthem <u>half-naked</u>.
> At the game, <u>John</u> sang the national anthem <u>in a kilt</u>.

In these next two sentences, the same adjective and propositional phrase are used to describe the object of the sentence *his drunk friend*.

> After the game, John found <u>his drunk friend</u> <u>half-naked</u>.
> After the game, John found <u>his drunk friend</u> <u>in a kilt</u>.

Obviously, context makes the difference in these cases. In the first two examples, a national anthem cannot be described as *half-naked* or *in a kilt*, leaving them with nothing to refer to other than *John*. In the second pair of sentences, one might very readily expect to find a drunk friend *half-naked* or *in a kilt*.

This associative ambiguity can fuel the sort of humor exemplified in an exchange between two characters in *Wizard of Id*, Spook (the perpetual prisoner in the dungeon) and Turnkey (the guard):

> SPOOK: Have you ever eaten squid fried?
> TURNKEY: Yes.
> SPOOK: How was it?
> TURNKEY: Better than when I was sober.

While the joke utilizes two meanings of *fried* ('cooked in a pan in oil' and 'drunk'), it also depends crucially on the associative ambiguity just described. Spook asks a question in which *fried* is intended to describe *squid* (and in which *fried* is understood to mean 'cooked in a pan in oil').

> Have you ever eaten <u>squid</u> <u>fried</u>?

Turnkey, in wanting to convey that he would never enjoy eating squid unless he were drunk, uses *fried* to mean 'drunk', and can do this because the sentence offers the possibility of associating the adjective with the subject, as in:

> Have <u>you</u> ever eaten squid <u>fried</u>?

So, while the lexicon provides the double entendre in *fried*, it is the associative ambiguity provided by the grammar that allows it to be used in this joke.

Verbs and their objects

Another source of ambiguity that does not involve alternative groupings of words is that which arises from a verb's having an optional direct object (a direct object is normally a noun or noun phrase, with no preposition, directly following the verb). Consider this exchange between Dolly and her little brother P.J. (from Bill Keane's *Family Circus*):

> DOLLY: Your socks don't match!
> P.J.:   Match what?

What's going on here is that *match* is one of those verbs that can take, or not take, a direct object. Accordingly, you can express the same thought with either of the following two sentences (the first being transitive and the second being intransitive):

> Your socks match your shirt.   (A matches B)
> Your socks and your shirt match.   (A and B match)

This is clearly not possible with all object-taking verbs. The sentence *Your dog bit your cat* cannot alternate with and have the same meaning as *Your dog and your cat bit*. The reason that *match* may alternate in this way is because it expresses a 'symmetrical' relation. That is to say that if 'A matches B' then it must also be the case that 'B matches A'. This leads to the option of both things showing up as sentential subjects, and the verb having no object. Some other symmetrical verbs are *meet* and *marry*. Thus:

> IF   Harry met Sally.
> THEN Sally met Harry.
> AND   Harry and Sally met.

Notice that the intransitive (non-object-taking) versions of *match* and *meet* require that the subject be plural. Accordingly, you can say:

> Your hat and your tie match.
> Your shoes match.
> They match.

but not, without further context:

> Your shoe matches.
> It matches.

So, if you asked *Does this tie go with my socks?*, someone might say *Yes, it matches* or *Yes, it matches them* or *Yes, they match*.

Going back to the exchange between Dolly and P.J., if Dolly had said *Your sock doesn't match*, then P.J. would have been correct to ask *Matches what?* if in fact he didn't know. Of course, even in response to *Your socks don't match*, P.J. could have asked sensibly *Match what?* if he thought she was telling him that his socks didn't match **something else**. However, since we normally take socks to match each other, P.J.'s response counts as funny.

There are other cases in which verbs can optionally not have an object, and which can serve as fuel for humor. Consider this exchange from *Shoe*, in which Cosmo is conducting a jailhouse interview of a career criminal:

> PRISONER: I've had a rough life . . . I cursed the day I was born!
> COSMO: Really? I didn't start until I was four.

The verb *curse* is one of those which can be used both in the sense of 'to invoke evil upon something' or 'utter curses or swear'. In the latter sense, it is intransitive and doesn't take an object. In this respect, the prisoner's statement is potentially ambiguous, meaning either the intended 'I invoked curses upon the day I was born' or the ridiculous 'I uttered curses from the day I was born'. Cosmo, of course, takes up the nonsensical meaning, replying that he didn't begin uttering curses until he was four.

It is interesting to look more closely at what it means for a verb to have an object (or not). Some verbs can optionally take objects, but we understand them to have objects even if they don't come with an overt one. For instance, *They ate lunch* has the object *lunch* and *They ate* has no object, but in both cases one cannot imagine them eating without their eating something. So, even when *eat* doesn't have an object, we still conceive of there being one. Note that while *eat* can occur without an overt object, other similar verbs cannot do so. So while you can say *They ate the pizza* or *They devoured the pizza*, you can only say *They ate* and not *They devoured*.

Some verbs that take optional objects are different from other verbs that take optional objects in that when the object is missing, we don't assume that there's something there. The verbs *throw* and *pass* contrast in this way with their indirect objects. You can say *He passed the ball to someone* or simply *He passed the ball*. In the second case, we assume that there was someone who he passed the ball to, even though it's not expressed. Otherwise, using the verb *passed* makes no sense. In this sense, the indirect object of *pass* is like the direct object of *eat*. We assume it exists even if it's not expressed. This contrasts markedly with *throw*. So, if you say *He threw the ball to someone*, the indirect object and intended recipient of the ball is expressed and assumed to exist. But if you say *He threw the ball*, there is no assumption that anyone was there to receive it (in contrast with *He passed the ball*). This difference is nicely encoded into the game of football (the American variety). You can only say that the quarterback *passed the ball* (whether it was received/caught or not) if there was an intended recipient. If there is no intended recipient, then the quarterback is said to have *thrown the ball away*, and in certain circumstances *throwing the ball away* is deemed 'intentional grounding' and results in a penalty. So, we can be quite sure that the National Football League is acutely aware of the contrastive semantics of *pass* and *throw*, whether they realize it or not.

Having considered verbs whose objects we assume exist even when they are unexpressed, it would be unfair not to also consider those verbs whose expressed objects don't seem to mean anything. Consider the verb *behave*, as in *John behaved*. Notice that you can also say *John behaved himself*, without changing the meaning of the sentence. In fact, in an act of *behaving* there can be only one participant – the person who is behaving (well or badly). You can't say *John behaved Ted*, or anyone else. So, if *behave* has an object, it invariably refers to the same person who is the subject. In other words, the object doesn't really mean anything, and is only there because the verb *behave* doesn't care whether it's there or not.

Right alongside *behave* is the verb *perjure*. And where *behave*'s meaningless object is (appropriately) optional, *perjure*'s meaningless object is (inexplicably) obligatory. The verb *perjure* means 'to lie under oath' and an act of perjury involves only the individual doing the lying. So, the sentence *Ted perjured himself* means 'Ted lied under oath'. As with *behave*, the object is meaningless and adds nothing. However, unlike *behave*, which is fine in the sentence *John behaved*,

Figure 5.1 *Dilbert and 'associative' ambiguity.*

you can't say *Ted perjured*. So, *perjure* not only takes a meaningless object, but insists on having it. In this regard, *behave* is like *eat*, in that each of their objects (meaningless and meaningful, respectively) are optional. *Perjure*, in turn, is like *devour*, in that they both demand to have an object expressed (even when, in the former case, it means nothing).

Using (and misusing) pronouns

Another kind of 'associative' ambiguity rests in the various interpretations that pronouns can have. Figure 5.1 shows an early *Dilbert* comic strip from 1994,[2] Dogbert is trying to help remove a cat off of Ratbert's head, and tells Bob the Dinosaur,

> I'll yank the cat off of Ratbert's head and you stomp on it.

The associative ambiguity here involves the referring possibilities of the pronoun *it*. Dogbert means for *it* to refer to the cat, as in

> I'll yank <u>the cat</u> off of Ratbert's head and you stomp on <u>it</u>.

Bob the Dinosaur understands *it* to refer to Ratbert's head, much to Ratbert's detriment,

> I'll yank the cat off of <u>Ratbert's head</u> and you stomp on <u>it</u>.

As Dogbert says afterward, he could have "phrased that better." Phrasing anything with pronouns can be somewhat treacherous, since pronouns are nothing but "variables" or "placeholders" for other things in the context of a conversation. So, in the sentence:

> John thinks he is a genius.

He is like a variable *x* that can be assigned a value. If *he* = *John*, then 'John thinks that John is a genius', and we can conclude some further things about John's modesty. On the other hand, *he* might refer to someone else in the conversation, based perhaps on prior context. So if the sentence in question were preceded by this:

> Harry is such a smart man.

then we would likely understand *he* = *Harry*, and take the sentence to mean 'John thinks that Harry is a genius'. Notice that a sentence containing a pronoun (i.e. a variable) cannot be interpreted as true or false unless we know what the pronoun refers to (i.e. the value of the variable).

Let's consider a mathematical analogy. If someone were to ask you whether this expression is true or false:

$$20 + x = 36$$

You couldn't really say, unless you know what *x* is equal to. If $x = 16$, then the expression is indeed true. But if $x = 10$, it would be false. Likewise with the sentence *He is a genius*. Suppose we know that Harry is indeed a genius and that John is somewhat full of himself. Then, if *he* = *Harry*, *He is a genius* is true. And if *he* = *John*, *He is a genius* is false. Thus, the meaning of *John thinks he is a genius* changes according to the value of *he*.

Just as pronouns require us to look backwards in a sentence (or discourse) to figure out what they refer to, so do elisions require us to look backwards in a sentence or discourse to figure out what is missing. So, if you ask me *Have you eaten lunch?* and I answer *I have*, you are entitled to fill in the missing words *eaten lunch* based on what has come before. That is to say, it would be daft for me to say *I have* in answer to your question, if what I really meant was *I have had coffee*. Of course, sometimes the available associations lead to more than one possibility for reconstruction. Consider this dialogue from a *Wizard of Id* comic strip:

> SIR RODNEY: The press says you're spending more on the military than the poor.
>
> THE KING: Hogwash! The poor spend twice as much on the military as I do!

The humor in this exchange relies on the fact that we don't necessarily know whether the noun phrase *the poor* following *than* in the first sentence is the subject or the object of what's missing.

In order to understand how this comes to be, we must first understand that Sir Rodney is eliding (or leaving out) part of what he means. This sort of elision is normal for almost any sentence that involves the expression of 'more X than Y'. For instance, rather than say:

> Sir Rodney likes dragon soup more than <u>the King likes dragon soup</u>.

one could and would probably say:

> Sir Rodney likes dragon soup more than <u>the King does</u>.

or:

> Sir Rodney likes dragon soup more than <u>the King</u>.

The last of these three sentences leaves out all but *the King* (the sentential subject) from *The King likes dragon soup*. Now, consider the next sentence:

> Sir Rodney likes dragon soup more than <u>he likes the King</u>.

This sentence could also be shortened to:

> Sir Rodney likes dragon soup more than <u>the King</u>.

in which the words *he likes* – that is, everything but the direct object – is elided. In the paraphrased joke above, when Sir Rodney says:

> The press says you're spending more on the military than <u>the poor</u>.

he leaves out the words *you're spending on*, in order to get the meaning:

> The press says you're spending more on the military than <u>you're spending on the poor</u>.

The King, for his part, takes Sir Rodney's utterance to have left out the words *are spending on the military*, and gets this meaning instead:

> The press says you're spending more on the military than <u>the poor are spending on the military</u>.

Of course, Sir Rodney could have made his sentence unambiguous by only leaving out the words *you're spending*, and leaving the preposition *on*, as in:

> The press says you're spending more on the military than <u>on the poor</u>.

But then, of course, we would not have had the joke.

Elision can also lead to ambiguity of a different sort: that is, "associative" ambiguity, or the kind that we saw in our discussion of pronouns. In a *Kudzu* comic strip from 2001, the main character Rev. Will B. Dunn is counseling a female parishioner, who first tells him:

> "We're a perfect match. I'm head over heels in love with him . . ."

and then bursts into tears, saying:

> " . . . and so is he!"

Normally, *and so is he* would be taken to mean, *and he's head over heels in love with me, too*. But her anguish suggests that what she really means is, *he's head over heels in love with himself, too*. Not too propitious for the relationship.

This joke is built upon a very common type of elision, involving variations on the expression *so . . .* , as in *so is he*, *so am I*, *so are you*, etc. An unremarkable example of this would be:

> John bought himself a new car, and <u>so did Dave</u>.

The expression *and so did Dave* replaces *and Dave bought himself a new car, too*. Of course, the inclusion of regular pronouns ("variables" as we saw earlier) leads to the potential for ambiguity. I could say either of the following:

> John bought his best friend a gift, and I bought his best friend a gift, too.
> John bought his best friend a gift, and I bought my best friend a gift, too.

In the first case, it is John's best friend that is getting two gifts. In the second case, John's best friend and my best friend each get a gift. Now consider this sentence:

> John bought his best friend a gift, and <u>so did I</u>.

This sentence is ambiguous in the sense that *so did I* could be interpreted to mean either *I bought his best friend a gift, too* or *I bought my best friend a gift, too*.

How does this happen? The way in which we get two interpretations out of this last sentence has to do with how the possessive pronoun *his* and the noun phrase *his best friend* get interpreted. One way of interpreting the meaning of *his best friend* is to understand that *his = John's*. On this interpretation *his best friend* means 'John's best friend':

> <u>John</u> bought <u>John</u>'s best friend a gift.
> <u>John</u> bought <u>his</u> best friend a gift.

Now, to get the other meaning, we have to understand that *his* could also refer to the subject of the sentence itself, as in:

> <u>John</u> bought GRAMMATICAL-SUBJECT's best friend a gift
> <u>John</u> bought <u>his</u> best friend a gift.

Watch what happens when these two ways of understanding *his* are used in the *so did I* sentence:

> <u>John</u> bought <u>John</u>'s best friend a gift, and I bought <u>John</u>'s best friend a gift, too.

> <u>John</u> bought <u>his</u> best friend a gift, and I bought <u>his</u> best friend a gift, too.

> John bought his best friend a gift, and so did I.

> <u>John</u> bought GRAMMATICAL-SUBJECT'S best friend a gift, and **I** bought **GRAMMATICAL-SUBJECT'S** best friend a gift, too.

> <u>John</u> bought <u>his</u> best friend a gift, and **I** bought **my** best friend a gift, too.

> John bought his best friend a gift, and so did I.

We refer to the interpretation of the first group of sentences as "strict identity," since the identity of the best friend stays the same throughout. In this case, *his* replaces *John's* throughout the sentence and we see that it is John's best friend for whom I also bought a gift. In the second case, since the GRAMMATICAL-SUBJECT is *John* in the first sentence and *I* in the second, *his* replaces GRAMMATICAL-SUBJECT'S in the first sentence and *my* replaces it in the second. This gives us the interpretation in which each of us bought a gift for our own friend. We call the interpretation in this second group of sentences "sloppy identity" because the identity of the best friend shifts depending upon who the subject of the sentence is.

These "strict/sloppy" associations are used quite often in constructing jokes. In a *The Middleton's* comic strip from 2005, Morris Middleton wishes Grimes a happy birthday, to which he replies:

> Thanks! Every year, on my birthday, I send my mother flowers. She loves it!

He goes on to suggest:

> You should try it.

to which Morris inquires:

> What's her address?

What is at play here is the meaning of the pronoun *it* in *She loves **it*** and *You should try **it***.

What Grimes means is that his (Grimes') mother loves his (Grimes') sending her flowers, and suggests that Morris should try sending his (Morris') mother flowers. Of course, this is a case of "sloppy identity" where the identity of the mother (Grimes' or Morris') shifts from one sentence to the next. What Morris (perversely) understands is the "strict identity" interpretation, where Grimes would be saying that his (Grimes') mother loves his (Grimes') sending her flowers, and suggesting that Morris should try sending his (Grimes') mother flowers too.

Yet another kind of identificational ambiguity arises from the difference between references to actual physical entities in the world and references to their qualities or properties. In this regard, if someone says:

> I wish I had her hair.

we normally understand that to mean 'I wish I had hair with the same properties or qualities as her hair'. We would not, at least normally, respond by saying:

> But if you had her hair, then she would be bald.

That interpretation could only arise from *having her hair* being taken to mean 'having the actual hair that grows out of her head'. The same potential ambiguity arises when I hold up a bottle of my best chianti and suggest:

> You should serve this chianti with the pasta you're planning to serve.

I am, most likely, not offering that particular bottle of wine to you to serve to your guest, but suggesting that you go out and buy a bottle of it for yourself. So, the distinction here is between "token" (a particular bottle of wine) and "type" (the kind of wine I'm suggesting). Similarly, above, I'm wishing for the "type" of her hair and not the "token" of it. In a *Shoe* comic strip, Cosmo asks a woman at the bar:

> What would you do if you had Donald Trump's money?

to which she answers:

> Duh . . . spend it before he noticed it was missing.

In this exchange, Cosmo is clearly referring to the "type" interpretation of *Donald Trump's money* (that is, its properties, and notable among them, its magnitude). The response shifts the reference to the "token" (that is, the actual money itself).

All the monkeys are not in the zoo and other semantic ambiguities

Moving more squarely into the realm of semantics, there is an entire domain of ambiguity . . . and of potential humor emanating from it . . . which arises out of the interpretation of expressions of quantity (such as *one*, *some*, *every*, *all*, along with numbers, etc.) and their interactions with other parts of a sentence. One of the most straightforward of these involves quantity expressions and negation (i.e. *not*). Consider:

> All the students are not present.

This can mean either that 'no students are present' (i.e. the entire group of all the students is not present) or that 'not all the students are present' (i.e. some students are still not present). *Dennis the Menace* takes advantage of this ambiguity by reporting to his mother, as they're bringing groceries into the house:

> I carried the egg carton and didn't break one!

The ambiguity here could be paraphrased as either:

> It is not the case that there's one egg that I broke. (i.e. I broke none)

or:

> There is one egg, such that I didn't break it. (i.e. I broke all but one)

Seeing that Dennis is pleased with himself, one would ordinarily imagine him to be meaning the first of these two interpretations. But in the next panel, holding a single egg and with the rest of the carton smashed in the background, he goes on to say:

> Here's the one!

Now we know that he is in fact meaning the second of the two interpretations, and is (implausibly) proud of that fact. Of course, it being Dennis the Menace, we more or less expected that.

To explain a bit further about the ambiguity of *I . . . didn't break one* [*egg*], let's understand that the 'not' in *didn't* and the 'one' in *one egg* each need to be interpreted relative to the other. We need to further understand that this can vary sometimes without respect to where the words are in a sentence. Consider:

> I did**n't** take **one** orange.

If *n't* (i.e. NOT) is interpreted before *one*, then it goes something like this:

> It's **not** the case [that there's **one** orange such that I took it].
> That is: It's not the case that I took even one orange.
> That is: I didn't take any.

If *one* is interpreted before *n't* (i.e. NOT), then it gets interpreted this way:

> There's **one** orange [such that it's **not** the case that I took it].
> That is: There's only one orange that I didn't take.
> That is: I took all but one.

This order of interpretation ambiguity arises not only with respect to *not* and quantity expressions such as *one*, but also between different quantity expressions in the same sentence. Consider how the order of interpretation of *100%* and *both* applies in the following dialogue (from a *B.C.* comic strip) between the baseball coach and two of his players:

> COACH: Last year you bozos only gave me 75%!
>   This year I want **100%** from **both** of you!
> PLAYERS: You got it coach! Put us down for 50% apiece!

When the coach says *I want 100% from both of you*, his intended meaning involves interpreting *both* before *100%*:

> From **both** (or each) of you, it is the case that I want **100%**.

In this case the desire for 100% applies separately to each player. The players, for their part, interpret *100%* first:

> There is an amount of **100%**, which I want to get from **both** of you collectively.

So, they reason that if they each contribute 50%, then the coach gets his desired 100%.

These sorts of quantity-quantity ambiguities are fairly common. If **every** student in my class studies **two** foreign languages, then it might be the case that:

> There are **two** foreign languages, say Spanish and French, such that **every** student studies them.

or perhaps:

> For **every** student, there are **two** foreign languages that that student studies (and perhaps not the same two for each student).

A Hickerson cartoon panel from some years ago provides a clear example of this ambiguity. The cartoon shows someone falling down a flight of stairs, with the following caption:

> In the United States a person falls down the stairs every 3.5 minutes.
> Bob IS that person.

Of course, the only sensible interpretation of the first sentence is one where the quantity expression *every 3.5 minutes* is interpreted ahead of *a person* (which could also have been rendered as *some person*).

> **Every** 3.5 minutes, there is **some** person (or other) falling down the stairs.

The Hickerson comic panel reverses this, by stating *Bob IS that person*, taking the meaning of *a person* (i.e. *some person*) first.

> There is **some** person such that he falls down the stairs **every** 3.5 minutes.

What this shows fairly clearly is that these ambiguities are available for use, even when one of the interpretations is thoroughly loopy.

Perhaps one of the best uses of this quantity-based ambiguity – one that has made rounds on the Internet – comes from a 2001 *Dilbert* cartoon in which the following exchange occurs between Dilbert and his date:

> DILBERT'S DATE: I believe there is one true soul mate for every person.
> DILBERT: He must be very busy.
> DILBERT'S DATE: I meant one per person . . . your way would be stupid.
> DILBERT: Can your soul mate be a monkey?

Where Dilbert's date means:

> For **every** person, that person has **one** soul mate.

Dilbert takes her comment to mean:

> There is **one** soul mate such that **every** person has him for a soul mate.

Notice further in this exchange that Dilbert's date doesn't specify that a *soul mate* need be a person, leading Dilbert to ask his question. This failure to specify on the date's part provides the opening for the second joke in this particular strip. Here, while the class of individuals denoted by *soul mate* includes all persons (i.e. humans) as possible candidates, it does not exclude (for Dilbert) monkeys and presumably other creatures.

The consideration of *soul mates* and *monkeys* leads to yet another sort of semantic lack of specificity (one which we will return to in our next chapter on pragmatics). As just noted, depending on one's beliefs about souls, a *soul mate* might or might not include individuals who are not human. Suppose you believe that non-humans (e.g. monkeys) can have souls. Suppose also that you believe that all humans have souls (a potentially debatable assertion given the way some humans behave). In this instance, you can say:

> If an individual is a person (is human), then that person is a potential soul mate.

You **cannot** say:

> If an individual is a potential soul mate, then that individual is a person.

In essence, the set of potential soul mates is larger than, and completely includes, the set of all people.

Let's see how this might lead to multiple interpretations. First of all, we can observe that smaller numbers of things are included in any larger number of the same things, such that if I have five pens, then I certainly have one pen. But if I have one pen, I don't necessarily have five. This is clearly shown by the fact that if I do have five pens, and you ask "Do you have a pen?" I am most likely going to answer in the affirmative and give you one to use. It would make no sense for me to answer "No, I have five," although there are circumstances in which that answer would be called for.

This shows up in a pre-April 15 episode of the *Cathy* comic strip in 2006, where she gets into an argument with her Certified Public Accountant (CPA):

> CATHY: If I'm in financial ruin, it's because of your advice!
> CPA: You ignored my investment advice . . . my prenup advice . . .
>   my savings advice . . . what advice did you ever take?
> CATHY: You told me to have a nice day, so I enjoyed myself all year . . .
>   and here I am: broke.
> CPA: I said "have a nice day," not "have 365 nice days"!!
> CATHY: See? Too vague. I deserve compensation.

Cathy's CPA, in telling her to have *a nice day*, has not told her not to have more than one of them. Just as 'having a pen' doesn't preclude my having five of them, 'having a nice day' doesn't preclude having many, many more.

In closing this chapter, and perhaps as a way to lead us into the sorts of discussion to be seen in the next, let us consider the case of words and phrases that can only be used in certain syntactic environments. In a 2002 episode of *Hagar the Horrible*, Hagar's wife, Helga, is scolding him:

> HELGA: I spend ALL my time doing housework . . .
>   and you won't even lift a finger to help.
> HAGAR: [holds up a finger]

Not only is Hagar ignoring his wife's complaint by taking her words literally – a point to be made in the next chapter – he's also (by his actions) suggesting a misuse of the phrase *lift a finger*. In this regard, he might have achieved the same effect by saying *OK, I will lift a finger to help*.

If you can say *He didn't lift a finger to help*, why is it that I can't object by saying *He did so lift a finger to help*? The reason for this is that phrases like *lift a finger* and *bat an eyelash*, along with words such as *ever* and *any*, can only occur in certain environments (such as following an *n't* [NOT]). They cannot occur in other environments even though we could understand what they would mean if they did. So, even though I think I understand the meaning of *He did so lift a finger to help*, I still can't say it.

So when can these items be used? And when can't they? Let's look at a simple contrast:

> John does**n't** have **any** money.
> **X** John has **any** money.

In the first sentence *any* is preceded by the negation *n't*. The second sentence is positive and has no negation in it. It's on account of this contrast that linguists have taken to calling words such as *any* 'Negative "Polarity" Items' (the metaphor here being to things – like batteries – that have a positive and negative pole). Of course, right alongside Negative Polarity Items, we also find Positive Polarity Items, such as *somewhat*, which can only appear in positive (non-negative) sentences:

> John was discouraged **somewhat**.
> **X** John was**n't** discouraged **somewhat**.

Negative Polarity Items can occur in the presence of most any negative word. That is, in addition to being used in sentences containing some version of *not* or *n't*, they can also show up in sentences having other negative-meaning words, such as *never* or *seldom* (in contrast with positive words such as *always* and *often*). Consider these sentences:

> John **seldom** has **any** money.
> John **never** has **any** money.
> **X** John **always** has **any** money.
> **X** John **often** has **any** money.

It is also the case that Negative Polarity Item can occur in questions:

> Does John have **any** money**?**

and in conditional (*if . . . then . . .*) sentences:

> **If** John had **any** money, then he would be able to afford his own apartment.

but only in the *if* part. Not in the *then* part:

> **X** If John didn't spend so much on his car, **then** he might have **any** money.

Notice, as we pointed out before, that this last sentence makes some sense. That is, we know what it's "trying" to mean, even if we wouldn't ever say it. This is an important fact, which will come up again when we look at language variation, and find that some dialects of English actually allow some of these "items" in positive sentences. *Anymore* works this way:

> **Anymore**, we try to use the stairs instead of the elevator.

Not surprisingly, dialects that use sentences like this are called "positive *anymore*" dialects. We will also see, in Chapter 10, that the "quirky" behavior of these "items" makes it hard for non-native English speakers to learn the restrictions on them, and results in occasional misunderstanding.

6 Meaning one thing and saying another

Indirect speech and conversational principles

HER! [GIRL VS PIG] BY: CHRIS BISHOP

The joke in this *Her!*[1] strip is quite well worn (at least as far as the bit in the first two panels goes). It relies on a well-established formula for humor: intentionally taking a statement at face value when the context makes clear that something else or more is meant. Variations on this include:

STUDENT:	Can I use the restroom?
TEACHER:	I don't know. *Can* you?

MAN TO NEIGHBOR:	Did you hear me pounding on the wall last night?
NEIGHBOR TO MAN:	Don't worry about it. We were making a lot of noise ourselves.[2]

And the granddaddy of all jokes of this kind:

CUSTOMER:	Waiter, there's a fly in my soup.
WAITER:	Keep it down, sir, or everyone will want one.

In all of these jokes, the first speaker is trying to do something with his or her utterance: request information, gain permission, or make a complaint. But instead of performing that action directly, each speaker takes an indirect path, using one kind of utterance to do the work of another. In the *Her!* strip, for instance, Girl uses a *yes–no* question to ask for more substantive information. That is, while she asks directly whether or not Pig 'knows' the time, what she really means is something like *What time is it?* or *Please tell me the time*. Similarly, in the "Fly in my soup" joke, the customer makes a statement about the condition of his soup as an indirect way of requesting that something be done about it. In most cases, the context of the utterance as well as an underlying assumption that conversation is a cooperative activity is supposed to make the first speaker's intentions clear. Meanwhile, the second speaker, equipped with an understanding of the context and a general willingness to cooperate, is supposed to respond appropriately. But it's often the case with humor that people are purposefully (albeit playfully) uncooperative and try to subvert the normative expectations. Thus in each joke, the second speaker responds to what the first person literally *says* instead of to what he actually *means*.

The gap between saying and meaning often arises when language is inserted into context. That is, there is often a difference between what a linguistic expression literally means in isolation, and what it means (or is used for) when inserted into a conversation. When we isolate a sentence and examine it in a vacuum, so to speak, the sentence has a more or less stable meaning. Inject that same sentence into a conversation, and its meaning might change – sometimes radically so. In our previous chapters, we considered the meaning of bits of language and linguistic expressions (words, phrases, sentences) objectively. Even though we encountered all kinds of ambiguities and competing interpretations in the sample jokes and cartoons we featured, we were primarily focused on the form of language itself and not on how people use it. In this chapter, we consider what people do with language, and how they do it. We will gain a more precise understanding of all this by considering language use from several perspectives. We will focus here on the notion of *deixis* (literally, pointing) to show how we use language to refer to things out in the world, on the notions of *indirect speech* and *speech acts* to show how we manage to use some kinds of expressions to do the work of others, and on the notion of *cooperative principles* to understand how we manage and manipulate multiple meanings within the use of a single expression.

Deixis

Deixis means "pointing to" or "specifying," and is a good place to begin our study of how language use depends on context. Because we (mostly) use language to talk about things in the real world, the manner in which linguistic expressions refer or point to people, things, times, and places is an important aspect of their use. In Chapter 5, we discussed one kind of pointing word – pronouns – where we described them as "variables" or "placeholders." In order to determine the value of these variables or placeholders, we have to figure out what they point to in the context of a conversation. Recall Bob the Dinosaur's mistake after Dogbert says to him, "Bob, I'll yank the cat off of Ratbert's head and you stomp on it." Bob understands *it* as pointing to Ratbert's head rather than the cat, and Ratbert suffers the consequences of that mistake. The men in the following jokes make similar blunders:

A man walks into a book shop and says, "Can I have a book by Shake-speare?" "Of course, sir," says the salesman. "Which one?" The man replies, "William."[3]

A guy phones the local hospital and yells, "You've gotta help! My wife is in labor!" The nurse says, "Calm down. Is this her first child?" He replies, "No! This is her husband!"[4]

In both jokes, there's deictic confusion – that is, confusion over what the pronouns point to (the indefinite pronoun *one* in the first joke, and the demonstrative pronoun *this* in the second). In most cases, context should make their references clear. For instance, when discussing literature, we typically recognize only one *Shakespeare*, the one whose first name is *William*. Given this, it would make little sense to ask *Which Shakespeare?* as if there were more than one that is relevant. With the second joke, context should again eliminate confusion. It should certainly rule out the unlikely domestic arrangement in which the first child of a woman would refer to his mother as his *wife*!

The kind of pronominal deixis that fuels the referential jokes we saw above typically involves "third person" pronouns and other such forms. Variable expres-sions, such as *he*, *she*, *that*, *them*, and *which one* can get their reference (that is, can point) in a variety of ways. Their meaning can be understood from the content of the conversation, as in *I met Mary in the lobby, and **she** is ready to leave*. They can get it from an act of actual pointing, as in *I would never go out with **him*** (said while gesturing toward said individual). It's often the case that when we use one of these, there are multiple interpretations possible (as in the Ratbert joke above).

There are also pronouns (variables) whose meanings do not lend themselves to multiple interpretations in a given instance of use (even though they are indeed still variables). The pronoun *I* means 'the one talking' and it points to different individuals depending on who is doing the talking, but is never ambiguous when used. The pronoun *you* refers to the one being addressed, or a group that includes the one being addressed. There can be some confusion with Standard English *you*, being that it is both singular and plural. And this has led to innovations, such as *y'all* (in the American South), *youse* (in New York and New Jersey), and *you'uns* (in western Pennsylvania) that specifically refer to "a group that includes the person being addressed" (we will discuss these variations in more detail in Chapter 9). The first person plural pronoun *we* has a stable meaning of 'a group that includes the speaker', but it too is sometimes subject to misunderstanding. If I say to you *We're leaving now*, am I including you in or excluding you from the group about to leave? We sometimes get around this ambiguity in English by contracting the pronoun *us* when we mean to include the addressees, as in *Let's eat*, and leaving it uncontracted when we mean to exclude them, as in *Let us eat in peace*. Many languages actually use two separate pronouns in these cases, one meaning '*we* including you' and one meaning '*we* not including you'. For many Chinese speakers, the first person plural pronoun *wŏmen* is exclusive and the first person plural pronoun *zánmen* is inclusive. The Chinese speaker would use *zánmen* in saying *Let's eat* and would use *wŏmen* in saying *Let us eat in peace*. Many other languages make similar distinctions.[5]

Obviously then, we won't expect to find many pronoun-reliant jokes (such as those above) that are dependent on first and second person pronouns. When the man in the book shop asks, *Can I have a book by Shakespeare?* we understand the *I* to refer to the speaker (and nothing more). Similarly, in the second joke, the *You* in *You've gotta help* refers to the person the frantic husband is addressing. These may seem trivial observations, but they reveal an important feature about diectic expressions: the point of view they imply is **anchored** with the speaker. Thus, when two people are speaking, the deictic center shifts with each turn of speech:

> SPEAKER A: I was wondering if you could lend me a hand.
> SPEAKER B: I would be glad to help you.

Although Speaker A and B both use the pronouns *I* and *you*, the people the pronouns point to change when the speaker does. In the first utterance, *I* refers to Speaker A and *you* to Speaker B, while in the second utterance, the references are the reverse.

In addition to pronominal deixis, we can find several other categories of deictic (or pointing) expressions. Recall the demonstrative pronoun *this* from the second joke above, as in *Is this her first child?*. It overlaps with another category of pointing words – that is, **spatial deixis**, or words and expressions that refer to places or spatial proximity relative to the speaker. Imagine if the nurse had responded:

> Is *that* her first child?

The nurse's use of *that* instead of *this* would sound unidiomatic in this context, but it might have prevented any confusion on the man's part. Why is that so? Because we use *this* to refer to things close to us, and *that* to refer to things distant (note how *this* and *that* can also serve as adjectives):

> Look at *that*. (distant from the speaker)
> Look at *this*. (close to the speaker)
> Look at *that* car. (distant from the speaker)
> Look at *this* car. (close to the speaker)

By saying *Is this her first child?*, the nurse allows for reference to the caller, since things that are *this* are part of the conversational context, while things that are *that* are removed from them. If someone calls and we're not sure who's speaking, we might say *Is this Frank?*, referring to the caller. We would never say *Is that Frank?* unless referring to some person removed from the conversation. So, if the nurse had said *Is that her first child*, she (or he) would have made clear to the caller that the child was not physically (or telephonically) close.

In addition to using *that* to indicate where something is, we can also use it to indicate where we would prefer something to be. *That* has the power to metaphorically push something away. Consider a parent placing an unwanted plate of brussel sprouts in front of her three-year-old. The toddler might say, *I don't want that!* While the sprouts are undeniably close to the child, her use of *that* makes clear her wish to put as much space as possible between the sprouts and herself.

There are also other pairs of words having to do with place, distance, and direction: *here* and *there, come* and *go, bring* and *take*, and the archaic forms *hither* and *thither*, and *yon* and *yonder*. As with personal deixis, the point of view is anchored to the speaker. If a speaker says *Bring that here*, we understand the *that* to be distant from the speaker and the *here* to be the space immediately around and including the speaker. Reciprocally, with *Take this over there*, the *this* is close to the speaker, while the *there* is relatively far from the speaker. Two spatially deictic terms – *come* and *here* – play a central role in a joke from Stephen Wright:

> I bought a dog the other day . . . I named him Stay. It's fun to call him . . . "Come here, Stay! Come here, Stay!" He went insane. Now he just ignores me and keeps typing.

English is fairly impoverished in regard to spatial pointing expressions, having just two kinds: 'near' (*this, these, here*) and 'far' (*that, those, there*). Other languages have more flexibility in this realm. Both Japanese and Spanish have regularly used expressions that mean, roughly 'here', 'there', and 'yonder'. Spanish has three third person pronoun types (*este* 'this', *ese* 'that', and *aquel* 'that there') and three locatives (*aquí* 'here', *allí* 'there', and *allá* 'yonder'). Japanese, as well, uses three types of demonstratives: *kono, sono*, and *ano: kono hon* means 'this book, the one close to the speaker'; *sono hon* means 'that book, the one close to the addressee'; and *ano hon* means 'that there book, the one distant from both'.

A third class of deixis involves words that refer to time. The most common temporal terms are adverbs such as *now, then, soon, before*, and *after*, and calendric expressions such as *yesterday, today*, and *next week*. Like personal and spatial deixis, the times communicated by these terms are anchored to the speaker. If Mary says, *I have to leave now, now* points to the immediate present (the moment she utters the sentence that contains the word). If she says, *I have to leave soon, soon* is understood, relative to the moment of utterance, as a time shortly following the statement. The following comment from a blog site leverages temporal deixis for comedic effect. The commenter is responding to a blog entry titled "Don't call me NOW" and has a little fun at the blog author's expense:

> So does "Don't Call Me NOW" mean your *now* or my *now*? Because my *now* is around 11:30 while your *now* was at 9:51 which is my *then*. But by the time you read this and give me an answer my *now* will be

your *then* and your *now* I haven't even gotten to yet. And unless we happen to be looking at your website at the [same] time, this could go on forever.[6]

The commenter is exploiting here the difference between encoding time (the time when an utterance is delivered) and decoding time (the time when it is received). In face-to-face conversation, these are virtually the same: a speaker says something and the listener hears it instantly. But with print, electronic, or recorded communication, the time between encoding and decoding can be seconds, minutes, or millennia (think of the difference between reading an email sent to you minutes ago and reading Homer's *Iliad*).

Calendric terms also convey information about time anchored to a time of utterance, a fact this riddle makes use of:

> Q: What is today if yesterday is tomorrow?
> A: The day before yesterday.

To process this riddle, the reader has to juggle two points in time for naming the same two days. Suppose that it is currently August 12. We can call August 12 *today*. We would also call August 13 *tomorrow*. Now suppose that we travel in time to August 14. From the perspective of August 14, August 13 is now called *yesterday* and August 12 can now be called *the day before yesterday*. What we see from this riddle is that every deictic word (including temporal deictics) needs to be anchored to some fixed point in the real world. Most people have little trouble doing this because they understand how temporal deictic terms work: the times they express are anchored to the moment of speaking. Those who fail to do this get scripted into jokes, as does Julie here below:

> JULIE: What time is it?
> COUNSELOR: Three o'clock.
> JULIE: Oh, no!
> COUNSELOR: What's the matter?
> JULIE: I've been asking the time all day. And everybody gives me a different answer.

Besides pointing to participants in a conversation, the things they are talking about, and the times when things are reported to be happening or have happened, deictic words can also be used to point to other words. This is to say that, since words themselves are things out there in the world, we often need expressions to refer to them (or back to them).

> Conversation #1
> KIND SPEAKER A: I like you.
> NARCISSISTIC SPEAKER B: I know that.
>
> Conversation #2
> KIND SPEAKER A: I like you.
> GRATEFUL SPEAKER C: How kind of you to say that.

As we can see by comparing these two conversations, there is a difference between a "state of affairs" (a situation) and the words used to describe it. In conversation #1, Narcissistic Speaker B's use of *that* refers to the situation or fact of Kind Speaker A's liking him. In conversation #2, Grateful Speaker C's *that* refers back to the actual words uttered by Kind Speaker A, *I like you*.

Referring back to words or expressions in this way is called discourse deixis (or sometimes anaphora). Other examples of discourse deixis include expressions like:

> *That* was a good joke.
> *The following example* proves ...
> Few will find *those arguments* compelling ...
> As noted *before*, deictic expressions are "pointing" expressions.

As all these examples suggest, discourse dexis can work like spatial deixis (*that* [*joke*], *those arguments*) or like temporal dexis (*before* and *the following* . . .). In the former case, the discourse is imagined as a space with locations we can point to. In the latter, the discourse is something that we experience in time, so that things can be said before, now, or later. The artist in the following joke uses a little deictic jujitsu on a critic who doesn't like his latest production:

> ARTIST: So what's your opinion of my painting?
> CRITIC: It's worthless.
> ARTIST: I know but I'd like to hear it anyway.[7]

The pronoun *it* spoken by the critic can refer to the painting (a physical object out there in the world) or to the critic's own opinion (some collection of words he has that describe what he thinks about the painting). The critic likely intends the *it* in *It's worthless* to refer to the painting. Meanwhile, the artist, understandably, prefers to understand the *it* as referring to the critic's opinion, and says that he would like to hear "it" anyway. By purposefully (and rather cleverly) misinterpreting the intended referent of the critic's use of *it*, the artist cuts the critic down while preserving his own high regard of his artistic production.

Confusion can also arise when it's not clear what part of the discourse the deictic expression points to, as in this exchange from the sitcom *Frasier*:

> FRASIER: The other day I was asked out by this twenty-two-year-old girl that I met in a mall.
> NILES: That *is* alarming.
> FRASIER: Well, I turned her down.
> NILES: No no, you were in a mall. Did anyone see you?

When Niles says *That is alarming*, Frasier takes his *that* as pointing to the expression *I was asked out by this twenty-two-year-old girl*. For Niles, however, *that* points to what he considers the real scandal, contained in the expression *I met* [*her*] *in a mall*, that Frasier was in a mall and, possibly worse, that someone might have seen him there.

Direct vs. indirect speech

Let's return to the *Her!* strip from the beginning of this chapter. You'll remember that its humor hinges on a distinction between direct and indirect speech. Girl says to Pig, *Do you have the time?* By itself, this question simply asks whether Pig *knows* the time; it does not explicitly request that he also share it with Girl. In most contexts, however, people would still understand Girl's *yes–no* question as a conventional (albeit roundabout) way for requesting the time. They would, in other words, understand Girl's question as a form of indirect speech. Pig chooses not to recognize it as such and, instead, interprets it as a direct question. As a result, he has a little fun at Girl's expense and, in return, earns Girl's disdain.

We probably side with Girl in this little exchange because we recognize, one, that Pig is being a jerk, and two, that Girl's indirect request is a thoroughly conventional way for asking the time. There are, of course, many situations that favor direct speech (for instance, a general issuing a command on the battlefield), but there are just as many, if not more, situations in which indirectness is the norm. And that seems to be the point of an installment of Simon Donald's *Mr. Logic* strip recounted here. The strip begins with Mr. Logic, an annoyingly literal-minded dweeb, entering a post office:

MR. LOGIC: Do you sell stamps?

POSTAL CLERK: How many do you want?

MR. LOGIC: I do not necessarily require any. I merely asked whether or not you sold postage stamps. However, I do at present require one first class stamp.

POSTAL CLERK: That's 16p please.

MR. LOGIC: You assume that I wish to make a purchase . . . I merely stated that I required a stamp. A purchase does not necessarily follow. However, I do at this point intend to purchase the stamp. Accordingly, I remit the sum of 16 new pence.

Throughout the strip, we find indirect speech as normative, while direct speech stands out as an aberration. For instance, the postal clerk understands *Do you sell stamps?* as a perfectly normal indirect way of saying *I want to buy some stamps.* And she responds accordingly, *How many do you want?* Mr. Logic, being a feckless user of direct speech, simply won't cooperate with such indirection. In his reply, he first insists that she accommodate his first question as a direct query about whether or not the post office sells stamps. He then announces that he needs one. The clerk takes this too as an indirect way of making a purchase. Mr. Logic again retorts that he was simply and directly informing her of his needs. And then goes on to announce that he is indeed about to make a purchase. At this point, a burly patron waiting behind him who has had enough of listening to this, headbutts Mr. Logic right in the kisser.

The dialogue in the *Mr. Logic* strip gives a clue as to how impossibly banal life would be without indirect speech. If we all conducted ourselves as Mr. Logic and used only direct speech, not only would the world be a more boring place, but we'd lose valuable resources that enrich our means of communication. So, how then do we use indirect speech? Perhaps most commonly, we use it to negotiate politeness. Or, to put it somewhat differently, indirectness helps us avoid, among other things, two sure signs of impoliteness: imposing too forcefully upon others or talking down to them. Consider these alternatives for getting someone to shut a window:

> Shut that window.
> Can you shut that window?
> I was wondering if you could shut that window.
> Did someone leave that window open?
> Brrr! It's cold in here.

These alternatives range from most to least direct – or, more simply, from direct to indirect. A speaker who chooses the most direct alternative, *Shut that window*, would seem to have little trouble either imposing upon someone else or talking down to him or her (the utterance is a command, after all). With the last and most indirect alternative, *Brrr! It's cold in here*, the speaker drops a hint and hopes the listener will pick it up. In this way, the appearance of either imposition or disrespect is minimized.

Beyond politeness, we also use indirect speech to test for shared knowledge or interests. Say you want to ask someone to the movies, but you're not sure if he or she is interested in going – or, at least, interested in going with you. To test for shared interest, while also reducing the embarrassment of being turned down, you might deliver – or at least, initiate – your proposal through indirect speech. So instead of saying *Do you want to go to the movies with me?*, you might say something like *I heard there's a good movie playing at the cinema tonight* or *How do you feel about romantic comedies?* Of course, using indirectness in situations like this hinges on the other person's noticing the indirect strategy. In an episode from *Seinfeld*, for instance, George Costanza totally blows it when his date, Carol, propositions him using indirectness. They're sitting in George's car outside of her apartment building:

> CAROL: So, thanks a lot for dinner. It was great.
> GEORGE: Yeah. We should do it again.
> CAROL: Would you like to come upstairs for some coffee?
> GEORGE: Oh no, I can't drink coffee late at night. It keeps me up.[8]

George completely misses the romantic implication of Carol's question and instead answers it as if it were a direct question about whether or not he'd

Table 6.1 *Sentence Types and Speech Acts*

	Assertion	Question	Command or Request
Declarative	**You left the window open**.	*I'm wondering if you left the window open.*	*I can't stand having that window open.*
Interrogative	*Didn't you leave the window open?*	**Did you leave the window open?**	*Can you please shut that window?*
Imperative	*Remember that you left the window open.*	*Tell me whether you left the window open.*	**Shut the window**.

like some coffee. A few minutes later, after Carol gets out of the car and goes in, George realizes his mistake and starts banging his head on the steering wheel.

Speech acts and performatives

By now, it should be clear that people use language to do things, such as asking for the time of day, trying to get a date, or requesting postage stamps. We also saw that certain kinds of utterances can do the work of other kinds. For instance, an interrogative can perform a command, and a declarative sentence can be used to ask a question. Let's consider this point a little more carefully. We can classify sentences into three general types:

Declarative	*The window is open.*
Interrogative	*Is the window open?*
Imperative	*Open the window!*

Each sentence type is typically associated with a particular kind of task:

Sentence Type	Associated Task
Declarative	makes an assertion
Interrogative	asks a question
Imperative	delivers a command or request

However, while each sentence type is directly associated with the tasks listed above, there are plenty of occasions on which each of these sentence types is used indirectly to perform one of the other above-named tasks. For instance, instead of saying *Please give me a glass of water*, which is a direct use of an imperative sentence to deliver a request, you might instead say *May I please have a glass of water?* or *I could really use a glass of water right now*. The first uses an interrogative sentence to indirectly deliver the request, while the second uses a declarative. In Table 6.1, we see that each sentence type can be used directly to

Figure 6.1 *Beetle and indirect speech.*

perform its associated task (shown in bold), or be used indirectly to perform one
of the other two (shown in italics).

It is often the case that when one person uses a sentence indirectly to perform
a "non-typical" action, the person being spoken to may intentionally misinterpret
what they say as direct speech. In Figure 6.1 Sarge[9] uses a declarative sentence
(*I'd like this pencil sharpened*) indirectly to make a request. Beetle, by saying *If I
was using it, I'd like it sharpened too*, intentionally misinterprets Sarge as having
made a direct assertion.

Further on in this chapter we will take a closer look at precisely how we
translate sentences into their indirect meanings. But first, let's have a look at
a special class of very powerful verbs that actually perform actions by merely
being spoken. If anyone doubts for a moment the power of speech, he or she need
only look at the effects of what we call 'performative' verbs. These words are,
in some ways, magical in that they explicitly name the action they perform. Here
are some examples of *performatives* used in utterances:

> I promise to mow the lawn.
> I order you to leave.
> I bet you five bucks that I can make this shot.
> I sentence you to 30 days in jail.

All of these examples have the form of a declarative sentence, but three features
set them apart from everyday, run-of-the-mill assertions:

(1)   They contain a performative verb (i.e. a verb that names the act it
         performs),
(2)   they have a first person (i.e. *I*) subject, and
(3)   they are in the present tense.

Furthermore, as we shall see below, they can only be used effectively in certain
appropriate contexts.

As noted above, a performative verb is one that performs the action it names.
In other words, when someone says *I promise*, or *I order*, or *I bet*, that someone
performs the act of promising, ordering, or betting. And that is an altogether

different thing from saying, for instance, *I mow the lawn*. Saying the verb *mow* doesn't perform the action its names. You actually need a lawn mower for that. Saying *I mow . . .* doesn't get the lawn mowed, unless you are some kind of wizard or genie whose utterances can magically alter reality.

Performatives also use the first person. In other words, only the person uttering the words can perform the action. For instance, if we said *Mary bets you $50 that Italy will win the World Cup*, that utterance doesn't constitute an actual bet. Mary, on hearing us, is likely to say *No, I don't!* It clearly doesn't commit Mary to paying you $50 if Italy doesn't win the World Cup or commit you to paying her the same amount if they do. For the bet to take place, Mary has to say ***I bet** you $50 that Italy will win the World Cup*.

Performatives also use the present tense. If Mary says, *I **will** bet you $50 that Italy will win the World Cup*, the future tense of the verb (*will bet*) merely proposes a bet – and doesn't constitute a bet in and of itself. Similarly, if Mary says, *Yesterday, I bet you $50 that Italy would win the World Cup*, then she's making an assertion about what happened in the past – perhaps, she's reminding you about the bet she actually did make with you yesterday and now it's time to pay up.

If you're not sure whether or not an utterance meets the first three requirements (performative verb, first person, and present tense), there's a little trick you can use to check. Insert the word *hereby* between the subject and verb, and see if it works as an utterance. Here are two utterances that pass the test:

> I **hereby** promise to mow the lawn.   This sentence performs a promise.
> I **hereby** order you to leave.   This sentence performs an order.

Here are three that don't:

> I **hereby** walk to the store.   *Walk* is not a performative verb.
> Mary **hereby** bets you that Italy will win the World Cup.
>   Performatives have to be in the first person.
> I **hereby** sentenced you to one year's probation.
>   Performatives must be in present tense.

Even if an utterance meets all the formal requirements of a performative (that is, if it uses the first person and has a verb that is both performative and cast in the present tense), it still might fail if it isn't used in an appropriate context. For a performative to succeed, it must match its context in several ways. First, and perhaps most fundamentally, there must be a procedure in place for performing the action a performative names. For instance, the utterance *I bet you* can perform the action its verb names because it's part of a more general, and conventionally recognized, procedure for wagering money (or other valuables) for or against the outcome of some event. Other utterances, although they may satisfy the formal requirements, can fall short of that status if there's no existing procedure to make them a real performative. Consider the utterance *I divorce you*, for instance. It uses the first person and present tense, and has a verb that looks like it could be a performative verb, but in most Western cultures there is no conventional or legal procedure that would allow one member of a married couple to divorce the other simply by uttering those words. In some cultures, however, the word *divorce* is in fact a performative verb. A Moslem man can dissolve his marriage by saying to his wife, with full awareness after much thinking and consideration, the words *talluqtuki* 'I have divorced you' or *anti taliq* 'You are divorced' (some require the words to be spoken three times, and some prohibit it). What is clear in this is that the performing depends not only on the meaning of the words themselves, but on who is saying them and whether the culture ascribes that particular power to the words in question.

Or consider this rather ridiculous example. After delivering a speech to the Republican National Convention in 2004, Zell Miller, the fiery (and somewhat crotchety) senator from Georgia, gave an interview to Chris Matthews. During the interview, Senator Miller grew increasingly angry with Matthews' line of questioning and, exasperated, Miller challenged – or, at least, indirectly challenged – Matthews to a duel:

> I wished we lived in the day where you could challenge a person to a duel.

Matthews and the other pundits on the panel erupted in laughter, and their delight must surely have sprung from the incongruity between Miller's very earnest challenge and the absence of any procedure that would allow him to bring it off. The interesting aspect of this exchange is that Miller could certainly have said *I hereby challenge you to a duel*. This utterance would meet, on the face of it, all the requirements of being a performative speech act. The only thing preventing it from working in this way is the fact that we now have laws that prohibit it. So, just as Islamic law empowers the verb *divorce* to perform that act, US statutes currently prohibit *challenge to a duel* from having the power it once had. Note that *challenge* is still a quite usable performative verb, as in *I challenge you to a game of one-on-one basketball*. It's only the locution *challenge to a duel* which comes under the revised statutes.

Even if a procedure is in place, a perfomative can still go wrong if the parts of that procedure are executed incorrectly or incompletely. If during a promise, for instance, the speaker says *I promise to . . .* and then mumbles the rest, the other participant might accuse the speaker of not performing the promise correctly. Or, if the performative is executed correctly, but one of the participants doesn't carry it out completely, the other participant might cry foul. Such is the case in an episode from *Seinfeld* when Kramer tries to renege on a bet he made with Jerry. Here's the background: Kramer announces that he's going to remodel his apartment by getting rid of all his furniture and, in its place, build "levels" with steps, carpeting, and lots of pillows – just like, Kramer says, "ancient Egypt." Jerry doesn't believe Kramer will do it. Kramer insists that he will, and just to show how serious he is, he bets Jerry "a big dinner with dessert" and Jerry accepts the bet. Some time later, Kramer says he's abandoned the remodeling project, and Jerry tries unsuccessfully to collect on the bet:

> JERRY: So, when do I get my dinner?
> KRAMER: There's no dinner. The bet's off. I'm not gonna do it.
> JERRY: Yes. I know you're not gonna do it. That's why I bet.
> KRAMER: There's no bet if I'm not doing it.
> JERRY: That's the bet! That you're not doing it.
> KRAMER: Yeah well, I could do it. I don't want to do it.
> JERRY: We didn't bet on if you wanted to. We bet on if it would be done.
> KRAMER: And it could be done.
> JERRY: Well of course it could be done! Anything could be done, but it is only done if it's done. Show me the levels.
> KRAMER: But I don't want the levels!
> JERRY: That's the bet![10]

Here, Kramer is treating the bet that he made as substantially less than a performative act. Having made the bet (performed the act) himself, he imagines that it is his prerogative to nullify it. But, contra Kramer's misunderstanding, performative acts once performed are actually out there in the world and have an existence independent of the person who performs them. Performatives are not performances, they create facts. Kramer can no more declare that he is not party to a bet than a just-married spouse can nullify *I do*.

In addition to procedural constraints, appropriateness to context also requires that a performative be uttered by someone empowered to do the act in a situation in which the act is licit. Take this potential perfomative, for instance:

> I sentence you to one month in the county jail and one year's probation.

It only works as a performative if it is spoken by a judge to a defendant in court following a guilty verdict. If the bailiff or court secretary or someone in the gallery blurts it out after the verdict is read, it occurs in the appropriate setting and at the appropriate time during the proceedings, but it still doesn't work because none of these people is empowered to deliver a sentence. Similarly, it also doesn't work if a judge says it to someone who has cut him off as he's leaving the courthouse parking lot. It's certainly uttered by someone who is empowered to deliver it, but it occurs in a setting in which the utterance isn't licit. A judge just can't roam around town sentencing people to jail.

In all of these examples illustrating appropriateness to context, we can say that the performatives misfired in some way. In other cases, a performative can go wrong when a participant behaves insincerely and says something that he or she doesn't intend or believe to be true. For instance, say a friend of yours bets you $20 on the outcome of this weekend's game. If, at the time this friend made this bet, he had no intention of paying up should he lose, then we could say the perfomative was made inappropriately. The same would be true if it was you, and not the friend, who had no intention of paying up at the time of the bet.

As promised, with the understanding we now have about the typology of speech acts, about direct vs. indirect speech, and about performatives, we can now take a closer look at precisely how we translate sentences into their indirect meanings. In order to perform specific speech acts successfully, certain contextual conditions need to obtain (the terminology for these is "felicity conditions").

For instance, in order for person A to request that person B do X, the following things must be true:

Person A has to believe that X has not yet been done;
Person A has to believe that Person B can actually do X;
Person A has to believe that Person B is willing to do X; and
Person A has to actually want X to be done.

So, if Joe asks Harry to take out the garbage, it must be the case that the garbage hasn't yet gone out, that Joe believes Harry can do it, that Joe believes Harry is willing, and that Joe actually wants it taken out. The request:

> JOE: Harry, please take out the garbage.

will make no sense and not be a successful speech act if (i) the garbage is already out on the curb, (ii) Harry is in a full body cast, (iii) Harry has never, ever helped with any household chore in the six months he's lived with Joe, or (iv) Joe has a garbage fetish and has been stockpiling the garbage in his room for the last month.

It is through these "felicity" conditions that we calculate the meaning of indirect speech acts. So, if Joe were to say to Harry *The garbage hasn't gone out yet*, he would (through the first condition shown above) be indirectly requesting that Harry take it out. If he were to ask *Harry, can you take out the garbage?*, he would be making the request by reference to the second condition. If he asked *Harry, would you mind taking out the garbage?*, he would be referencing the third. And, if he said *Harry, I really would like to have the garbage taken out now*, he would be relying on the last.

Notice that our interpretation of an utterance (that is, our understanding of what speech act is being performed) fundamentally depends upon the condition of the context. For instance, one of the conditions necessary for the performance of a promise to do X is that:

Person A believes that Person B actually wants X to be done.

A promise turns automatically into a threat (using the very same utterance) if:

Person A believes that Person B **does not want** X to be done.

It is in this way that if one says *I'm going to tickle you* to our youngest child Isaac (who likes to be tickled), it is a promise. The same utterance spoken to our oldest Elijah, who hates it, turns into a threat.

The following dialogue from *The Office* illustrates what a key role these conditions play in negotiating the space of speech acts.

> DWIGHT SCHRUTE: OK. I'm going to have to search your car. Give me your keys.
> RYAN HOWARD: I am not giving you my keys.
> DWIGHT SCHRUTE: Don't make me do this the hard way.
> RYAN HOWARD: What's the hard way?
> DWIGHT SCHRUTE: I go down to the police station, on my lunch break. I tell a police officer (I know several) what I suspect you may have in your car. He requests a hearing from a judge and obtains a search warrant. Once he has said warrant, he will drive over here and make you give him the keys to your car, and you will have to obey him.
> RYAN HOWARD: Yeah, let's do it that way.

Here, Dwight is making a threat. A necessary condition for threats, as we noted above, is that the hearer does not want the act done. This is the nature of the metaphor *Don't make me do this the **hard** way*. In this way, Dwight's threatening to do it the hard way is supposed to mean 'hard for Ryan'. However, as it turns out, what Dwight describes would be hard for him, not necessarily for Ryan, and Dwight doesn't account for that. On hearing that the *hard way* is actually hard for Dwight but not for Ryan, Ryan is happy to accept the conditions promised in the threat, since they no longer meet the grounds for being one.

Cooperative Principles of conversation

Now that we know how indirect speech acts are performed and how we come to calculate the context-specific use to which our utterances are put, we can plug this into a discussion of creative ways to use language, starting with the engine under the hood, the Cooperative Principle. H. P. Grice made the reasonable and not surprising assertion that communication depends on cooperation. In this regard, he suggested that speakers are expected to:

(1)   Relevance
        Be relevant (that is, stay on topic)
(2)   Quality
        Say what they know to be true (that is, not lie or make up stuff)
(3)   Quantity
        Give the right amount of information (that is, not too much or too little)
(4)   Manner
        Be clear (that is, organize their thoughts, use shared vocabulary, etc.)

These four points are called the cooperative maxims or principles. They are not exactly laws rigidly governing conversation (as we'll see below, speakers depart from them frequently), but they do serve as a set of default expectations for most conversations. If, for instance, you asked your roommate *Have you seen my car keys?*, you would expect her answer to be relevant to the topic or purpose of your question, such as:

> I saw them on the kitchen table.

But not:

> The capital of North Dakota is Bismarck.

You would also want her answer to convey what she knew to be true and not contain falsehoods. If she had in fact seen your keys on the kitchen table, you would expect her to say so and not say *They're behind the couch* or *The landlord must have stolen them.* You would also expect her answer to give the right amount of information and not say too little, such as:

> I've seen them.

or too much:

> I saw them on the kitchen table approximately four or five inches from the right edge, spread out in a fan-like pattern, with the ignition key pointing slightly north by northwest.

Finally, you would expect her to be clear and not obscure:

> I spied their glitterings on the four-posted eating platform.
> Iway awsay emthay onway ethay itchenkay abletay. (Pig Latin)

nor disorderly:

> The kitchen table on, them I saw. (Yoda-speak)

Sometimes speakers don't follow the principles, and there are different ways in which this can come about. A speaker can, for instance, tacitly **violate** the maxim of quality (that is, lie) or quantity (by not providing the information actually requested, but leading someone to believe that they are doing so). An example of the latter is found in a recent *Hi and Lois* strip, where Dot asks her brother Ditto:

> Have you seen my doll today?

He answers, *Nope*, but in the next panel thinks to himself (and the reader) . . . *(but I did see her yesterday when I stuffed her in a boot in Mom's closet).* Clearly Ditto has engaged in deception by answering the question truthfully (in a literal sense), but providing less information than would be needed to answer his sister's request, and thus not implicating himself.

It is also the case that a speaker may simply and explicitly **opt out** of cooperating. This happens frequently when one person asks another for information that the second person is either not willing or not permitted to reveal. So, if one were to ask a neighbor whether they got a raise this year and how much they earn, the neighbor might readily and reasonably respond by saying any of the following:

> It's none of your business.
> I don't feel comfortable answering that.
> If you'll forgive me for not answering, I'll forgive you for asking. (per *Dear Abby*)

Opting out occasionally can take a humorous turn, as we see from the following Brian Kiley joke:

> I went to a bookstore today. I asked the woman behind the counter where the self-help section was. She said, "If I told you, that would defeat the whole purpose."

Here, the bookstore clerk opts out of answering the patron's question (refuses to cooperate) in order to make a dig at the customer.

The most creative utilization of the conversational principles occurs, however, in the **flouting** of the maxims. Flouting a conversational maxim, as opposed to merely violating it, involves violating it in an ostentatious way, so as to communicate to the listener that the maxim is being disregarded. Most often, the flouting of a maxim carries with it an additional, non-explicit message, above and beyond the literal meaning of what is being communicated. To use an example from Grice, imagine that a student came asking for a letter of recommendation, and the professor wrote a letter as follows:

> "Dear Sir, Mr. X's command of English is excellent, and his attendance at tutorials has been regular. Yours, etc."

One would take this letter to be a negative assessment of the student's abilities, even though nothing explicitly negative is found in it. The reason for this is that the letter blatantly flouts the maxim of quantity, giving far less information about the student than is normally warranted in such a letter. The failure to provide information in sufficient quantity will lead a reader of this letter to presume that no additional positive information about the student can be had (under the aphorism, "if you can't say something nice, don't say anything at all").

The flouting of maxims plays a key role in communicating difficult messages without being explicit, in expressing sarcasm, and in jokes that rely on these. The sitcom *Frasier* features a good deal of dialogue that relies on the flouting of conversational maxims. The cast includes the two Crane brothers, Frasier and Niles, both psychiatrists, along with their working-class father, Martin, a retired cop. In the following exchange between Martin and Frasier, Frasier's answer appears to violate the maxim of relevance:

> MARTIN: I just need a comfortable place to park my fanny.
> FRASIER: How about Florida?
> MARTIN: I heard that.

Martin here is just looking for a place in the room to sit down, and Frasier's answer appears completely irrelevant. This invites Martin to calculate what message Frasier might be trying to get across, and leads to the conclusion that Frasier (who would fondly wish for his father to move out) is suggesting that Martin should find himself a place to sit down (i.e. to live) in another state.

In another exchange, here between Frasier and Niles, Frasier is talking to Niles about his estranged wife, Maris, and it is Niles' answer that flouts relevance.

> FRASIER: By calling her so many times, you give her all the power! You're much better off coming from a position of strength!
> NILES: Don't pour that sherry on your shirt: it will stain.
> FRASIER: What?
> NILES: Oh, I'm sorry. I thought this was the portion of the afternoon where we give each other patently obvious advice.

Niles' response to Frasier's advice is patently irrelevant to the preceding conversation, leading Frasier to remark on it (*What?*). It is here that Niles connects the dots for Frasier, suggesting to him that the "relevance" of Frasier's remark and his answer to it is that they both constitute patently obvious (and from Niles' perspective, unwanted) advice. In Niles' second comeback, he makes a statement which is blatantly false (flouting quality in this case) and thereby sarcastic.

The flouting of quantity also frequently plays a key role in jokes and other humor. The following two examples, like the professor's letter above, rely on the blatant delivery of less than the requisite amount of information:

> When is the best time to go shopping? When the stores are open.

Here, of course, the answer is obvious and uninformative. The only possible way of understanding the answer to this question is to take it as sarcasm. Similarly, in an episode of the *Shoe* comic strip, a patron in Roz's diner asks Shoe:

> How's the meatloaf here?

to which he responds:

> Well, Roz gets upset if I criticize her cooking, so I'll try to be positive . . . . It's boneless.

Given that meatloaf is, by definition, boneless, Shoe's response is completely uninformative, flouts quantity, and has the characteristics of the "letter of recommendation" that we cited, above.

Similar flouting of quality for comedic effect is also occasionally found, and can serve the familiar function of delivering a message of sarcasm. In the following exchange between Niles and Frasier, Frasier's answer clearly violates quality because it obviously misrepresents his knowledge about his brother's profession:

> NILES: Who knows why anybody does anything?
> FRASIER: [*looks incredulously at him*] Remind me again what you do for a living.

Frasier's comment here is designed to cast aspersions on Niles' rhetorical question, suggesting sarcastically that being a psychiatrist should enable him to know something more about the world than his question would indicate.

Flouting of maxims is a great comedic tool, and shows up in a host of genres. A classic musical routine featuring jokes set to music is the Arkansas Traveler, a fiddle (or banjo) tune played to a monologue (or dialogue) that depicts a conversation between a local musician sitting out on his porch and a lost traveler who has stopped to get directions. The repartee varies from performance to performance, but typically includes exchanges such as the following. Each of these relies on some aspect of flouting conversational maxims to make a joke:

TRAVELER: Hey there, mister. Where's this road go to?
FIDDLER: Well, since I've been livin' here, it ain't gone nowheres.
           (flouts quantity and relevance, ignores the 'leads to' meaning of *goes to*)
TRAVELER: Mister. You've lived around here all your life?
FIDDLER: Nope. Not yet.
           (flouts quantity and relevance, ignores the implied 'until this moment')
TRAVELER: Hey, mister. How far is it to Little Rock?
FIDDLER: I don' know, but there's a heck of a big'un down there in the corn field.
           (flouts quality and relevance, ignores the proper name meaning of *little rock*)
TRAVELER: Mister, you know I don't believe there's much between you and a fool.
FIDDLER: Nope. Just the front yard there.
           (flouts relevance, intentionally substitutes *distance* for *difference*)

These jokes are, unsurprisingly, much more entertaining with the musical accompaniment, which the reader can find on the website.[11]

Presupposition

Before closing out this chapter, it is essential that we discuss one additional aspect of language in the context of its use. Presuppositions are the off-stage mechanisms that support, enhance, and embellish the making of assertions. It's the way that we get to say, with a given utterance, more than we are actually asserting. For instance, if one says:

It's raining outside.

then one has simply asserted that it is raining outside now, with no accompanying suggestion of what may or may not have been going on until now. But if the utterance is changed to:

> It's still raining outside.

the new utterance not only asserts everything that the previous one does, but it also carries with it the implicit suggestion that it has been raining outside prior to this point. Note, however, that the addition of the word *still* does not actually assert anything about it raining before. It is presented as a "given." We can see how this is so when we try to deny the utterance. If you were to reply to the statement *It's still raining outside* by saying *No, it isn't*, you would only be denying that it is raining now and would be saying nothing about what happened before. In order to challenge the "presupposition" carried by the word *still*, you would need to explicitly challenge it, saying something like *No, it's not and it wasn't raining before now either*.

Questions that contain (unwelcome) presuppositions are what we call "loaded questions." They can't be answered simply and directly without accepting the unwanted baggage. For example, if you haven't been angry at all, there is simply no way that you can answer the *yes–no* question:

> Are you still angry?

without (falsely) admitting that you were angry previously. Neither *no* nor *yes* will make it go away. Lawyers are notoriously adept at positing such questions, such as:

> When did you stop embezzling funds from the office travel account?

They frustrate witnesses, when they are successful (and the judge tells the witness to "just answer the question"), and earn approbation from judges when they are caught ("you're leading the witness").

Presuppositions can also find their way into humor, as this snippet of dialogue from *Monty Python and the Holy Grail* shows. Here, King Arthur asks a serf named Dennis about the resident of a nearby castle:

KING ARTHUR:	Old woman!
DENNIS:	Man!
ARTHUR:	Man. Sorry. What knight lives in that castle over there?
DENNIS:	I'm thirty-seven.
ARTHUR:	I – what?
DENNIS:	I'm thirty-seven. I'm not old.
ARTHUR:	Well, I can't just call you "Man".
DENNIS:	Well, you could say "Dennis".
ARTHUR:	Well, I didn't know you were called "Dennis".
DENNIS:	Well, you didn't bother to find out, did you?

Arthur's utterance *Old woman!* is merely designed to get the serf's attention. Of course, the presuppositions carried by this statement are that the person being addressed is a woman, and is old. Dennis challenges the first of these immediately, and gets an apology from Arthur. Thinking that this is the end of it, Arthur goes on to ask a question. Dennis, for his part, is having none of it, challenging Arthur's use of the word *old*. And so it goes, with Arthur locked into a conversation about presuppositions, and never getting his question answered.

In this chapter, we've covered a lot of ground: from deixis (or pointing words), indirectness, speech acts, performatives, conversational maxims, to presuppositions. Throughout we've seen the many ways in which the meaning of an utterance depends on its context of use. In fact, we've shown just how crucial this link between utterance and context is. In the next chapter, we build on this work and examine not only individual utterances but collections of utterances fitted into larger structures (or discourses), showing how their meanings and functions also depend on the contexts in which they are used.

7   Fitting the pieces together

The structure of discourse

A dog will stay stupid. That's why we love them so much. The entire time we know them, they're idiots. Think of your dog. Every time you come home, he thinks it's amazing. He has no idea how you accomplish this every day. You walk in the door, the joy of this experience overwhelms him. He looks at you, *He's back, it's that guy, that same guy!* He can't believe it. Everything is amazing to your dog. *Another can of food? I don't believe it!*

–Jerry Seinfeld[1]

This bit from Seinfeld's stand-up routine might seem loosely put together. Just some guy talking off the cuff about dogs and their owners. But actually, it's fairly well organized. Consider its overall design. It begins with a general statement about dogs and their stupidity and then illustrates that point with a specific example – that is, the dog's reaction (or overreaction) to its owner. This two-part structure – a general point followed by an example illustrating that point – gives the Seinfeld excerpt its overall shape. It also serves as a framework into which smaller structural elements fit. For instance, *Think of your dog* serves as a transition between the general point and specific example, and the example itself takes the form of a narrative: it's a story recounting how a dog will typically behave when its owner returns home. And within this narrative, we can find smaller structural units, including repetitions of words, quotes, even another general-to-specific pattern: *Everything is amazing to your dog* (general point); *Another can of food? I don't believe it!* (example illustrating that point).

We could go on analyzing other structural elements in the Seinfeld bit (and we will give those elements a closer look in a minute), but if we left it at that – if we limited ourselves to looking only at its verbal form or shape, then we'd only have a partial understanding of how it all works. To complete the picture, we also need to consider how its structures interact with its context, including: who the speaker is, who the audience is, what their assumptions and expectations are, and where, when, and how they interact. Take the general-to-specific pattern again. It's a fairly common structure and appears in all kinds of speaking and writing – humorous and otherwise. But Seinfeld's use of it is constrained by context, particularly who he is and what his audience expects from him. Seinfeld is, of course, a comedian, and his audience expects him to be funny. So it's not enough for him to follow a general-to-specific pattern – or any other pattern, for that matter. He must do so in a way that provokes laughter. If he had opened with

A dog will stay stupid and then gone on to talk about canine intelligence, he'd have followed the general-to-specific pattern, but it wouldn't have been funny, and wouldn't have worked. He doesn't do that, of course. He knows his role and knows what his audience wants. So he presents a monologue that both has a definite structure, and is appropriate to the context in which it appears.

Structure and context – these are the two elements that figure most prominently as we take a look at **discourse** (which is what we call language use above the level of the sentence). In the previous chapter on pragmatics, we examined the sentence in the context of its use. In this chapter, we go a step further and examine how sentences fit together into longer structured texts, and how those structured texts function in the contexts in which they're used. We'll begin by looking at structure by itself, and while our examples mostly involve humor, the structures they illustrate are identical to what is found in all kinds of discourse. We then look at context and how speakers, listeners, and physical settings affect the shape and interpretation of discourse. We end the chapter with a look at genre – a notion that brings structure and context together.

Structure

The Seinfeld bit, as we saw, employs a general-to-specific pattern that gives it its overall shape or design. But there are, in addition to this, many other structural parts and devices that work on a smaller scale to form links between and across sentences. And like the general-to-specific pattern, these smaller units of organization are common to many kinds of discourse – not just stand-up comedy. Some of these smaller units include using repetition and pronouns, moving from information already known to listeners to new information, developing a topic through conventional conceptual patterns, and following various conversational patterns.

Repetition

Let's start with repetitions, which come in at least two forms. First, there are simple repetitions of words. In the Seinfeld bit, *dog* appears three times, while *amazing* and *guy* each appear twice. These repetitions help hold the discourse together. The repetition of *dog* helps give the discourse its central focus, keeping the listener's attention on that creature and its behavior. The repetition of the word *amazing* helps to reinforce the simple-minded nature of the dog's response to his owner. And the repetition of the word *guy* in *it's that guy, that same guy* helps to emphasize the informal familiarity of that relationship. Another form of repetition involves using synonymous or backward-referring expressions to recall something already mentioned. The sentence *they're idiots* repeats the idea expressed earlier as *A dog will stay stupid*. And later in the discourse, the noun phrase *this experience* stands in for *You walk in the door*. Much like the simple repetition of words, synonymous and backward-referring expressions help bind the passage together. They not only link back to other locations in the discourse, but also allow the speaker to introduce further details about the characters and events being described. They further allow the speaker (as we've seen) to reinforce particular attitudes toward the characters being described.

Pronouns

As in any discourse, other links are forged by pronouns. Recall from Chapter 5 that pronouns are, essentially, variables. They have no meaning on their own. Because of this, pronouns are the most basic tools for holding bits of discourse together since, in order to understand what they mean, listeners must refer back to the words they stand in for (that is, their antecedents). Consider the pronouns in this portion of the excerpt:

> Think of your dog. Every time you come home, he thinks it's amazing. He has no idea how you accomplish this every day. You walk in the door, the joy of this experience overwhelms him. He looks at you . . .

If you were to circle each pronoun in this passage and draw a line from it back to its antecedent, the result would look something like a web, with each strand connecting one part of the passage to another. There are three things being referred to here: *you* (the listener), *your dog*, and what is happening (*you come home*). The possessive *your* and the subject pronoun *you* (repeated four times) all point back to YOU (the listener). The three instances of *he* and one instance of *him* all refer to *your dog*. Finally, the *it's* and the *this* refer to what is happening *you come home*. So, in this passage, through the use of pronouns, Seinfeld is able to refer to these three things a total of thirteen times in the excerpt above containing thirty-eight words (without sounding repetitious).

Known to new information

Another common structural device involves arranging information within successive sentences in predictable ways. Typically, the order of information presented goes from what the listeners already know to what is new to them. Consider these two alternatives:

> (A) A dog will stay stupid. That's why we love them so much.
> (B) A dog will stay stupid. We love them so much because of that.

In both cases, *that* refers back to the first sentence, namely the claim that *a dog will stay stupid*. However, in A the word *that* comes first, and in B it comes last. If given a choice between A or B, most listeners or readers would prefer A. Why? Because A preserves the flow of information from known to new, and B disrupts it. Since the assertion *a dog will stay stupid* was introduced in the first sentence, *that* acquires the status of known information in the second, while the new information is *we love them so much*. In A, the information flows from known (*that*) to new (*we love them so much*). In B, it goes the wrong way, from new to known.

In extended samples of discourse this known-to-new pattern often results in interlocking chains of information, with each new sentence beginning with information from previous ones before moving on to the new stuff. The following passage comes from the same bit about dogs and their alleged stupidity. As you read it, think about how the information is staged within and across sentences:

> Dogs want to be people. That's what their lives are about. They don't like being dogs. They're with people all the time, they want to graduate . . . . That's why the greatest, most exciting moment in the life of a dog is the front seat of the car. You and him in the front seat. It's the only place where your head and his are on the exact same level. He sits up there, he thinks, *This is more like it. You and me together, this is the way it should be.*[2]

In the second sentence, the pronoun *That* picks up information from the first sentence before moving forward to the new information – which, in this case, is *what their lives are about*. Sentence three begins with the pronoun *They*, which is known information referring back to dogs, while *don't like being dogs* introduces new information about dogs. The two clauses in sentence four also begin with known information (*They* again), and then each goes on to deliver even more new information about dogs. And so the pattern goes throughout the rest of the passage: known to new, known to new, known to new.

This known-to-new pattern offers comedians a structure which they can work to their advantage. In other words, they can approach the organization of their sentences as they might approach the construction of their jokes – that is, by saving the new and surprising information for the end. Seinfeld adopts this strategy in another selection from his stand-up routine:

> There are many things you can point to as proof that the human is not smart. But my personal favorite would have to be that we needed to invent the helmet. What was happening, apparently, was that we were involved in a lot of activities that were cracking our heads. We chose *not* to avoid doing these activities but, instead, to come up with some sort of device to help us continue enjoying our head cracking lifestyles. The helmet.[3]

As you read through this passage, where does the humor seem to spike? Where is the humor most concentrated? Although each sentence is not a full-blown joke, Seinfeld approaches each as if it were, treating the ends of his sentences as if they were punch lines. What if Seinfeld had delivered his bit in this way, with the known and new information flipped around:

> The human is not smart, and there are many things you can point to as proof. That we needed to invent the helmet would have to be my personal favorite. Our being involved in a lot of activities that were cracking our heads is

what was happening, apparently. To continue enjoying our head cracking lifestyles, we chose to come up with some sort of device – the helmet – instead of avoiding these activities.

In addition to being clunkier than the original, this version dampens, if not destroys, the humor. It does so because it mismanages how the information is positioned. In our altered version, the humorous material either appears at the beginning of sentences or is buried in the middle. The original works so well because Seinfeld places the new and surprising information – *the human is not smart*, *to invent the helmet*, *cracking our heads*, and *head cracking lifestyles* – at the end of his sentences, and as any comedian would tell you, that's where the zinger should go.

Conceptual patterns

You might have noticed that the overall structure of the "helmet" passage mirrors that of the "dog" one. In other words, Seinfeld begins with a general statement – *the human is not smart* – and then follows that with a specific example illustrating that point: the invention of the helmet. But this pattern is only one among many other structures for organizing larger stretches of discourse. We've already mentioned narrative, but there's also comparison-and-contrast, description, problem-and-solution, and so on. These conceptual structures offer speakers and writers fairly conventional ways for developing a topic, and like the general-to-specific structure, they give longer stretches of discourse a recognizable shape. Here's Chris Rock using a problem-and-solution pattern (note that this example comes from 1997, before Barak Obama came on the scene):

> We still need a black leader. What are we going to do?
>
> They import basketball players from Africa. How about bringing in one of those kings? They ran a country. We need a leader who already ran something. But we never get that guy. We get the *next* guy. Martin Luther King got shot – Jesse was standing next to him.
>
> "Let's use him."
>
> As far as I'm concerned our leader doesn't even have to be black. Let's get Pat Riley. He's led a lot of black men to the championships. Maybe he can take us to the promised land.[4]

The first two sentences introduce a problem, and the rest of the discourse considers possible solutions. Like narrative and the general-to-specific pattern Seinfeld uses, the problem-and-solution pattern is already part of most of our linguistic repertoires. When we encounter structural patterns like these, we are free to focus less on the how a given speaker or writer structures their observations and more on the observations themselves.

Conversational structure

So far we've looked at samples of discourse delivered by a single speaker, but discourse involving two or more speakers can also have structure. Take your standard conversation. It typically begins with some kind of opening routine – an exchange of *hello*s, for instance, or introductions by name, or perhaps some ritual opening like *Nice weather we're having*. Following this would be the body of the conversation, and following that would be some kind of closing routine, like an exchange of *goodbye*s. Here's an example of the structure in full. It comes from the sitcom *Seinfeld* and involves Jerry's arch nemesis, Newman, who sees Jerry and his girlfriend Rachel making out at the theater during *Schindler's List* (a film about the Holocaust). The next day, Newman drops by Jerry's apartment where Jerry's parents (Helen and Morty) are staying for a visit. Once he wheedles himself inside, Newman shares his scandalous news:

NEWMAN: Hello Mrs. Seinfeld
HELEN: Hello, Newman. Jerry's not here. [goes to shut the door on him]
NEWMAN: Uh ah [stops her from closing the door; walks in]
          Having a nice trip? [walks over, grabs a Junior Mint, smells it then puts it in his pocket]
HELEN: Wonderful, we went to the theater last night.
NEWMAN: Oh the theater. Because I was wondering.
HELEN: Wondering what?
NEWMAN: Why I didn't see you at Schindler's List with Jerry.
HELEN: Well we already saw it.
NEWMAN: Oh, well it's a good thing for Jerry that you didn't go.
MORTY: [getting up from the table and coming over] Why is that?
NEWMAN: Well he really seemed to have his hands full if you know what I mean.
HELEN: I'm afraid I don't.
NEWMAN: Him and his little buxom friend Rachel were going at it pretty good in the balcony.
MORTY: What?
NEWMAN: What, do I have to spell it out for ya? He was moving on her like the storm-troopers into Poland.
HELEN: Jerry was necking during Schindler's List?
NEWMAN: Yes! A more offensive spectacle I cannot recall. Anyway I just really came up to get some detergent.
HELEN: Jerry sends his laundry out.
NEWMAN: [laughing] Oh ho right. Well very nice seeing you folks and by the way you didn't hear this from me.
          Tata [runs down the hallway laughing].[5]

This exchange has all the structural ingredients of a typical conversation. It begins with Newman and Helen trading *hello*s, and then, before Helen can cut the conversation short by saying *Jerry's not here* and closing the door, Newman keeps it going by asking a seemingly innocent question, *Having a nice trip?*

With this question, the body of the conversation begins. It ends with Newman performing a standard closing routine: *Well very nice seeing you . . . Tata.*

Within this overall structure, there are other patterns of organization. Note how the conversation progresses as a series of turns: Newman says something, then Helen says something, then Newman says something, then Helen says something, and so on. This turn-taking pattern is common to most conversations and keeps them from being free-for-all's with everyone speaking at the same time. Note also how these turns fall into paired utterances. Newman says *Hello*, and Helen says *Hello*. Newman asks a question, and Helen answers it. Helen asks a question, and Newman answers it. Linguists call these paired utterances **adjacency pairs**, or two utterances spoken by different speakers in which the first utterance creates a strong expectation that the second one will follow. In addition to greeting–greeting pairs (*Hello – Hello*) and question–answer pairs (*Having a nice trip? – Wonderful*), there are offer–acceptance/denial pairs (*Have a Junior Mint? – Yes, thank you* or *No, thank you*), request–acceptance/denial pairs (*Lend me a hand – Sure* or *Sorry, I can't*), and leave-taking pairs (*Goodbye – Goodbye*). Each member of a pair may be performed directly (as in all the examples we just used), or indirectly, as Newman and Helen do towards the end of the excerpt where there is a request–denial pair: *Anyway I just really came up to get some detergent* (indirect request) and *Jerry sends his laundry out* (indirect denial).

Adjacency pairs contribute greatly to the organization of conversations. In fact, they exert such a powerful influence that when the first member of an adjacency pair is not followed by an expected second member, the first speaker is likely to think that something has gone wrong. If Helen had refused to answer Newman's question *Having a nice trip?* and remained silent instead, Newman would have received overwhelming evidence that his presence was unwelcome, although Helen trying to cut the conversation short from the get-go by closing the door on him should have been a tip-off. We might even say that joking itself is structured by an adjacency pair formula. Telling or cracking a joke would be the first member of the pair, while laughter would be the second. If a speaker delivers a joke and the listener doesn't laugh, then that speaker knows that his or her joke has flopped.

Context

So far we've focused on how discourse is structured, but to understand discourse fully, we also need to consider its context. As suggested in previous chapters, context refers to everything that surrounds a discourse and plays a role in interpreting its meaning and effects. These external factors include such things as who the speaker and listener are, what they know or believe, and where, when, and how they interact. Take any of the examples we used in the previous section. Their meanings and effects all depend, at some level, on context.

The conversation between Newman and Jerry's parents, for instance, would be difficult to understand if viewers don't have certain kinds of knowledge: (1) that the relationship between Newman and Jerry (and, by proxy, his parents) is an antagonistic one, (2) that *Schindler's List* is about the Holocaust, (3) that the Seinfelds are Jewish, (4) that a guest who takes food (the Junior Mint) without being offered is rude, (5) that tattletailing on a friend to his parents is a underhanded thing to do, (6) that World War II began with Germany invading Poland, and so on. In the rest of this section, we'll look at some other ways that context impinges upon the meaning and function of discourse.

Who's talking to whom

Let's start with speakers and listeners – particularly the roles they play while interacting and the pre-existing identities they bring to an exchange. Look around you and you can't help but find people playing various roles through discourse. This is most obviously the case in fairly standardized encounters – encounters in which we can predict, at least in a general sense, how the talk will go: a customer places a dinner order with a waiter, a patient consults with her doctor about some ailment, two lovers whisper quietly in the corner of a room. Each of these encounters comes with a rough script that participants tend to follow. A customer at a restaurant would say something like *I'll have the filet mignon*, while the waiter might follow with *How would you like that? Rare, medium, or well done?*, and so on. Even in less standardized interactions, people still take on roles. Consider this joke in which a little old lady sees an old man on a park bench and sits down next to him:

> LADY: Are you a stranger here?
> MAN: Sort of. I used to live here years ago.
> LADY: So, where have you been?
> MAN: I was in prison – for murdering my wife.
> LADY: Really? So you're single . . . ?[6]

Throughout this series of question–answer pairs, the lady adopts one role for herself and assigns another to the man: she's the questioner, and he's the questionee. If she had said nothing when she sat down or begun with a statement rather than a question – say, an observation about the weather like *Nice day* – she would have given the man more options in how to respond. Instead, by asking a question and taking on the role that comes with that speech act, she assumes a measure of control over the encounter, prompting the man to speak and determining the topic of their conversation (that is, the status of the man as either a stranger or a resident). The man's on-topic reply shows his willingness to play the role he's been assigned. Consider the difference if he had remained silent or said, *Leave me alone* – both of which, to varying degrees, would signal an unwillingness to participate. He doesn't, and in complying with her request for information he indirectly encourages her to continue in her role as questioner – which she does even after learning that he murdered his wife. A revelation as startling as this one might shock most listeners into silence and thus end the exchange. But not this lady. For her, it's an opportunity!

The identities of the two people featured in this joke are also crucial in understanding their exchange. The joke plays on several stereotypes about men, women, and old people in general. The supposed aggressiveness of men and beliefs about prisons being mostly populated by males make the information about this man's murdering his wife and his subsequent prison stint seem more plausible. On the flip side, a stereotype about single women (especially older single women) being desperate for husbands seems also at work here. So powerful is the lady's desire for a husband that the joke invites us to believe it can cause her to gloss right over the man's horrendous crime. Imagine if the roles of the lady and man were reversed, and the man asked the same questions of the lady and she responded with the same answers as the man:

> MAN: Are you a stranger here?
> LADY: Sort of. I used to live here years ago.
> MAN: So, where have you been?
> LADY: I was in prison – for murdering my husband.
> MAN: Really? So you're single . . . ?

Does the joke work as well? What if the lady and man were young – say teenagers or young professionals? Would the joke work in either of these cases? Probably not, and we can chalk up the failure of either alternative to the power that identity has in the meaning and effect of discourse.

Speakers

These possible revisions of the lady–man joke suggest another important point about the relationship between speakers and discourse. The identity of a speaker not only influences how we interpret what that speaker says but also limits what he or she can say in the first place. In other words, who we are – the social and professional roles we occupy – affects what we say. For instance, we expect doctors to sound doctorly, mothers to sound motherly, teachers to sound teacherly. Comedians are also expected to sound comedian-ly, but their role also gives them more freedom in what they say and how they say it. They traffic in humor, and humor comes with an understanding that its speakers are not being serious and are only playing. Plus, humor often depends on surprising listeners or undermining their expectations, including how your everyday person would talk or behave.

But even here there are limits – particularly in the area of racial or ethnic humor. The unwritten rule seems to be that comedians can crack jokes about their own ethnic or racial group: whites about whites, blacks about blacks, Jews about Jews, Hispanics about Hispanics, and so on. If the comedian's group is also a minority, then jokes about members of the majority group are usually fair game: a black comedian, for instance, is relatively free to joke about whites. Comedians in a minority group may also have more freedom to target members of other minority groups: Carlos Mencia (a Hispanic comedian) often tells jokes at the expense of blacks and Asians. What you're not likely to see much of – at least in mainstream American culture – are whites telling jokes about minority groups. The logic here is that white comedians belong to a group that already wields considerable power in our culture. So a white comedian who makes fun of minorities is, in effect, throwing salt into an open wound and reinforcing various kinds of social inequality.

Listeners

Listeners also influence the discourse a speaker produces. In other words, what we say also depends on who we are talking to. Linguists call this phenomenon **audience design**, a phrase that captures well the process by which speakers tailor their discourse to suit or even match the identities of their listeners. A good, if somewhat hyperbolic, example of audience design is Larry the Cable Guy, a comedian who presents himself as a good ol' boy from the south. What many of his fans might not know is that his real name is Daniel Whitney and that he was born in Nebraska – not Tennessee or Alabama. In his early career as a comic, during the 1990s, he spoke using a more or less mainstream dialect (you can find videos of these performances on YouTube). But around 2000, perhaps in the wake of Jeff Foxworthy's success, he decided to tap into the large and lucrative market for southern or redneck humor. So he adopted a pronounced southern dialect to match the way his target audience speaks. Apparently, it worked. He's a staple of the Blue Collar Comedy Tour, and his catch-phrase *Git-R-Done* has gained national recognition.

But not everyone tailors their discourse towards their listeners in such a calculating and complete fashion as Larry the Cable Guy. Many speakers may not even be aware that their speech shifts depending on who they talk to. We probably all know someone who is a linguistic chameleon – that is, someone who, after spending extended periods of time with a particular group of people, begins to take on their speech habits, including what they typically talk about as well as their pronunciation, word choice (slang or jargon), and even their sentence structures. But it's not always a case of a near-complete linguistic transformation. In fact, it's more typical for these shifts in discourse to be short-lived and to last only as long as we are in contact with the listener who prompted the shift in the first place. For instance, we may speak more formally when interacting with figures of authority (teachers, bosses, ministers, rabbis), and the subjects of our discourse may match their interests or concerns (talk about school with teachers, work with bosses, and so on). With friends and relatives, our discourse may shift toward a more familiar or colloquial level and be about more everyday things and events. Likewise, parents may talk to their newborn using baby-talk and then shift to their regular way of speaking when talking with each other. We even knew a guy who always shifted into a southern dialect whenever he talked to his dogs. They were hound dogs, and we suspect that he thought a southern dialect best suited their hound-doggy temperaments.

The where and when of discourse

Setting or occasion also influences discourse. In other words, what we say and how we say it often depend on where we are and at what time we are there. In a library, we use hushed tones to ask for the location of a book. At a ballpark, we cheer loudly for the home team and boo the visiting one. Before a religious service, we might chat casually with our neighbor, but once the service starts, the chat stops and our discourse turns to prayer and psalm. At work, we might be all business, but when five o'clock rolls around, we might speak more freely and jokingly with our co-workers as we head out for the day. As all of these examples suggest, we expect certain kinds of discourse to occur in certain places at certain times. So strong are these expectations that comedians, cartoonists, and scriptwriters often turn them toward humorous ends. That is, they'll play with and undercut these expectations with characters who say the wrong thing in the wrong place at the wrong time. Just think of Michael Scott from the US version of *The Office*. In one episode, after Scott performs a horrendously inappropriate imitation of Chris Rock (an imitation that includes Scott – a white male – using the N-word), a consultant is brought in to deliver a seminar on racial diversity in the workplace. During the seminar, Scott tries to take over from the consultant and run the session. For their opening activity, Scott suggests, *Everybody say a race that you are attracted to sexually*. In the workplace, and especially in the workplace during a seminar on racial diversity, Scott's comment is doubly inappropriate – it's both racist and sexist. And it only gets worse from here, with Scott saying and doing increasingly inappropriate things. Matters come to a head when Scott performs a racist caricature of a convenience store owner of East Indian descent to a co-worker with the same racial background. She slaps him and thus delivers the most appropriate action in the episode.

The channels of discourse

Discourse is also influenced by the media, or channels, through which we interact. In other words, what we say and how we say it often depend on whether we're speaking with someone face-to-face, talking on the phone, writing a letter, sending a text message, yelling through a bullhorn, or broadcasting on radio or TV. We can group language-based media into three major categories:

- Media that rely on **speech**: face-to-face conversation, telephones, radios, recordings.

- Media that rely on **text**: books, letters, newspapers, magazines.
- Media that rely on some combination of speech and text – we'll call this **speech/text**, and it includes Instant Messaging, email, blogs, computer message boards.

While this categorization ignores predominately visual media (photographs, films, video games), it does allow us to consider important differences within each of these broad categories based on whether or not a given category member allows for a visual component. In face-to-face discourse, for instance, a lot of information is exchanged through visual cues as well as through speech. We gesture with our hands, we frown, we raise our eyebrows, we lean into or lean back from our listener. We also refer to things that we and our listener can see, touch, and manipulate (recall our discussion of deixis from the previous chapter): *Bring that over here*. Other kinds of spoken media lack this visual dimension, and the discourse that gets transmitted through them is affected as a result. For instance, when calling an acquaintance on the phone – someone who isn't able to recognize us by our voice alone – we usually begin by identifying ourselves (*Hi. It's Mary*) because the person on the other end can't *see* us and may not recognize our voice through a less than perfect connection. We also generally avoid statements like *Bring that over here*, unless the *that* and the *here* have already been mentioned explicitly in the preceding discourse. Because speakers talking on telephones can't see one another, there are also opportunities for all kinds of deceptions, tricks, and pranks: from concealing a frown or rude hand gesture to calling a bar and asking to speak with Maya Normusbutt.

The discourses of textual media are more permanent than speech. With text, we have a written or printed record, while speech (unless recorded) evaporates into the air into which it's spoken. Textual media also allows writers to plan and revise their discourse before sending it to its audience, while spoken discourse is produced in the moment and, once uttered, cannot be unuttered. But what text gains in permanence and planning, it loses in immediacy and in all the paralinguistic resources (gesture, volume, inflection) available in face-to-face discourse and (to a lesser extent) in telephonic speech. Text can make up for at least some of these losses by adding visual enhancements, like pictures, charts, diagrams, and so on. Some books are purely text – like those giant Victorian novels you read in your literature classes. Others use various kinds of graphics to boost the text. Newspapers add photos, children's books add pictures and drawings, and product instructions use diagrams, figures, and visual warnings to ensure that some chucklehead doesn't use his hair dryer in the shower.

Speech/text is neither speech nor text, but a combination of the two. It's typically created through digital media, such as email, cell phone texting, and instant messaging and chat. And while it shares features with text (it's typed, for instance, and can be revised and edited), it often aspires to the immediacy and sounds and even visual cues of face-to-face speech. Here are some features common to speech/text discourse:

Figure 7.1 *Emoticons.*

- Phonetic, rather than standard, spellings: *wanna* instead of *want to*, *boyz* instead of *boys*, or *gnight* instead of *good night*.
- ALL CAPS to imitate shouting: *WOOT*.
- Running words together to imitate a hurried pronunciation: *nonononono*.
- Ellipses to indicate pauses: *hmmm . . . I'm not sure.*

These are all good examples of the hybrid nature of speech/text because they use typography (a feature of text) to capture the sound and feel of spoken discourse. Another example of hybridity includes all those acronyms that developed in the fast-paced medium of Internet chat and instant messaging – acronyms like *lol* (laughing out loud), *bbl* (be back later), and *tyvm* (thank you very much). Acronyms such as these offer users ways to shorten text so they can deliver it at a rate that comes close to matching the speedy exchanges of speech. And what about emoticons? Originally, they were rather ingenuous ways of manipulating symbols and characters found on most keyboards so that users could incorporate facial expressions (a feature of face-to-face discourse) into text: **:-)** for a smile, **;-)** for a smile and a wink, and **:-(** for a frown. Their purpose was to compensate for the limits of text and convey the attitude or tone of a comment in a fairly economical way. Now, most email and Instant Messaging software include lists of prepackaged graphical emoticons – such as the ones in Figure 7.1.[7]

These graphical depictions of facial expression and gesture may be visually appealing and offer users a greater range of attitudes and tones to convey, but they may lack the imaginative spirit that inspired the original text-based symbols.

Genre

In the previous section, we saw how setting can influence discourse: using hushed tones in the library, or hooting and hollering at a ball game. But some settings or occasions are so common that people have developed thoroughly conventionalized responses to them. A funeral, for instances, calls for a eulogy, a major sporting event typically comes with sports commentary, a wedding gift prompts a thank-you letter. These conventionalized responses are called genres, and understanding what genre a sample of discourse belongs to often reveals important information about its meaning and effects.

Genres in general

What, then, are some common genres? In literature, the three main genres are poetry, drama, and fiction, and each of these divide into subgenres: poetry into lyric and epic, for instance; drama into comedy and tragedy; and fiction into short story, novel, and novella. The three main genres and their subtypes have been with us a long time, but in an increasingly complex world, we've come to recognize many more kinds of discourses: the research report, sermon, advertisement, political speech, business letter, shopping list, movie review, email, science fiction novel, and so on. Instances of humor can also be classified according to genre: jokes, cartoons, stand-up, sitcom, parody, graffiti, comic novel, limerick, etc. Just like many of the genres we mentioned above, the genres of humor often divide into subcategories. Jokes, for instance, include the canned, "did-you-hear-the-one-about" variety and those that speakers generate off-the-cuff in the flow of everyday conversations (we can call this latter type "witticisms" or "spontaneous jokes" for lack of a better word).

Genre brings structure and context together. In other words, genres are partly defined by a set of features that we can point to within a discourse, such as subject matter, style, and organization. But they also depend on context. Consider the humble shopping list. It's a genre of discourse whose structure meets the needs of a particular situation. Say you are about to send your spouse to the grocery store, and you need some kind of mechanism to help him remember what items you want him to buy. The shopping list is a good solution. It's a scrap of paper on which you list the desired items, typically in a vertical column with one item per line (see Figure 7.2).

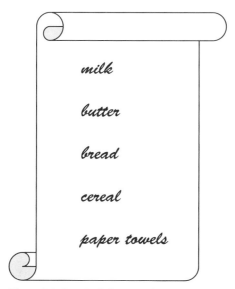

Figure 7.2 *A typical shopping list.*

There's no need to present items within full sentences – in fact, doing so would needlessly slow you down as you wrote the list and then, later, interfere with your spouse's ability to read it as he moves through the store's busy aisles. Here's the same shopping list cast as another genre of discourse – a narrative:

> When you get to the store, you'll first need to pick up some milk. Walk down aisle seven. You'll find it at the end, along the back wall. Be sure to pick up a gallon of the stuff (last time you only got a half-gallon's worth, and we ran out by the middle of the week). Then you'll also need to pick up a stick of butter – it'll be in the same aisle as the milk, so you shouldn't have far to look. With these dairy items taken care of, turn left and walk down to the bread and cereal aisle where you'll pick up . . . what else? Bread and cereal. Ha-ha! Make sure to get wholewheat bread and a box of Captain Puffy Corn Pops. After you get these, go one aisle further to where paper products are and get a roll of paper towels – extra absorbent ones, because we know how messy you can be.

This story may be a mildly entertaining read, but its structure hardly suits the context for which it's designed. If your spouse walked through the grocery store with this narrative in hand, he'd have to pick through all that prose to find the items you want him to buy. Perhaps you could use a highlighter for each item. But why do that when the shopping list is better tool for the job?

There's another sense in which genres depend on context. When we compose or read a particular discourse, we depend on our knowledge of how similar instances of the same kind of discourse have been fashioned in the past. In other words, our past knowledge of a genre (its structure, style, subject matter, and the situation to which it responds) becomes part of the context of our writing or reading it. The genre of the shopping list, for instance, doesn't have to be reinvented every time we plan a trip to the store. Instead, we call on our past experiences with shopping lists and use it to compose or process the one before us.

Genres of humor

As an illustration of how we might analyze any given genre, let's end this section (and chapter) by considering a few genres of humor. As you'll remember from earlier chapters, almost every instance of humor depends on some form of incongruity, or the collision of dissimilar frames of reference. Most, if not all, genres of humor will share this feature. How those incongruities are realized, however, will vary from one genre of humor to the next. Consider the canned or prepackaged joke. The subject matter of such jokes covers the full range of human experience: there are jokes about lawyers, death, marriage, sex, politics, driving, age, schools, dumb blondes, sports, ethnic and regional groups, and so on. But individual jokes will typically develop in predictable ways, and it is this predictability in organization that lends the joke some of its stability as a genre. There are two-part jokes that consist of a set-up followed by a punch line:

> I'm not afraid to die. I just don't want to be there when it happens.[8]
>
> I don't plan to grow old gracefully. I plan to have face-lifts until my ears meet.[9]
>
> I tried to walk into Target, but I missed.[10]

There are also three-part jokes. Some of these build on the two-part structure by inserting a sentence or two that carries the set-up forward, while increasing listeners' anticipation for the punch line:

> I had plenty of pimples as a kid. One day I fell asleep in the library. When I woke up, a blind man was reading my face.[11]

Other three-part jokes involve either a single character repeating an action three times or three characters performing the same action one after the other. There's usually some variation with each repetition, and the third and final one typically serves as the punch line. Here's a single character performing three actions:

> A man walking on the beach finds a strange looking bottle. He picks it up, and just for the heck of it, he rubs it. To his surprise, out pops a genie who says, "For releasing me from this bottle, I will grant you three wishes. But there's a catch. For each of your three wishes, every lawyer on the planet will receive double what you ask for. What's your first wish?"
>
> The man says, "I'd like a Ferrari." POOF! A Ferrari appears in front of him, and the genie says, "Now every lawyer on the planet has been given two Ferraris. What's your second wish?"

> "I'd like a million dollars," says the man. And POOF! One million dollars appears at his feet. "Now every lawyer is two million dollars richer," says the genie. "What's your final wish?"
>
> "Well, I always wanted to donate a kidney."

Now three characters, three similar actions:

> Three mice were sitting in a bar trying to impress each other. The first mouse says, "Whenever I see a mousetrap, I lie on my back and set it off with my foot. When the bar comes down, I catch it in my teeth bench press it twenty times to work up an appetite, then take the cheese." The second mouse replies, "Yeah, well, when I see rat poison, I collect as much as I can, take it home, grind it up into powder, and add it to my coffee each morning . . . " The third mouse yawns, looks at his watch, and says, "Sorry guys, I don't have time for this bullshit. I gotta go home and screw the cat."[12]

The three-part structure is so common, here's a joke that plays on it using a two-part structure:

> A priest, a rabbi, and a minister walk into a bar. The bartender says, "Is this some kind of joke?"[13]

Although the first sentence reads like the introduction to a three-part joke (like the three-mice one above), it's actually the set-up for the punch line in a two-part joke.

The relatively basic structure of most canned jokes makes them easy to remember and thus a good fit for the contexts in which they typically appear – that is, in everyday conversations. In these informal and largely unscripted contexts, the canned joke works as a set-piece of sorts, and its two- or three-part structure serves as a mnemonic device, helping speakers recall them on the fly. Moreover, a goal of many conversations is enjoyment (the pleasures we seek in the company of others), and canned jokes answer that aim in an economical and time-tested form. Even if listeners don't laugh at a speaker's joke, it may give them an opportunity to rib that speaker for telling such a groaner and thus contribute to the overall enjoyment of the conversation. Finally, we should note how a canned joke might fit into the context of an ongoing conversation. Speakers will often frame their canned jokes with some kind of introductory comment: "I heard a good one the other day . . . "; "That reminds me of a joke . . . "; "Did you hear the one about . . . ?" With statements such as these, the joke teller signals that a joke is one the way, while securing listeners' attentions and priming them for some kind of amusement. Then comes the telling of the joke itself. Ideally, this is followed immediately by the laughter of other participants. If they don't laugh, then the speaker will know that something has gone wrong – either they didn't understand the joke or they didn't think it was funny.[14] If they do laugh, then that response typically ends the joke, and the conversation can resume. But it sometimes happens that the telling of one joke will trigger the telling of others.

In other words, a joke told by one participant in a gathering will serve as an invitation (or excuse) for others to share their own.

Although we've just seen how the canned joke might fit into a broader conversational context, the canned joke is itself relatively self-contained. In other words, canned jokes can circulate widely and appear in many different conversational contexts. Not so with the witticism, or spontaneous joke. It's more thoroughly bound to the context in which it appears. Unlike the canned joke, which comes with its own set-up and punch line, the witticism typically involves a speaker riffing off the utterances of others and using them as opportunities to joke. In the following exchange from *Seinfeld* the sitcom, Jerry is at a train station picking up Rachel, his girlfriend (one of many throughout the series' run):

> RACHEL: The train was so crowded. I had to sit in the seat facing the wrong way.
> JERRY: Oh, I like that. It's like going back in time.

Rachel's utterance is a complaint, and typically it would be followed by an expression of sympathy or understanding – something like, *Oh that's awful*. Not so with Jerry. He sees Rachel's complaint as an opportunity to crack a joke, and in seizing that opportunity, he transforms Rachel's complaint into the set-up for a punch line which he delivers in the form of a witticism.

Another genre of humor, stand-up comedy, differs from both canned and spontaneous jokes. Perhaps the most significant difference involves the roles the participants play. With your garden variety joke or witticism, the joke-teller typically shares the floor with other participants. Those participants will usually allow the joke-teller to hold the floor long enough to tell his or her joke, but once it's completed, control of the floor may pass to another speaker who might comment on the joke just told, share a joke of his or her own, or change the topic altogether. In stand-up, by contrast, the roles of participants are more rigidly defined. Typically, the comedian holds the floor (or stage) for the entire performance, while the audience grants that comedian their attention and offers feedback in the form of laughter and applause. Occasionally, a heckler may try to take control of the floor, but a skilled comedian can, with a quick barb or witty retort, shut that heckler down and resume the role of principal speaker.

In terms of the structure of stand-up, most performances begin with an emcee or an off-stage announcer introducing the comedian to the audience. The audience applauds, while the comedian enters the stage from the wings. The comedian then greets the audience, usually with some acknowledgement of the city or venue in which the performance takes place (*It's great to be in Chicago*). Then the routine begins. As for the routine's structure, some comedians may just string together a number of canned jokes with mostly functional transitions between them. Or (and this is more typical of recent comedians), they can move Seinfeld-like: deliver a general observation, expand on it, transition to another general observation, expand on it, and so on. Another possibility appears in the following excerpt from the beginning of Wanda Sykes' stand-up routine. Throughout her performance, Sykes weaves together short narratives, and while none of these have a punch-line per se (they are not jokes in the strict sense), they do include a number of laugh lines that (if the audience's reactions are any indication) build in terms of their relative funniness:

ANNOUNCER: [off-stage] Ladies and gentlemen, put your hands together for Miss Wanda Sykes.

AUDIENCE: [applause and loud cheers]

SYKES: [over applause] Thank YOU ... Thank you SO much ... Thank you, thank you ... Nice ... Thank y'all so much. Thank y'all so much. You're very cool. Good to be here in Seattle. Good to be here.

AUDIENCE: [cheers]

SYKES: This is nice because I never know what to expect. You know, because people say anything to me. I hear, "Wanda!" I did one show and this lady yelled out, "Wanda! I love you!" I was like, "Thank you. Love you too." And then she goes, "I named my dog after you!"

AUDIENCE: [laughs]

SYKES: That's not cool. I don't want to hear, "Wanda shit on the rug again today."

AUDIENCE: [laughs]

SYKES: "Wanda, stop sniffing that dog's ass."

AUDIENCE: [laughs louder]

SYKES: "Wanda pregnant. We gotta get that bitch fixed."

AUDIENCE: [laughs even louder]

And so ends the first segment of Sykes' routine (after this she transitions into another narrative about a similar encounter she experienced while traveling by plane). The laugh lines come at the end of the segment, where Sykes imagines what this adoring fan might say to her dog named Wanda. As in a canned joke, the laugh lines come in a group of three, with the third one serving as a climax of sorts. But if anything, the laugh lines look more like witticism than the parts of a canned joke. The fan's remark *I named my dog after you* provides Sykes with her set-up, and she spends the rest of the segment riffing off of it. In other words, Sykes creates a narrative context (the story about the adoring fan) in which she can deliver what appear to be witticisms (even if those witticisms have been scripted in advance).

And what else can we say about that narrative context? It looks strikingly similar to the actual context in which Sykes is performing. She walks on stage and is greeted by a concert hall full of adoring fans. After thanking those fans, Sykes launches into a story about one fan in particular. The difference is that the flesh-and-blood fans in front of Sykes are behaving appropriately. They're cheering, applauding, laughing – they're doing a good job of playing their role within the genre of stand-up. The fan in Sykes' narrative, however, comes close to crossing a line; in fact, naming her dog after Wanda borders on being a bit creepy. By making that fan the subject of her comedy and by enlisting the actual audience members into laughing at her, Sykes indirectly reminds those members about appropriate forms of behavior between audience and performer. In short, the structure and substance of Sykes' comedy, at least in this instance, is about its context.

8   "Kids say the darndest things"

Children acquiring language

For Better or For Worse®   **by Lynn Johnston**

Children acquiring language are continually forming hypotheses and making guesses about how to use it. In the *For Better or Worse*[1] comic strip shown above, we see this process in action. Here, April's class is about to learn to draw faces, and she is invited by her teacher to *make a face*. She then commences to show in her own way that she already knows how to. What she knows about the expression *make a face*, though, is its idiomatic meaning, discussed back in Chapter 4. The literal meaning goes straight past her.

What the comic strip does not show is that children come into the world specially prepared (that is, innately enabled) to acquire language. The acquisition process (and we call it "acquisition" instead of "learning," because it is so very distinct from typical "learning" – such as learning arithmetic or piano) begins before birth and continues at least into early adolescence. It involves "acquiring" all the different sorts of linguistic knowledge that we have discussed up until this point – knowledge of language sounds, word meaning and structure, sentence grammar, and how to use and interpret language in contexts. This chapter will go through some of the main aspects of child language acquisition, relating their acquisition when appropriate to points made in earlier chapters.

It was some forty-five years ago that Eric Lenneberg set forth the hypothesis that aspects of children's linguistic abilities are the product of innate endowments, rather than being developed through exposure to their environment.[2] In the nature versus nurture debate, Lenneberg's ideas tilted toward nature, suggesting that acquiring language was for a child much more like "learning" to walk than it was like learning to play a piano. Language, like other "biologically controlled" behaviors, is seen to emerge before it is necessary, is not the result of conscious decision on the part of the child, and is not triggered by external events. Further, unlike the case of an adult learning a second or foreign language, direct teaching and practice has little effect, there is a regular sequence of developmental milestones, and there is a period within which language acquisition must occur if it is ever to occur (a so-called "critical period"). These ideas were quite revolutionary at the time, standing in opposition to the then widely accepted "radical behaviorism" of B. F. Skinner (which held that all behavior, including language, was the direct result of positive/negative reinforcement – that is, conditioned by the environment).[3] In this book, we largely operate under the assumption that Lenneberg (and later Noam Chomsky) were correct about the nature of language acquisition. But it should be noted that a good portion of what we present here is independent of that.

The development of phonology (speech sounds)

Children begin to acquire speech sounds long before their first word. In fact, as recent research has shown, they have internalized the general intonation patterns of their parents' language before they exit the womb (a recent study found that the pitch of newborn cries – rising or falling – matched the sentence intonation patterns of their German- or French-speaking parents, something that they could only have picked up by eavesdropping in utero).[4]

By six months, babies can tell the difference between the sound [b] as in *beat* and the sound [p] as in *peat*. You might be asking yourself how can anyone possibly know that, or figure that out?! Well, knowing that babies will suck on a pacifier faster if they are stimulated by, or interested in, something, researchers[5] set about to find out if babies were excited by (that is, noticed) different language sounds. This involved repeating one sound until they were bored with it, and then suddenly changing to a different sound. Imagine a voice over a loudspeaker doing something like this . . .

[p] – [p] – [p] – [p] – [p] – [p] – [p] – [p] – [p] – [p] – [p] – [b] – [b] – [b]

What they found was that the babies' sucking rate increased dramatically when the voice changed from saying [p] to [b]. They did the same for other contrasting language sounds . . . but not so for non-language sounds, indicating that they are acutely sensitive to language sounds and their patterns. What is amazing about this is that they are sensitive to all language sound differences, whether or not the sounds are part of their parents'/caretakers' language or not.

Between the age of six months and twelve months (usually before they utter any actual words), something else happens. Babies gradually stop paying attention to language sounds and sound differences that are not part of their native (parents' or caretakers') language. It's as if they come into the world equipped with the tools to learn any language and then, between six and twelve months, dispose of the phonological tools that won't be needed to learn the language to which they are being exposed. They do all this before they use their toolkit to actually produce any words. By about eighteen months, now having started to utter words, they have begun to realize that sound differences are meaningful. That is, they know that switching phonemes can change the meaning of a word (for instance, children at this age demonstrate the ability to distinguish between two dolls named *Bock* and *Pock*).

It is a few months after they're born (roughly four months) that babies start to develop the ability to make language sounds. We call it "babbling" and all babies do it. The babbling sounds that babies produce are pretty universal too. At four months of age, they have yet to figure out which language sounds belong to the language that they're "supposed" to be acquiring, so the range of sounds that they produce is pretty large and goes beyond what they'll produce later on. Even deaf children "babble." That is, they spontaneously produce gestures with their hands that are possible sign language gestures (as opposed to random non-language movements). And they all do it, showing that human infants are specially endowed for language. By about twelve months, they are beginning to produce words, and their sounds are restricted to those that "belong" to the language they're acquiring.

Of course, while they are acquiring the sounds of their language and learning to produce them, they don't acquire them all at once. Some sounds are harder to produce than others, and some combinations of sounds are difficult as well. Take "r" sounds, for instance. "R" sounds are hard, and they're not very stable. There are languages, such as Korean, that don't distinguish between "r" and "l" sounds, and speakers of these languages have trouble producing the "r" sound of English. Many languages produce very different "r" sounds than English. Think of the trilled "r" sound of Spanish, or the "r" sound of French that is produced in the back of the mouth. So, it's no surprise that "r" sounds are some of the last ones acquired. Parents often worry (sometimes excessively) about a child who is still referring to bunnies as "wabbits" well into first or second grade. For instance, one of the author's sons, Isaac Dubinsky, at age five, would frequently want to see how he looked in the "mewer" and loved "Kewewius" George. Now, at age six, he looks in the *mirror* and watches *Curious George*. We rarely see children that can't manage their "m" sounds (such as in *mama*, *more*, and *mine*), but "r" sounds, "th" sounds, and "sh" sounds are among the hardest for English-speaking children and some of the last to be acquired.

Almost all children and their parents are aware of this. It is this awareness that contributes to the enormous popularity of a recent children's classic by Helen Lester, titled *Hooway for Wodney Wat*.[6] It's about a rat named Rodney, who is in first grade at a primary school for "wodents." In a very familiar scenario, "Wodney" is teased mercilessly by his classmates on this account.

> Hey, Rodney! Where does a train go?
> [in a whisper] On the twain twacks.

When a new, very aggressive student, Camilla Capibarra joins the class, everyone is afraid (capibarras being very large rodents). But Camilla gets her comeuppance from Rodney in a game of "Simon Says." Rodney's classmates, who can understand (or translate) Rodney's "w" sounds as "r" sounds, are able to follow Rodney's commands.

> Wodney says "Wake the leaves!"

> [His classmates set about with rakes, while Camilla tries unsuccessfully to wake them up.]

Finally, to everyone's relief and delight, Rodney commands:

> Wodney says "Go west!"

> [His classmates lie down for a rest and Camilla stomps off in the direction of the sunset.]

"Wodney," having defeated and exiled the class bully, is now their hero and is not teased any more. Children delight in this book, and typically can't hear it enough times.

So, besides the difficult sounds mentioned above, what else do children have trouble with? Well, aside from pronouncing *rabbit* and *love* as "wabbit" and "wuv", *fish* as "fis," and *three* as "free," they also have trouble with piles of consonants. When two or three consonants are at the beginning or end of a word, they frequently only produce one of them. Thus, *spoon* becomes "poon," *from* is pronounced as "fum," and *bump* comes out like "bup."

Now, having said this, it is important to remember that "perception precedes production." Children are able to distinguish sound contrasts well before they are able to successfully produce them. Remember that babies have likely learned which sounds "belong" to their language, before they actually begin to produce words with them. Likewise, just because a child says "fis" instead of *fish*, one should not assume that s/he can't hear the difference between the "s" and the "sh" sound. It is likely the case that s/he can. As a case in point, a neighbor of ours (Nathan, five years old), having trouble pronouncing the consonant grouping "fl," would refer to his sandals as "bip bops." The following exchange illustrates quite effectively the difference between his ability to hear sounds, and his ability to produce them:

> ADULT: Are you wearing sandals, Nathan?
> NATHAN: No, they're bip bops.
> ADULT: You're wearing bip bops?
> NATHAN: No, they're bip bops.

ADULT: Bip bops?
NATHAN: No, not bip bops, bip bops.
ADULT: Oh, flip flops.
NATHAN: Yes, bip bops.

The development of word meaning

Aside from the rapidity with which babbling morphs into speech sounds, one of the most formidable aspects of children acquiring language is the speed with which they expand their vocabulary. At eighteen months, children have use of, on average, about 50 words. From that point on, they acquire about 10–12 words a day, with noun-like words being the most frequent, followed by adjectives. This continues apace, such that by age six, they have acquired nearly 14,000 words.

Now the process of word acquisition is, like the acquisition of language sounds, an imperfect and bumpy process. Children do not acquire new words completely in the first instance, as an adult might do, looking up a word in a dictionary. It is natural for a child to mistake a word they've never heard before as an instance of a similar sounding word that they already know. And this tendency results in lots of Lady Mondegreens (laid him on the greens). Cartoon humor of this sort abounds. In a 2002 edition of Robb Armstrong's *Jump Start*, Jojo Cobb announces to his school pals that he intends to nip a problem "in the butt." And again, young Isaac (Dubinsky) determined it to be hilarious at one point that some people might have "butt-teeth." Clearly, *butt* is learned by preschoolers long before the words *bud* or *buck*. Other examples abound, in a 2001 *Family Circus* panel, Jeffy is shown asking his mom if he can have some more "marble-ade" on his toast. Presumably, Jeffy has some knowledge about the affix *-ade* (as in *lemonade*, *Gatorade*, *Kool-Aid*, etc.) and also knows the word *marble*. As far as he knows, he has never heard the word *marmle*, so *marble* (with the bilabial sound [b]) is a reasonable and meaningful substitute for *marmle* (with its own bilabial [m] sound).

While they eventually learn the new words, and self-correct their vocabulary, their misuse of words is sometimes inexplicable and sometimes enlightening, but always entertaining. For instance, it was never certain why Isaac came home thinking that some of his classmates had "head-lights" in their hair, other than that *lice* and *lights* sound so similar and he hadn't a clue what *lice* were. On the other hand, when he took to calling the upper bed in his room a "bump bed" (rather than a *bunk bed*), he had an explanation for it, saying that it was a "bump bed" because you would bump your head on the ceiling if you jumped on it.

Some of children's mondegreens arise from a misunderstanding of where words do or don't end. Too many young children to count have, on arriving in the airport in South Florida, wondered whether this was Grandma's Amie (she called it "my amie"). Rick Detorie, in a cartoon strip *One Big Happy*, offers a twist on this as he has eight-year-old Ruthie ask her Grandma Rose, "How was Addle?"

> GRANDMA: Addle?
> RUTHIE: Yeah. Didn't you go to see somebody named Addle?
> GRANDMA: Uh ... I was out of town, but ...
> RUTHIE: Yes, you said you were going to see Addle.
> GRANDMA: Oh, Seattle!
> RUTHIE: Yeah ... Is Addle a boy or a girl?

And Bill Keane, the creator of *Family Circus*, puts a classic mondegreen into Dolly's mouth, as she tells her brother: "Mrs. Clarke is reading us *The Ugly Duckling* by Hans Christian and her son."

Even when children learn a new word, it takes additional time to learn to use it correctly. Two of the most common tendencies they exhibit are overextending or underextending the use of the word. In the case of overextensions, the child uses the word or expression to refer to a wider range of things than it is supposed to be used for. For instance, the word *dog* might be used for all four-legged animals, or *ball* could be used for any round object (such as a balloon or an egg, etc.). Overextensions are based on similarities in appearance or function (perceptual similarities). Isaac, for instance, would often ask:

> Please scratch my back ... right there under my "ankule" [ankle]. No, the other "ankule."

Apparently, for a while ... at least until he learned the separate word *shoulder* ... he used *ankle* to refer both to the place where his arm joined his body and to the place where his foot joined his body. In another instance, Isaac took to using the word *spicy* both for spicy-hot foods and for anything that overstimulated the inside of his mouth. For this reason, *very spicy* was overextended to include highly carbonated soda pop, and on one occasion (complaining of a sore throat) he said "I have a very spicy throat." Just as is the case with pronunciation, comprehension runs ahead of production. A child will normally overextend in production even when they understand (receptively) the meaning of a word. For instance, the child may correctly point only to dogs in a picture even while using the word for other four-legged animals.

Underextensions involve using a word to refer to fewer things than it would otherwise be used for. A child might use the word *kitty*, for example, only to refer to the family cat and not apply it to other cats (this would be the inverse of the overextended use of *kitty* to refer to all cat-like creatures including lions and tigers). One child was reported to have used the word *car* only to refer to cars that were moving outside on the street. That is, parked cars were not recognized as cars, and neither were cars that the child was riding in. This entertaining example of underextension was found in an exchange between Art Linkletter and a child on his classic television show, *Kids say the darndest things*:

ART: With Thanksgiving and all, we're supposed to be thankful. What are
you thankful for?

BOY: I'm an American.

ART: Ahhh, you are an American? That's good. I'm glad you're thankful
for that. You know what an American is? What is an American?

BOY: Someone who lives in California.

Another interesting example of underextension we can point to evolved out of
Isaac Dubinsky's misunderstanding of the word *lemonade*, when he was five.
Unlike Jeffy (above), he had no familiarity with the affix *-ade*, but he did know
the word *made*. And since lemonade was a drink that was "made" for him
and because it was "yellow," he christened it with the mondegreen *yellowmade*.
His reanalysis of the word made for a natural underextension. *Yellowmade* (as
opposed to *lemonade*) only referred to the yellow kind. Pink lemonade (since
pink-yellowmade would not be sensible) became *pinkmade*. And in an interesting
application of this pattern, rainbow slushies (ice-drinks) were called *rainbowmade
slushies*.

As children do acquire new words and figure out their meanings, they use
what they already know (words, pieces of words) in order to understand what
they don't. They pattern new words after words the already know. They take
their understanding of words' parts to construct meanings of the whole. And
sometimes they just make things up or guess.

Another important, and unsurprising, fact about their learning of words is that
they learn simpler concepts first. Their acquisition of spatial and dimensional
terms provides a good illustration of this. For example, the words *big* and *small*
are the least complex dimensional term because they can refer to any aspect of an
object's size. They are, predictably, acquired before other such terms. Words like
tall, *high*, *long*, and *short* are more complex than *big* or *small* in that they refer to
size along a particular dimension. These are learned next. After these come pairs
of words like *thick* and *thin*, *wide* and *narrow*, *deep* and *shallow*. These pairs of
words distinguish themselves in that they refer to size along one dimension but
along a less important dimension of the object that they measure. Consider the
case of a pencil or a crayon. We would notice and focus on its length (whether
it is long or short) before noticing its thickness (whether it is thick or thin). The
same principle would apply to a pond or a wading pool. We would first notice
or evaluate whether it is big or small, and only secondarily notice whether it is
deep or shallow. Accordingly, words like *deep* and *thick* are usually learned after
words like *big* or *long*.

It is also the case that the words that actually name a dimension are learned
before their partners. When you look at a pond, you might ask how deep it is and
not how shallow it is. When asking about height, we ask how tall someone is, not
how short they are. Accordingly, *deep* is usually acquired before *shallow* and *tall*
before *short*. What happens when a child has acquired one member of a pair and
not the other? Well, for a short while, they may use the one word they know for

both meanings. Isaac at age six had acquired the word *until* (as in *You can stay up until eight o'clock*) but not its opposite, *since*. When he needed to use a word that had the meaning of *since*, he substituted *'til*, complaining on the occasion in question: *I haven't played Wii 'til yesterday.*

As mentioned above, children pattern new words after words they already know. In a *Family Circus* panel from 2006, Bill Keane has Dolly ask "My friend Robin is Canadian, Mommy. Where is Canadia?" If Americans live in America and Californians live in California, then Canadians must logically live in Canadia. This construction of words through analogy is extremely useful and productive for children learning new words. Often, their creations are more logical and systematic than what the language offers them. As an example of this, consider the following exchange between Isaac Dubinsky and his dad (who was attempting to instruct him on the formation of fraction words).

> DAD: Ok. If we take a pizza and cut it into eight slices, each slice is an eighth. Now, what if we cut it into four slices? How much is each slice?
> ISAAC: A fourth.
> DAD: And what if we cut it into two slices? How much is each slice?
> ISAAC: A twoth [pronounced "a tooth"]

Isaac's word *twoth* is much more sensible and systematic than the irregular (and somewhat arbitrary) expression *half*.

Children also take their understanding of words' parts to construct meanings of the whole. In an old Calvin and Hobbes strip, Calvin asks his mom:

> CALVIN: Is hamburger meat made out of people from Hamburg?
> MOM: Of course not! It's ground beef.
> CALVIN: I'm eating a COW?
> MOM: Right.
> CALVIN: I don't think I can finish this.

Calvin's fascination with the prospect of eating people from Hamburg aside, his ideas about the meaning of *hamburger* are a sensible (albeit morbid) calculation of what it might mean. Isaac Dubinsky at age six had a first-grade project which involved finding out about a Native American tribe. He chose to report on the Pawnee, who inhabited central Nebraska and Kansas, until being forced onto reservations in first Nebraska and then Oklahoma. When he gave his report, his parents were surprised to find out that the Pawnee lived on the *great airplanes*. He had reasonably concluded that the Great Plains were some sort of way of getting around in the air. It's not certain whether he still thinks that.

Children learn words extremely quickly, as we have suggested. A single meaningful exposure to a new word can cause a child to recalibrate what they know about the world. In an experiment conducted in the 1970s,[7] early elementary school children were asked to describe a blue cafeteria tray (a color they knew) and an olive-colored one (a color they didn't know). Without instruction, they variously identified it as either *green* or *brown*. The experimenter then asked them to select the *chromium* tray (a word unknown to them). They uniformly picked the olive one, knowing that the blue one wasn't wanted. After a week, they were retested. They did not, after only a single exposure, remember the word *chromium*, but they did remember that the olive tray was neither green nor brown.

Of course, familiarity with a word (and even remembering to use it) does not guarantee that it will be used correctly. The process of coming to understand the precise meaning and usage of a word takes a long time, and many exposures to it. Children's (and young adults') misuse of words is legend, and shows up time and again in their writing. George Miller and Patricia Gildea[8] report some good examples of these in their 1987 *Scientific American* article.

> Me and my parents correlate, because without them I wouldn't be here.
> > [correlate = be related to one another]
> I was meticulous about falling off the cliff.
> > [meticulous = very careful]
> Mrs. Morrow stimulated the soup.
> > [stimulate = stir up]

We find plenty of examples of this sort of humor in cartoons as well. Bill Keane's *Family Circus* comes through for us once again, in 2000 and 2009. In the first, Jeffy turns to his older sister Dolly in a movie theater and informs her that:

> "The movie won't start until they turn the dark on."

And in the second, Dolly complains to her mother:

> "Mommy, my socks don't agree with each other."

In one case, Jeffy has simply extrapolated quite logically to get the opposite of the expression *turn the light on*. And in the second, Dolly has reasonably extended the meaning of *agree* to include *match*.

This sort of thing occurs with very great frequency in the use of "idioms" (multiple-word expressions that have single-word-like meanings . . . for example, *kick the bucket* = 'die'). Children can err in either direction. They can misinterpret an expression that is meant to have a literal meaning, and think that the idiom is intended, as April does in the cartoon at the beginning of this chapter with *make a face*. They can also take an idiom and mistakenly interpret or use it literally. In a 2002 *Dennis the Menace* cartoon, we find Dennis on his scooter, standing alongside a car with a flat tire, helpfully observing to the owners: *Yep. Looks like it got the wind knocked out of it*. His misapplication of the idiom *got the wind knocked out of it* is quite reasonable, even if it is wrong. There is nothing about the expression in and of itself that suggests that its use should be restricted to creatures that breathe.

Finally, children will quite often invent their own words for things, when they don't know what something is. These inventions are usually rather insightful and make some sort of sense, even if they are not really words. Two examples come to mind. Isaac, on being brought down to the school district track with his brother when he was five, decided that he wanted to run sprints with his parents. He likely heard them refer to what they were doing as *running wind sprints* (which involves short successive sprints, such that one winds up getting winded), but having no idea what *sprint* meant, he decided that he was going to run *wind blows*. Given that "blow" is what the wind does and that it does it right past your head when you run fast, his invention made perfect sense. On another occasion, Isaac's father was trying to see whether he considered *nose* a plural noun (like *toes*). What came out of this exchange was an (unexpected) lexical invention:

DAD: How many toes do you have?
ISAAC: [counts toes] . . . Nine.
DAD: How many on each foot?
ISAAC: [counts] one, two three four five . . . I have ten toes.
DAD: How many nose do you have?
ISAAC: One.
DAD: You have one no?
ISAAC: It's a nose, daddy. I have one.
DAD: What are these two things? [points to nostrils]
ISAAC: They're sniffles.
DAD: Oh yes, that's right, they're sniffles.
ISAAC: Yes! I guessed right. I knew it.

Isaac's delight at inventing a word and getting approval for it was palpable, and in fact, it was a good word for the things that you "sniff" with. His dad didn't have the heart to tell him that they're *nostrils*, and so they're *sniffles* now.

Syntactic development

If acquiring language were simply a matter of working out the sounds of a language and using them to produce words, this chapter would be done. But in addition to learning words and using the sound system of a language to understand them and produce them, children have to learn how to organize words into grammatical phrases and sentences. This involves both getting the words in the right order and using grammatical affixes to indicate things like present and past tense (for instance).

Grammar does not emerge at the outset, since there isn't much use for it. That is, it takes a while before children are producing strings of words that are long enough for grammar to be relevant. Beginning somewhere around twelve months of age and for about six months following, children express themselves using one word at a time. This is appropriately called the "one-word" stage, and it is marked by the use of one-word utterances to express sentential types of meanings (these are called "holophrases" in an allusion to the word *holistic*). Children accomplish this feat by choosing the most informative word that applies to the situation being commented on and just saying that. Here are some examples of one word used to express an entire thought:

> "more"   = give me more candy
> "up"   = pick me up
> "allgone" = the milk is all gone
> "alldone" = I am all done

Beginning at about eighteen months, they transition into something called the "two-word" stage, which involves (no surprise here) two-word utterances. These two-word expressions usually follow predictable patterns. Here are some examples of the most common two-word patterns:

> agent + action   "baby sleep"
> action + object   "kick ball"
> action + location   "sit chair"
> possessor + possession   "mommy book"

From this point, children begin combining longer and longer strings of words (three and more). While these utterances are more like grammatical sentences than the one- and two-word expressions that precede them, it is hard to maintain that children at this stage are really utilizing grammar yet. For one thing, these three-word and larger utterances typically don't have grammatical bits such as the tense affixes that attach to the verb (*-s* and *-ed*), and small grammatical words such as *to* and *the*. Here are a couple of examples of multiword expressions typical of this stage (the missing "grammatical" bits are underlined in the translations):

> "Car make noise" = The car makes a noise.
> "I good boy"   = I am a good boy.

In order to use grammatical affixes, such as past tense *-ed*, children have to solve a number of problems. One of the most basic of these is figuring out that the suffix exists. Notice that past tense *-ed*, while consistently spelled as "ed," is pronounced in three distinct ways depending on what verb it attaches to. In the past tense of *hate*, the suffix is pronounced as a whole syllable [ɛd]:

> hate + ed = [heytɛd]

In the past tense of *spoon*, it has only the sound [d]:

> spoon + ed = [spuwnd]

And in the past tense of *poke*, it sounds like [t]:

> poke + ed = [powkt]

So, first off, the child has to figure out that [ɛd], [d], and [t] at the end of verbs all mean "past tense." This problem is greatly complicated by the fact that not all verbs even use this suffix to form the past tense. In fact, the most common ones, and the ones a child is most likely to hear a lot, don't:

eat	–	ate
go	–	went
drink	–	drank
come	–	came

It is for this reason that, once a child has worked out the fact that there is a single past tense verb ending -*ed*, they use it for everything, including the verbs that aren't supposed to have it:

eat	–	eated
go	–	goed
drink	–	drinked
come	–	comed

   After they have worked out what the past tense ending is, they also have to figure out where to put it. You might think that this is simple – it goes at the end of the verb. But it's not always easy to figure out which is the verb, or which verb gets the ending. Consider these facts:

> *feel* is a verb, as in: *I feel happy.*
> *like* is a verb, as in: *I like it.*
> *like* is also an adjective, as in: *He is just like Sam.*

So, in the sentence *I feel like it* which word is the verb? An adult has presumably worked out that in this sentence it is *feel*. So, the past tense is *I felt like it.* But Isaac, at age six, considered both words to be verbs, and attached the past tense ending to the last one:

> I feel lik**ed** it.

The same thing happens with other verb endings, such as the present tense -*s* that goes on the end of verbs when the subject is *he* or *she*. Consider the words *skate* and *board*. *Skate* is a verb, and *board* is a noun. *Skate-board* is a noun, as in *I have a skate-board.* And we know that *skate-board* can also be used as a verb, as in *He skate-boards in the park* (notice that the -*s* ending attaches to the entire complex verb *skate-board*). Now, while an adult might know this, a child could still be thinking that the -*s* goes on the verb, not the noun. Watching a clip of *The Simpsons*, Isaac observed:

> Look! Bart [Simpson] skat**es** board naked.

This sort of "where do I attach the ending" confusion extends to the -*ing* ending as well. Being told to sit down on one occasion, Isaac announced:

> But I am sit downing!

One might ask, why would he do that? *Down* obviously isn't a verb! But consider the problem that *sit down* presents. Yes, *sit* is a verb, as in *I sit*. But it rarely comes by itself. Usually we hear, *sit* + a location (as in *sit here*) or *sit* + a direction (as in *sit down* or *sit up*). Add to this, the fact that there are so many verb plus preposition combinations in which the preposition loses its basic meaning when it combines with the verb (becoming a verb + preposition compound verb).

look up	as in, *look up the word*
beat up	as in, *beat up the monster*
mix up	as in, *mix up the letters*
calm down	as in, *calm down the baby*
cool down	as in, *cool down the soup*
slow down	as in, *slow down the car*

So . . . *sit down* might well be another one of these compound verbs. And Isaac has yet to learn to put the verb ending on the verb part of the verb–preposition compound verb, sticking it at the end of the entire compound instead.

In addition to figuring out grammatical suffixes (such as, past and present tense on verbs, plural on nouns), children also have a lot of very complex grammatical sentence patterns to figure out. Consider what goes into forming the negative of a sentence. First of all, there are three negative words that mean roughly the same thing but which are pronounced differently: *no*, *not*, and *n't*.

I have **no** candy.
I do **not** have candy.
I do**n't** have candy.

The word *no* is used in front of nouns, while *not* and *n't* are used with verbs. But the words *not* and *n't* are sometimes placed after the verb:

She is **not** here.
She is**n't** here.

Sometimes between two verbs:

They have **not** left.
They have**n't** left.

And sometimes they alternate:

I do **not** have any candy.
I do**n't** have any candy.
I have**n't** any candy.

The whole situation is very confusing. So what is a child to do? Well, like everything else they go through stages in which they gradually approximate the correct adult patterns.

In the first stages of learning negation (18–25 months), they use *no* at the beginning of sentences:

> No baby sleep
> No I drink milk

Later, at about 26–42 months, they place the word *no* inside the sentence:

> Baby no sleep
> I no drink milk

Finally, sometime after age 3½, they begin to use *not* and *n't* in ways that look more like adult speech:

> Baby don't sleep
> I not drink milk

There are, in addition to negation, many other complicated grammatical patterns to learn, and these take time to master. It is common, for instance, for passive sentences not to be learned until sometime between grades 1 and 3. The reason for this is clear, once we understand what passive sentences do. First off, we should note that it is typical in most sentences for the agent/actor/doer in a sentence to come before the verb, and for the patient/undergoer to come after, as in:

> Sally hit John.
> The dog bit the baby.

Passive sentences disturb this basic order, by placing the patient/undergoer in front of the verb.

> John was hit (by Sally).
> The baby was bit (by the dog).

Learning to decode these passive sentences involves learning that the subject of such a sentence is the verb's (typical) object. In a way, learning to understand (and use) passive sentences is a little like trying to process the arrangement of items in a room while hanging one's head upside down off a sofa.

It is not only passive sentences which present this dilemma. English presents different possible orderings for verbs of "giving" and "sending." Sometimes the thing given or sent comes right after the verb, with the recipient following right after that:

The teacher gave	a book	to the boy.
	thing-given	recipient
Mom sent	a message	to John.
	thing-sent	recipient

Sometimes the recipient follows the verb directly, with the thing-given or thing-sent coming after:

The teacher gave	the boy	a book.
	recipient	thing-given
Mom sent	John	a message.
	recipient	thing-sent

Not only is the first order more basic and more common, but it also has more information to help a child understand it. The recipient has the preposition *to* marking it out. In the second order, neither noun phrase is marked in any way to help someone figure out what's going on. For this reason, the second order is particularly hard to deal with when either noun could be a recipient:

She sent	the boy	to the teacher.
	thing-sent	recipient
She sent	the teacher	the boy.
	recipient	thing-sent

Children have problems with this pattern, just like passive, and acquire it late. Isaac, for instance, was not able to understand or produce the second pattern at age five. On hearing the following sentence out of a children's book:

> "Sammy shows his friends the train track"

Isaac concluded that *the train track* was a description of *Sammy's friend*:

> "The train track is his friend."

Even with prompting:

> "What did he show?"

Isaac still persisted in asserting:

> "Sammy shows [his friend the train track]"

In other words, it was easier for him to ignore the fact that *show* is missing an object and ignore the plural ending on *friends*, than to understand the "thing-shown plus recipient" order of the sentence. He simply could not get the meaning "Sammy shows the train track to his friends" out of this sentence.

In another instance, rather than produce the quite often heard expression *remind Mommy something*, he produced the normally ungrammatical:

> I need to remind something to mommy

preferring the "thing-reminded plus recipient" pattern that he had never heard anyone else say to the "recipient plus thing-reminded" pattern that he didn't understand.

Isaac's attempts to contend with other complex patterns are also informative. At age six, trying to juggle past tense, negation, and the formulation of a question in one sentence was particularly trying. Wanting to know the reason that some people did not come to a party his parents hosted, he asked:

> Why didn't some people didn't came to the party?

Notice here that *did* (the past tense of *do*) shows up twice (once before and once after the subject) and that the verb *came* also has past tense. The negation *n't* also shows up twice. So, instead of having past tense once and negation once, Isaac uses both in every conceivable position (presumably just to be sure). Of course, he is helped along in this regard by the fact that the position of negation itself isn't entirely fixed in adult speech. Either of the following are possible:

> Why did**n't** some people come to the party?
> Why did some people **not** come to the party?

In producing possessives, Isaac (from age four) had a predilection for placing a possessive pronoun first (a reasonable place for it, in most instances). So inclined was he in this regard that he regularly produced *my by self* in place of *by myself*, as in

> ISAAC: I do my by self.
> DAD: You want to do it your by self?
> ISAAC: Yes, my by self

More recently, at age six, he had to juggle two possessives at the same time. A particular folder, belonging to his brother, was (appropriately) *Elijah's folder*. This folder was also *his favorite*. Two possessives, *Elijah's* and *his*. What to do? An adult might solve this problem by putting one of the possessives after the noun, as in:

> This is my favorite folder of Elijah's.

However, having not yet figured out the trick of displacing one of them, Isaac was forced to put both in the front, and produced:

> That is my Elijah's favorite folder.

Finally, there was an instance where Isaac tried to deal with a sentence that contained a relative clause inside another modifying phrase. Hearing the sentence as part of the dialogue on a children's show he was watching (*Arthur*), he may have understood it but he was unable to repeat it. The background is that Arthur accidentally makes a hole in a lampshade and feels bad about it. His annoying little sister D.W., in order to cause him more discomfort, walks into the living room, loudly greeting the hole in the lampshade and reminding everyone how it got there. She says:

> Hi, lampshade with a hole in it that Arthur made!

Notice that there are two descriptors here, the *lampshade* is the one *with a hole in it*, and the *hole* is the one *that Arthur made*. Lining these up, we see that the descriptor *that Arthur made* modifies a word that is inside the descriptor of the *hole*. Here, we've underlined the first combination and boldfaced the second, to make it clearer:

<u>lampshade</u>   with a **hole** in it   **that Arthur made**

Thinking that D.W.'s line was funny (and therefore presumably understanding it), Isaac tried to repeat it, saying:

Hi, Lampshade that Arthur made a hole in it!

Notice how he shifted things around, to eliminate the double-embedding pattern (even though he produced an ungrammatical sentence in the process).

A guide to "caregiver speech" (how adults talk to children)

This chapter would not be complete without a discussion of how adults talk to children. That adults speak differently to children is undeniable. Think for a moment of how you might say *Hi!* to another adult, versus how you might say the same thing to a two-year-old child. In the latter case, your utterance is likely to be higher pitched, more melodic, spoken closer to the addressee, and possibly accompanied by a touch on the shoulder or hand. This said, we address two matters: precisely how adult speech to children is different and why it is this way.

The reasons for specially tailored speech to children (called "caregiver speech") are pretty straightforward. Children are not always aware that you are addressing them, as much of what they hear consists of unfamiliar sounds that they largely don't understand. So, caregiver speech is designed to get and hold a child's attention, and to give children input that they can (mostly) understand.

Parents and other adults who are skilled at talking to children will typically provide them with slow, carefully articulated speech, will use exaggerated intonation and stress, will have longer pauses between sentences or phrases, and will speak in a higher-pitched tone. All of these special manners of speaking improve the clarity of the adult's speech, and also help to get and keep the child's attention. Alongside these phonetic attention-getting devices, adults will come closer to a child when speaking to them and also touch them on the arm or shoulder. Given that so much talk goes on that is not directed toward, or understandable to, a child, it is most helpful to the child to know when speech is being directed to them.

In addition to being designed to get and keep attention, caretaker speech also assists children's acquisition in other ways. It usually consists of more restricted vocabulary – that is, words that are likely to be familiar to the child (*doggie* instead of *collie* or *poodle*, or *truck* instead of *tractor-trailer*). From a grammatical perspective, caretakers tend to use complete sentences:

> "Would you like a piece of cake?"

instead of:

> "Cake?"

and short sentences:

> "Give me the blue Lego! . . . Ok, now give me the red one!"

instead of:

> "Give me the blue Lego first, and then afterwards hand me the red one."

It is also the case that speech addressed to children will contain more imperatives and questions:

> "Look at the horse!"

instead of:

> "There's a horse out there in the field near the barn!"
>
> "Do you see the boat?"

instead of:

> "You can see a boat right out there in the harbor."

Imperatives and questions, like higher-pitched speech, have the effect of getting and keeping a child's attention, as well as encouraging a verbal response on the part of the child.

Beyond that, caregiver speech tends to involve more repetitions and shorter conversational turns than commonly seen in adult–adult interaction. In addition, adult conversations with children tend to focus on the "here" and "now," it being difficult for children to process utterances that rely on reference to other time frames and distant places. Confusion about temporal reference is quite common, and nicely illustrated by a question Isaac, aged six, asked about the meaning of the word *tomorrow*.

> Mr. Rod said that Nathan could come over tomorrow.
> How does tomorrow get to be today?

References to place can be equally confusing, and are sometimes the point of jokes about children's language understanding. In a 2006 *Family Circus* panel, Billy's mom scolds him for opening a box of cookies in the supermarket, saying:

> You're not to open it till you get home.

Billy responds, saying:

> But on the box it says, "Open here."

An older *Dennis the Menace* strip uses a similar device. While Dennis is at his friend Joey's house, playing in the living room, the phone rings. Dennis asks:

> DENNIS: Shouldn't you tell your mother the phone is ringing?
> JOEY: She's takin' a bath.
> DENNIS: Then you better answer it!
> JOEY: I can't! It might be a stranger!
> DENNIS: What difference does that make?
> JOEY: Lotsa difference! I'm not supposed to talk to strangers!...You answer it!
> DENNIS: Well okay...Hello?
> CALLER: Hello, may I speak to your mother please?
> DENNIS: She's not here.
> CALLER: What time do you expect her home?
> DENNIS: She's home right now!
> CALLER: But...but you said she **wasn't** there!
> DENNIS: I didn't say she wasn't **there**! I said she wasn't **here**! [hangs up]
> JOEY: [to Dennis] But why would anyone call **here** for **your** mother?
> DENNIS: I dunno. Grownups are hard to figger out.

While adult speech is specially crafted to facilitate children's acquisition of language, there is one thing that adults typically do not do – provide grammatical correction. Caregivers typically correct accuracy (false or incorrect statements) rather than grammar. Even when adults, atypically, attempt to correct children's grammar, it serves little to no purpose, since correcting grammar doesn't work. As we have seen, children go through specific stages independently to learn (deduce) the grammatical patterns for themselves. And until they're ready to move to the next stage, they usually cannot even process grammatical corrections and will understand them to be about something else. Here is a classic (textbook) interaction between a child and a father who is trying to get the child not to combine *other* and *one* in front of a noun (reported by Martin Brain, and cited in *The Language Instinct*).[9]

> CHILD: Want other one spoon, daddy.
> FATHER: You mean, you want the other spoon.
> CHILD: Yes, I want the other one spoon, please daddy.
> FATHER: Can you say "the other spoon"?
> CHILD: Other...one...spoon.
> FATHER: Say "other."
> CHILD: Other.
> FATHER: "Spoon."
> CHILD: Spoon.
> FATHER: "Other spoon."
> CHILD: Other...spoon. Now give me the other one spoon?

As this exchange shows, the child (while anxious to please her father) is impervious to grammatical instruction that she cannot process. A 1999 panel from *Family Circus* illustrates the same situation. In it, P.J. and his mom are watching the babysitter walking up to their front door.

P.J. says to his mom:

> Her's my favorite sitter.

To which his mom answers:

> **She's** my favorite sitter.

and P.J. affirms:

> Mine, too.

A final word: child language acquisition, television, and parenting styles

We would be remiss if we did not at least mention the positive and negative effects of environmental factors on children's language acquisition. The brief message to be given here is that if you want children to learn language, you must expose them to lots of it (by talking to them). And you should not imagine that exposure to television counts in any meaningfully positive way as exposure to language.

A child's brain is only partially developed at birth, with neurological development continuing apace after birth for at least 18–24 months. Even if one believes, as we do, that children are innately equipped to acquire language, it is still the case that language acquisition requires lots of linguistic interaction. That is to say, both nature and nurture each have their own roles to play.

This immediately takes us to the matter of exposure to television. Television does *not* provide input that greatly aids language development. As far back as 1998, in an article by Dr. Jane Healy,[10] it was reported that "Too much television – particularly at ages critical for language development and manipulative play – can impinge negatively on young minds in several different ways" including:

- Higher levels of television viewing correlate with lowered academic performance, especially reading scores . . . partially because the compellingly visual nature of the stimulus blocks development of left-hemisphere language circuitry.
- The nature of the stimulus may predispose some children to attention problems . . . fast-paced, attention-grabbing "features" of children's programming . . . deprive the child of practice in using his own brain

> independently, as in games, hobbies, social interaction, or just "fussing around."
> • "Mindless" television or video games may idle and impoverish development of the brain's pre-frontal cortex (its executive control system), which is responsible for planning, organizing and sequencing behavior for self-control, moral judgment, and attention.

These observations and accompanying research led the American Academy of Pediatrics to recommend that children below the age of two should not be watching television at all, and that television exposure after that be kept to a necessary minimum (that is, no more than an hour a day).[11]

Proof that speaking, being spoken to, and interacting with adults helps a child learn language was amply provided in a 1995 study by Betty Hart and Todd Risley.[12] In their research they followed forty-two families with children, divided by social class. There were thirteen professional families, twenty-three working-class families, and six on public assistance. They carefully monitored, in each family, the average number of words per hour addressed to children beginning at thirteen months of age up until thirty-six months. Their findings showed that working-class parents spoke approximately twice as many words per hour to their children as did parents on public assistance, and that parents in professional families spoke almost twice that. The averages, by group, were:

Professional	–	2,153
Working class	–	1,251
Public assistance	–	616

Their key finding involved correlating this factor with children's vocabulary development. They found that the children in the lowest group (at thirty-six months of age) had an average working vocabulary of around 500 words. This compared with a 50% larger working vocabulary for working-class children, and a 120% larger working vocabulary for the children of professional parents. The numbers are as follows:

Vocabulary of children at age 36 months:

Professional	–	~1100
Working class	–	~750
Public assistance	–	~500

In a second study, Hart and Risley further determined that these measurable differences in vocabulary skills, observed at three years of age, persisted at least through third grade (that is for at least an additional 6–7 years).

As they observed, there is a time-line for physical and cognitive development (that is, the window of opportunity to provide children with stimuli that will positively affect their development is time-bound). Early intervention, between one and three years of age, can partially or fully reverse the negative effects of a deficient home environment. However, on the sobering side of this optimistic observation, Hart and Risley calculated that forty hours/week of substitute care would be needed to make up for the deficits experienced by children of public assistance families. The lesson here, gleaned from the American Academy of Pediatrics advice combined with the Hast and Risley Study, seems to be: turn off the television and talk to your children.

9   Variety is the spice of life

Language variation

'I'm droppin' all my 'G's for a while.'

If variety *is* the spice of life, then the man featured in this cartoon[1] is looking to kick things up a notch. He's sporting a T-shirt, jeans, and western-style boots and hat – clothing we commonly associate with a cowboy. All he needs to complete his transformation (or so he thinks) is to alter one element of his speech: omitting the "g"s at the end of such words as *walking*, *talking*, and *laughing*. He's already omitted the "g" in *droppin'*, so he must think he's well on his way. But is he? His wife doesn't seem impressed, and why should she be? Clothing is certainly one way to display our identity to others, but at the same time, it's somewhat superficial and too easy to manipulate (to paraphrase an old expression: "The man is all hat and no cattle"). The way we speak is usually a more reliable guide. But the trouble with our would-be cowboy is that he mistakes one feature of language (the dropped "g"s) for an entire way of speaking. To sound bona fide, he needs to master an entire language variety. In other words, you can't change your linguistic identity as easily as you can change your clothes. And just as one item of clothing won't do the trick on its own, neither will one single feature of language (such as droppin' "g"s). He's surely gonna haveta start learnin' a mite bit more 'bout this way o' talkin' if he's gonna fool anybody.

So what is a language variety? It's not the same as a language, such as Spanish, English, or Japanese. Or to go to another extreme, it can't be boiled down to a single language feature. Rather, a variety is a specific way of speaking or writing within a given language, one that has recognizable features at every level of that language, including:

*   How it sounds.
*   What words it uses.
*   How it combines sounds and words into larger patterns.
*   How it uses those sounds, words, and patterns in specific situations.

We'll look at each of these levels more closely in a bit, but before we do, we need to say a bit more about the nature of varieties and how they are classified.

Types of varieties

You often hear people use the words *dialect* and *accent* to mean roughly the same thing as we do here by *language variety*. Are the terms interchangeable? Strictly speaking, no. *Accent* is too narrow and actually refers only to variations at the level of sound, such as *droppin'* vs. *dropping*. It thus ignores variations at other levels of a language, including vocabulary, syntax, and language use. *Dialect* comes closer in meaning to *variety*, but it also has its limitations. For one, even though it can refer to differences at every level of the language (and thus avoids the shortcomings of the word *accent*), it's most commonly used to refer to regionally based variations, as in *southern dialect* or *northwestern dialect*. While regional variation is certainly important, it's not (as we'll see in a minute) the only source of language variation. For another, *dialect* is sometimes used pejoratively – that is, to imply a negative judgment about the way someone speaks, as in: "She should use proper English, and stop talking in dialect." The term thus ignores how every distinguishable variety is just that, a variety. What some might refer to as "proper English", or more accurately Standard English, is itself a variety. And so we will try to use (as much as possible) the term *language variety* or, more simply, *variety* when discussing what some might call a dialect. It's relatively neutral in meaning and thus avoids the negative baggage that comes with *dialect*. Plus, it more readily allows for other sources of variation beyond that of region.

Having finished up this little bit of terminological house-keeping, let's consider the different ways language varieties are classified. The first is, as we already hinted, based on location or region. English, for instance, is a language spoken around the world, but as we move from country to country, we encounter different national varieties: British English, American English, Canadian English, Australian English, Hong Kong English, South African English, and so on. If we narrow our focus to any one of these countries, we'll find regional varieties in each. In the United Kingdom, there's Scots English, Irish English, Welsh English, and British English. In the United States, we have different varieties spoken in the northeastern, southern, midwestern, western, and Pacific parts of the country. And within each of these areas, there are many local varieties that may share some characteristics, yet are nevertheless distinct. A native of London, for instance, doesn't speak the same variety as someone raised in Liverpool or the rural regions of Yorkshire. Nor does someone from Charleston (South Carolina) sound very much like someone who grew up in Knoxville or the Texas Panhandle.

Beyond regional varieties, we find differences based on social factors such as class, ethnicity, gender, age, and even profession. Let's consider the first of these: class. It's often associated with someone's level of education, occupation, and social status. Differences in class are quite often reflected by, or reinforced through, differences in how people speak. In the sitcom *Frasier*, much of the humor derives from mostly class-based collisions among its central characters. You have the two Crane brothers, Frasier and Niles; both Harvard graduates, both psychiatrists, and both reasonably wealthy. As a means of displaying evidence of their social achievements, they speak a variety we commonly associate with the upper reaches of society. They also frequently butt heads with their working-class father, a retired cop, Marty Crane, who enjoys fried corn snacks and cheap beer. Also in residence is Marty Crane's live-in therapist, Daphne Moon, who speaks a working-class variety of Manchester English, and whose duties in the Crane household often resemble those of a maid. Given these descriptions, try to match up the following quotes from *Frasier* with the character who speaks them:

> Oh geez, the disposal's jammed! [*to Niles:*] Yeah, stick your hand down there, see what's stuck, will ya?[2]

> Oh, will you look at that. What a comfy chair! It's like I always say, start with a good piece and replace the rest when you can afford it.[3] [1.1]

> He was livid, thank you. But I pointed out that the emissions from his oversized vehicle endangered the health of anyone passing through the lobby, and I won the day.[4]

Can you tell which quotes go with which character? What specific linguistic features tipped you off? How do they reveal the class of their speaker?

There are plenty of other social factors influencing language variation. They include ethnicity, gender, and age. Ethnicity refers to the culture in which people are raised, and members of any ethnic group often express their identity in how they speak. In the States, we find African American English, Spanglish, Yiddish English, and so on. Gender may also express itself through language variation. Men, for instance, might avoid words and phrases they think sound too feminine such as *darling*, *precious*, or *fabulous*. Women, for their part, typically have a far wider repertoire of color terms than men. To the average man, *azure*, *indigo*, *sapphire*, and *teal* are all *blue*. And women have different styles of talking than do men. They are more often found to prefer styles of conversation in which participants work towards goals in a collaborative, rather than a competitive, fashion. Finally, there are differences in speech related to age. Teenagers are particularly good at coming up with words and phrases that help define them as a group while keeping their parents in a perpetual state of confusion: *chillaxin, emo, wanksta.* Throw into this mix the ways teenagers often communicate electronically through instant and text messaging, and you have a near impregnable code. As we saw in Chapter 7, instant messaging (and other forms of speech/text) is filled with acronyms such as *LOL* ['laughing out loud'], *ROFL* ['rolling on the floor laughing'] and *BF4L* ['best friends for life'], typography to suggest features of oral speech like volume ("OMG IM TYPING!!!!!!!"), and phonetic spellings and spellings that mix letters and numbers ("ur a n00b" ['you are a noob (newbie)']).

It's important to remember that all of these differences are social and cultural in origin and not rooted in biology. Take the American comedian Henry Cho, for instance. He is the son of Korean immigrants, but he grew up in Knoxville and is a native speaker of a variety of English characteristic of East Tennessee. His stand-up routine often plays on this apparent incongruity, poking fun at people who expect him (based on his racial characteristics) to speak a certain way:

> I'm an Asian with a Southern accent. To a lot of people, that right there is funny. I am full-blooded Korean. I was born and raised in Knoxville, Tennessee. So I'm South Korean.

The pun on *South* in *South Korean* captures well the circumstances of Cho's upbringing: the son of Korean immigrants, but also a southerner. And Cho himself is a walkin', talkin', joke tellin' example that undercuts any notion that the varieties we speak are somehow genetically determined.

Although variety may be the spice of life, there is an underside to language variation. Because varieties reveal differences among groups of people, they are often used (unjustifiably) to discriminate. As we mentioned earlier, every language has a "standard" variety, a form of the language that is either taken as the norm or regarded more highly than other varieties within the same language. In English, the standard variety is the one that you learn in school, read in books and magazines, and hear on the nightly news. Varieties that deviate from this standard are often viewed as incorrect or inferior, and people who speak nonstandard varieties are typically judged to be less intelligent, unsophisticated, and poorly brought up. Such beliefs are implicit in the following joke by Jeff Foxworthy, a southerner who often pokes fun at his own way of speaking:

> Nobody wants to hear their brain surgeon say, "Al'ight now what we're gonna do is, saw the top of your head off, root around in there with a stick and see if we can't find that dad burn clot."[5]

This joke plays on the stereotype that speakers of Southern American English are somehow slow or stupid, and it's a specific instance of the notion that "dialects" are inferior, along with their speakers. But Standard English is just as much a language variety as all the rest. It is merely one that has acquired, for many different historical and sociological reasons, a higher status in our culture. There is nothing about it that makes it inherently superior to any other variety.

The Foxworthy joke hints at one final category of language variety: that based on profession. Our confidence in doctors, lawyers, academics, computer technicians, and even plumbers and car mechanics derives, at least in part, from their ability to speak the language of their professions. In the Foxworthy joke, it's not just that the doctor speaks Southern American English (although that's a big part of it); it's also that he uses folksy vernacular language where we would expect medical terminology – for instance, *cranium* instead of *head*, *explore* instead of *root around*, and *thrombosis* instead of *dad burn clot*. Of course, if any of these professionals get too caught up in their language variety or use it to lord it over the rest of us, then they too might become the target of some well-deserved ridicule. Such was the case with the elementary school teacher who, too deeply steeped in her own muddy educational jargon, submitted a request for "behavior modification reinforcers." When her principal asked her what the heck these were, she sheepishly replied, "Lollipops."

How varieties sound

When our would-be cowboy said that he'll be droppin' his "g"s for a while, he made a commitment to altering how his speech will sound – at least, in terms of how he'll pronounce words ending in *-ing*. As we noted before, this change by itself does not add up to a distinct language variety. Nor is dropping one's "g"s unique to varieties of the Southwest or even the South more generally. This same feature is found in many nonstandard varieties of English, including African American English and several working-class varieties spoken in the Northeast. Nor is this even truly dropping the sound "g" so much as it is changing the last sound in a word that has the *-ing* ending. This change in sound is from one made by lifting the back of the tongue to the roof of the mouth to one made by pointing the tip of the tongue at the gums behind the teeth (compare the pronunciation of *dropping* vs. *droppin'* and see if it isn't true). But regardless of whether this change involves droppin' a sound or changin' a sound, what distinguishes the speech of cowboys from these other varieties is how this one feature occurs together with other features of pronunciation to form a set. As we noted before, this set of sounds is sometimes called an *accent*, and if we are going to use that term at all, it really only applies to how varieties sound.

Besides dropping some "g"s, varieties also often vary according to whether or not they include an "r" sound in certain words. British English and varieties of Eastern New England, for instance, drop "r"s in such words as *yard* and *car*, pronouncing them as "yahd" and "cah." We've all heard this little ditty to illustrate the sound of a Boston accent: "Pahk the cah in Hahvahd yahd." Those same speakers will sometimes also add "r"s where, in standard American English, no "r" appears: for instance, "idear" for *idea* and "Warshington" for *Washington*. The Internet offers several Boston or New England "automatic translator applications" that capitalize on these sound differences for mild comic effect: for instance, "Ba ba" for the guy who cuts your hair, "Had licka" for strong spirits, and "Pete sir" for the round Italian pie with tomato sauce and cheese.[6]

Varieties also differ markedly in the pronunciation of vowels. Speakers in the Midwest, Eastern New England, and parts of Western Pennsylvania pronounce *cot* and *caught* as if they were the same word, while speakers in other parts of the country distinguish between the two vowel sounds. In Southern American and in African American English, the vowels in *pin* and *pen* have merged into the same sound. That's why you'll sometimes hear members of these communities say "stick pin" or "ink pin" instead of just "pin," so their listeners will know what kind of "pin" they mean. Other sounds are produced by gliding from one vowel to another. Compare the "o" sounds in "bob" and "boy." In "bob" there's only the one vowel sound; in "boy," however, the sound involves gliding from an "o" to an "i." Many Southern dialects leave out the glide to the second vowel while lengthening the first one, so that a word like "time" (which includes a glide from "a" to "i" in standard pronunciation) comes out as "taahm." On the flip side, the same Southern speaker might add a vowel sound (and even an extra syllable) with some words. As Jeff Foxworthy says, "If all your four letter words have two syllables, then you might be a redneck." Some commonly heard examples of this include the "redneck" pronunciations of the words *damn* as "daa-um" and *shit* as "shee-it."

Another example of variation at the level of sound involves the placement of syllable stress within a word. When speakers of English utter a word with more than one syllable, at least one of those syllables is stressed more than the others. So with a word like *police*, most Standard English speakers place the stress on the second syllable, as in *po-LICE*. However, speakers of African American English and several Southern varieties place the stress on the first syllable, as in *PO-lice*. Similarly, while standard speakers pronounce *theater* with the stress on the first syllable (as in *THEE-a-ter*), many Southerners will stress the second syllable: *the-A-ter*. Differences in syllable stress are not limited to varieties within the States; they also exist across national varieties. British comedian Eddie Izzard capitalizes on several of these differences in part of his stand-up routine. Riffing off the old saying, "Britain and America are two countries separated by a common language," Izzard offers several examples:

> We do pronounce things in a different way . . . You say "aLUminum," and we say "aluMINium." You say "cenTRIfugal"; we say "centriFUgal." . . . You say "basil" [long "a"]; we say "basil" [short "a"]. You say "herbs" [the "h" is silent]; we say "herbs" [the "h" is voiced] because there's a fucking "h" in it.[7]

The last two examples (*basil* and *herbs*) are differences in vowel and word pronunciation, not stress – but the stress-based examples do set up the punch line nicely. Izzard might also note that while Americans say *soccer*, the rest of the English-speaking world says *football* because you kicked the ball with your bloody feet. But that's a difference in vocabulary and belongs in the next section where we talk about language variation at the level of the lexicon.

Variable vocabularies

> "I want to shake off the dust of this one-horse town. I want to explore the world. I want to watch TV in a different time zone. I want to visit strange, exotic malls. I'm sick of eating hoagies! I want a grinder, a sub, a foot-long hero! I want to LIVE, Marge! Won't you let me live? Won't you, please?"[8]

Homer Simpson's wanderlust, his desire to hit the road and see and experience different places and things, is undercut by the bland similarity among the destinations and activities he lists. Does TV programming differ all that much from one time zone to the next? And aren't all shopping malls pretty much the same? There is one way, however, that Homer can measure the extent of his travels, and that is by the names the locals call the sandwiches he hopes to eat. Even though *hoagie, grinder, sub,* and *hero* all refer to roughly the same kind of sandwich (a bread roll stuffed with meat, cheese, lettuce, and tomatoes), Homer could actually chart his location by the use of these terms from region to region. People from Pennsylvania and Southern New Jersey call them *hoagies,* while in New England they're *grinders.* In New York, Homer would be ordering foot-long *heroes.* And if he makes it down to New Orleans or Miami, he'd be served *poor boys* and *Cuban sandwiches,* respectively. Everywhere else across the US, he'd be getting *subs* or *submarine sandwiches.*[9]

This little quote from *The Simpsons* illustrates another general feature about language variation: different groups of speakers sometimes use different words to name the same things. Staying for the moment with food items, what do you call a sweet carbonated beverage that comes in a can or bottle and is served chilled or over ice? Your answer will likely depend on where you (or your parents) grew up. If you answered "coke," chances are that you're from the South, where people are known to go down to the store for some "orange cokes." If you said *pop,* we'd bet that you're from the northern half of the country (the Great Lakes region, the Midwest, the Rockies, or the Pacific Northwest). Speakers who call the stuff *soda* hail from a variety of places, including the mid-Atlantic region or New England, eastern Wisconsin, southern Illinois or eastern Missouri, southeastern Florida, Arizona, and California. These regional differences are set out in the map shown in Figure 9.1, which is based on a 2003 map created by Matthew T. Campbell.[10] Campbell's map is far more detailed, for those who are interested, showing the relative use of these terms in each county. Notice that the regional tendencies are unmistakable. Each of the three different terms really has its own turf. At the same time, it's also worth noting (if one goes to Campbell's source map) that the borders between these categories can be pretty squishy and poorly defined

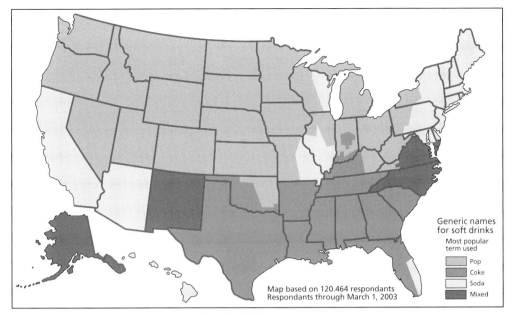

Figure 9.1 *Generic names for soft drinks.*

(much more so than in the rendition we've provided here). Finally, it is important to keep in mind that these are only tendencies. That is, not *all* those in a *soda* region use that term. In many of the areas characterized as *soda*, *pop*, and *coke*, only about 50 percent of the population use the term in question.

Differences in vocabulary can lead to some pretty comical encounters, especially when two speakers of different varieties have the same word or expression in their vocabularies but use it to refer to different things. Consider this exchange from the sitcom *Frasier* between Frasier and Daphne:

> FRASIER: Hello, Daphne. Is Dad here?
> DAPHNE: No, I haven't seen him since he knocked me up this morning.
> FRASIER: What?
> DAPHNE: Knocked me up. Woke me up. It's an English expression. What does it mean here?
> FRASIER: Oh, something else. You'd definitely be awake for it.[11]

This miscommunication results from lexical differences across two national varieties. In British English, *knock up* can mean 'to **knock** on the door in order to wake **up**', while in American English it means 'to get someone pregnant'. Frasier, not knowing the British meaning of the phrase, and Daphne, being unfamiliar with the second meaning, sets up the miscommunication between them, and Frasier's wry response to it. But misunderstandings of this sort can also occur between speakers who share a national variety but come from different regions within the same country. We once knew a man from the Northeastern United States who moved to Texas. On the day he arrived (and after settling into his new apartment), he walked to nearby drugstore to buy a few incidentals – a toothbrush and whatnot. After he paid for them, the cashier (a native Texan) asked, "Would you like a sack with that?" Somewhat startled, the man replied, "No thank you. A bag will be fine." What threw the man was the word *sack*. Where he came from, the word carries the connotation of 'big', as in a *sack of potatoes* or a *sack of grain*. In Texas, however, *sack* can refer to a small paper or plastic container for carrying store purchases (hence some Texans call convenience stores *sack an' go's*). Several years later, this same man moved to South Carolina, and once again, while shopping for a few home necessities, he had a puzzling exchange with a store employee. The man was walking down an aisle, his arms over-burdened with items he had picked off the shelves, when an employee saw him struggling and asked in a helpful tone: "Would you like me to get you a buggy?" Puzzled, the man asked, "What would I do with a buggy?" to which the employee replied, "Put your things in it." This response only confused the man further because, for him, a *buggy* was something you placed a baby in or, perhaps, hitched a horse to – neither of which made sense to him in this context. It was only later that he learned that, in South Carolina, *buggy* is a term for what he had always known as a *shopping cart*.

Differences in vocabulary are not limited to regional affiliations. They can also indicate a speaker's social or cultural membership. Perhaps the most famous example of an English word (actually two words contracted) carrying social connotations is *ain't*. At some time or another (most likely in elementary school), we've probably been on the receiving end of this little bit of grammatical snobbery: "Ain't ain't a word because it ain't in the dictionary." *Ain't* is a variant of such standard forms as *is not, are not, has not,* and *have not*. Originally a contraction of *am not* as in "I ain't deaf," the use of *ain't* has widened to include other pronouns as in "She ain't finished," and "They ain't here." What is interesting about this contraction is that, in its original usage, it has no alternative. There is simply no other way to contract *am not* other than *ain't* since *amn't* doesn't exist. Having expanded in its use to coexist alongside other usable contractions, where both *he isn't* and *he ain't* can replace *he is not, ain't* has acquired a particular social status, and is now typically associated with particularly informal or lower-class speech, although its frequent occurrence in pop culture (music lyrics, TV shows, sports broadcasts) may be making it less stigmatized among many speakers. As for the schoolyard taunt, "Aint ain't a word . . . "? Well, most dictionaries these days do include an entry for *ain't*, even if they follow it with a long note warning speakers and writers to use it only in colloquial or informal settings. Beyond that, most folks have no trouble understanding statements like "They ain't here," so its status as a word seems pretty much secure.

At the other end of the social spectrum, we have words that suggest a speaker's elevated social status. These are typically polysyllabic words with Latin or Greek origins, or they might include words borrowed from French, Italian, or British English (a high-prestige variety in America). Think again of Frasier Crane and the words that characterize his speech. Here's another sampling:

> What trenchant criticism!
> Pompous and sanctimonious am I?

Words like *trenchant*, *pompous*, and *sanctimonious* all fall into that $10 word category. When used appropriately, they suggest the erudition of their speaker. The risk, of course, is that that same speaker might come off as pompous and sanctimonious, and if he were to use them inaccurately, then that would surely mark that speaker as a poseur.

Cultures also have words that help define their members as a group. African American English, for instance, includes such words and phrases as *buggin'* ('acting or thinking crazy'), *call herself* or *call hisself* ('try but not succeed', as in "She call herself a teacher"), and *grill* ('caps worn over teeth', but also figuratively for 'face' or 'personal space'). Cajun English has *lagniappe* ('something extra'), *making groceries* ('grocery shopping'), and *zydeco* (a folk music style of southern Louisiana). Yiddish English has *chutzpah* ('nerve' or 'guts'), *mazeltov* ('good luck' or 'cheers'), *shlemiel* ('a fumbler'), and *shlemazel* ('an unlucky person'). The different meanings of these last two words are captured nicely in this joke:

> What's the difference between a *shlemiel* and a *shlemazel*?
> A *schlemiel* spills the soup on a *shlemazel*.

And we would be remiss here not to mention a recurrent character from *Saturday Night Live*, Linda Richman (a.k.a The Coffee Talk Lady), played by Mike Myers, who imitates a New York Jewish variety and, in the process, introduced late night audiences everywhere to the Yiddish term *verklempt* in the saying, "I'm a little *verklempt*." For those of you who are not Yiddish speakers or "knowers," *verklempt* means 'emotionally overwrought' . . . which is clearly too large and highfalutin' a mouthful to be used by The Coffee Talk Lady.

Finally, we have words belonging to various professional varieties – that is, words and technical terms used by doctors, lawyers, computer specialists, and so on. For this class of varieties, vocabulary is arguably their most distinctive feature. Perhaps that's why we hear so many complaints about professional jargons – that is, using jargon-laden speech or writing as a kind of polysyllabic smokescreen (recall the elementary school teacher who requested "behavior modification reinforcers," otherwise known as "lollipops"). But professional vocabularies do serve some important functions. For one, they offer members of a profession a kind of shorthand, a highly economical way of referring to complex concepts or processes without having to explain or refer to every aspect of those concepts or processes. For another, they help members of a profession establish their credibility (recall Foxworthy's joke about the southern brain surgeon). An installment from the *Non-Sequitur* comic strip suggests how an ill-chosen word can threaten a professional's reputation. The installment asks, how can you "tell your attorney worked too long in juvenile court"? It then depicts a court scene in which the lawyer for one side stands to address the judge, "The defense moves for a do-over." The more professionally appropriate word, of course, would be "retrial," but this lawyer, so steeped in the language of his former pint-sized clients, uses a word from a language variety of the school playground. As a result, he puts his request in jeopardy.

Variable grammars

Imagine that our would-be cowboy mastered a western accent and added to his vocabulary words that characterize a western variety. He'd be further along than he was when he started – that is, further along than just droppin' some "g"s. But he'd still have a ways to go. He'd also have to learn new ways of combining some of those sounds and words into phrases and sentences. In other words, he'd have to learn the grammatical features that help define western speech. A good place to start might be with *y'all*. At first, you might think that *y'all* is a matter of word choice or vocabulary. In a way it is, but it's also a grammatical feature. Let us explain. Standard English makes no distinction between the singular and plural versions of the second person pronoun:

	Singular	*Plural*
First person:	I am	we are
Second person:	**you are**	**you are**
Third person:	he, she, or it is	they are

In a Standard English sentence like "Are you from Texas?" there's nothing in the form of the utterance itself that indicates whether *you* refers to one person or to more than one person. Now, at one time, until a few centuries ago, English had a perfectly useful and respectable second person singular pronoun, *thou*. So, speakers of Shakespeare's time could ask one person if they were cold, "Art thou cold?," or more than one person, "Are ye cold?" For a number of reasons, *thou* fell into disuse and *you* filled the place of both *thou* and *ye*, leaving English speakers without a way to distinguish between singular and plural in the second person.

To make up for this gap, many nonstandard varieties have come up with ways to mark a difference between the singular and plural forms. Some varieties use the verb to signal the difference, so that "Is you from Texas?" is singular, while "Are you from Texas" is plural. Other varieties mark the difference in the pronoun itself – that is, by adding something to the second person plural form. In New Jersey and New York (and in some British and Australian dialects), speakers "pluralize" the *you* to form *youse*, as in *youse guys*. In the South, speakers contract the *you* and add *all*, so that "Are you from Texas?" is singular, while "Are y'all from Texas" is plural. In southwestern Pennsylvania, and the near surrounding area, people use the form *yinz*, as in "Are yinz from Pittsburgh?"[12]

This form, like *y'all*, has evolved from the addition of a plural words to *you*, going from *you ones*, to *you'uns*, to *youns*, to *yuns*, to *yinz*.

There's a joke of sorts that has confused the issue. Here it is: "Remember: 'y'all' is singular, 'all y'all' is plural, and 'all y'all's' is possessive plural." Southern humorist Roy Blount Jr. doesn't buy this formulation. While criticizing one of its proponents, Maureen Duffin-Ward, Blount explains why *y'all* is always plural, if only implicitly:

> People in the South do indeed sometimes seem to be addressing a single person as "y'all." For instance, a restaurant patron might ask a waiter, "What y'all got for dessert tonight?" In that case "y'all" refers collectively to the folks who run the restaurant. No doubt the implication of plurality is hard for someone who didn't grow up with it to discern. It may even be that Duffin-Ward has heard a native speaker, in real life, violate deep-structure idiom by calling a single person "y'all." That would be arguable grounds for saying that "y'all" is singular on occasion. But how can she have missed daily instances of people unmistakably addressing two or more people as "y'all"? When a parent calls out to three kids, "Y'all get in here out of the rain," does she think only one child is being summoned? ("All y'all" is of course an extended plural: "Y'all listen up! I mean all y'all." Often it is pronounced "Aw yaw.")[13]

All y'all may indeed work, as Blount says, like an "extended plural," but our own experiences living in the South suggest another distinction, one that's based on the number of people referred to by the pronoun: *y'all* for a few people, *all y'all* for a gaggle.

Although some of y'all might think *y'all* sounds like uneducated speech, it is a thoroughly functional feature, making clear a distinction absent in the standard variety – that is, between the singular and plural forms of the second person pronoun. Other departures from Standard English are also functional. One of those is the double negative. In grammar school, we were taught to avoid sentences like "I don't have no money," and say or write this instead: "I don't have *any* money." The reasoning was that the two negatives (*don't* and *no*) cancel each other out and result in a positive. So what the first sentence "logically" means is "I do have money." But only a smart aleck would take this as the sentence's actual meaning. In fact, double negatives are common in many varieties of English, including Scots English, Black English, Southern English, and many earlier versions of English (Shakespeare, for instance, often used them). They're also found in other languages, such as Spanish where *No tengo nada* 'I don't have nothing' is actually standard. So even though double negation is nonstandard, it is still commonly and frequently used in casual conversation with precisely the same meaning as its single negation counterparts.

SPEAKER A: Can you lend me a buck?
SPEAKER B: I told you, I don't have no money.

The double negative in Speaker B's answer means precisely the same thing as *I don't have any money*, and is only marked as being less formal. There are nearly no cases in which the two negatives would be understood to "cancel each other out." In the above conversation, if Speaker A were to respond, "Oh, so you do have money," he would be considered a wise ass and might find himself looking up at Speaker B from the floor.

Other syntactic differences between varieties can be found in the verb phrase. Speakers of African American English, for instance, use *be* to indicate actions that repeat or persist over time (also known as the habitual or recurrent present): "She be sick all month" or "He be joking all the time." To indicate an action or condition going on right now, speakers of this variety would say, "She sick," meaning 'she is sick right now' omitting the verb *be* entirely, or "He joking," meaning 'he is joking right now' and again omitting the verb *be*. In some Native American varieties, speakers add the -*s* to the *be* form itself, as in *I hope it* **bes** *a girl* and *They* **bes** *doing all right*.[14] In Southern English, speakers will sometimes double up on modal or auxiliary verbs, as in *It might could work* and *I might could go with you*. Speakers of Standard English would use one modal or the other: either *I might go with you* (it's a possibility) or *I could go with you* (I am able to). But neither of these options in Standard English really captures the meaning of *I might could go with you*, which in Southern American English means something like, *I may be able to go with you but I'm not really sure*.[15]

Variable uses and style-switching

Let's say our would-be cowboy has learned the sounds and meanings of words characterizing a western variety. Let's say that he's also learned how to combine those sounds and words into phrases and clauses other speakers of the same variety would recognize as meaningful. He still has one more level of language to consider: that is, how speakers use language in specific situations to accomplish various goals. Most, if not all, varieties do similar things with language: ask questions, give information, make promises, tell stories, start and end conversations, and so on. But speakers of different varieties often have different ways of accomplishing these goals, including a tacit understanding about when and where they might even be undertaken. These differences in how, when, and where speakers do things with language also help distinguish one variety from another.

Consider how speakers of the same variety greet one another. Texans (and other Southerners) might say, "Howdy" (in Appalachian English, they call this greeting ritual "swapping howdy") or "How'ya doin'?" Philadelphians and New Yorkers might trade "Yo's," while speakers of African American English might greet each other with "What's up?" or even more briefly "'Sup." Leave-taking, or saying goodbye, also differs from variety to variety. A Texan, for instance, might borrow a term from Spanish and say, "Adios," while a speaker of British English might make his exit with a "Cheers, mate." There may also be considerable variation in greetings and closings depending on other factors such as age, gender, status, and occupation. Older speakers might prefer a more formal closing, as in "Goodbye," while younger speakers might opt for the more informal "Catch you later" or simply "Latah."

There are many other pragmatic differences across language varieties: for instance, different expectations about what topics are appropriate to discuss in certain situations, how fast or loud a speaker should talk, how long pauses should be between utterances, and so on. We'll come back to many of these differences in the next chapter on language and culture. There we'll see that these differences don't simply distinguish one language variety from another. Instead, they point to deeper, more profound differences across cultures.

In the meantime, let's close this chapter with a brief look at style-shifting – that is, when a single speaker switches from one language variety to another. Many, if not all, of us can speak more than one variety, and when we do shift between varieties, we do so to serve various purposes. One of these is to adapt to – or forge a link with – our listeners. A Southerner, for instance, who has lived in the North for many years and has, as a result, lost many features of her home variety may switch back to that variety when visiting home or interacting with other Southern speakers. Similarly, a speaker of African American English may shift to a more standard variety at school or at work, understanding that the way she speaks at home can be perceived negatively in mainstream culture. Reciprocally, a white teenager might adopt features of African American English to sound "cool" and fit in with others in his circle of friends. In other cases, speakers might switch varieties to distinguish themselves from their listeners. Imagine if that same Southerner living in the North switched to her home variety on certain occasions. She may do so in order to show her difference from those around her – to stand out from the crowd, so to speak – and preserve a connection to her regional home and its traditions and culture.

Dialect switching is a staple of stand-up comedy. When telling jokes and funny stories featuring characters who speak nonstandard varieties, comedians will often shift roles and adopt the "voices" of those characters. Margaret Cho, for instance, speaks a West Coast variety with hints of Valley Girl speak, but she often shifts into Korean English (or a kind of Pan-Asian English) when portraying Asians. From her stand-up routine:

> I almost married this Irish American guy, and we got really close to getting married. I even went down to meet his family, and they lived in Sarasota, Florida. And I was really worried before I went there. I asked him, I said, "Are there going to be any Asian people there?" And he was like, "No." And I said, "OK. Then could you just drop me off at the dry cleaner then? Because I don't want to be the only one!" I mean, I love his family, but they were

kind of too nice to me. So the whole time I just felt really like, [shifting into an Asian English dialect and bowing repeatedly] "Dis is my host famary. I come from Asia . . . America is numbah wuh-un . . . Tank you Mistah Eddie's fahther."[16]

The British comedian Eddie Izzard also switches frequently between varieties, ranging in his stand-up routine from several American varieties through different regional varieties in England. Sometimes Izzard will even deliver parts of his act in French and German (but that's a topic for another chapter). In the following bit, he imagines a conversation between Darth Vader and Luke Skywalker spoken in Cockney English:

> "'Ello. Look, I'm Lord Vader and just pay ah-bloody-tention, ah right? Luke, Luke, the force is strong with you."
> "Is it?"
> "Yea."
> "Well 'oo told you that?"
> "Uh . . . some bloke . . . . Yes, he said the force is really rather strong with you."
> "Well how strong?"
> "As strong as a small pony."
> "Oh, that's quite strong, that is."[17]

In both of these examples, Cho and Izzard switch varieties as part of their comedic bits. The disjunction between their normal speaking variety and the ones they take on during those bits works well to heighten the humor. But that disjunction also reflects broader cultural differences among different groups of people. And it's to these differences that we turn in our next chapter.

10 Cross-cultural gaffes

Language and culture

> I'll never forget the first time my mother-in-law met my dad. Me and my dad went down to Arab [a small town in Alabama]. We get out of the car at the house. My future mother-in-law walks out and says "Hey" to me. I swear to you all, she looks at my dad and goes, "HEL-LO . . . MIS-TER . . . CHO . . . HOW . . . ARE . . . YOU?" My dad's like, "What is she doing?" [I say,] "Well, she thinks she's speaking Korean." –Henry Cho[1]

Henry Cho's dad and future mother-in-law come from different linguistic and cultural backgrounds. His dad is Korean, but has lived and worked in the States for many years (at least since the mid-1960s), and has had plenty of time to become quite fluent in English. The future mother-in-law, on the other hand, is a white woman who's spent her entire life in the small rural Alabama town of Arab. She is, in other words, a bit provincial. Meeting Mr. Cho for the first time, she assumes, given that he looks foreign, that he probably doesn't understand English, and to compensate she speaks to him as she would to any foreigner, slowly and loudly (Americans have a reputation for thinking that anyone can understand English if they just speak slowly and loudly enough). Notice by way of contrast, how she greets Henry with the more normal and more familiar "Hey." As it turns out, however, the joke is on her. When Mr. Cho asks, "What is she doing?" he shows that he can speak English just fine, although he remains a bit puzzled over the mother-in-law's behavior – that is, her attempt, as Henry playfully puts, to speak Korean.

In a roundabout way, though, Henry Cho's mother-in-law is not too far off the mark. When people from different cultures interact, misunderstandings emerge as much as from how things are said as from *what*. Of course, folks will stumble over unfamiliar pronunciations, words, and sentence structures (and we'll discuss some of those ways in a minute). But more frequently, interlanguage trouble occurs at the level of pragmatics and discourse – that is, in how utterances function within the context of a given speech event or broader social occasion. These difficulties reveal the close relationship between language and culture. Two speakers may share knowledge of a grammar (the meaning of words and how they are combined to form phrases and clauses), without necessarily having much command of the cultural conventions followed in putting that grammar to work in specific situations. Mr. Cho doesn't need Henry to translate the meaning

Table 10.1 *Linguistically Relevant Cultural Categories*

Criteria	Examples of Cultural Group
Geography or Nationality	Western, Asian, Japanese, American
Region	New England, Southern, Midwestern
Age or Generation	young, old, baby boomers, Generation X
Ethnicity or Race	African American, Jewish, Latino, Slavic
Gender	women and men
Social Status	working class, middle class, elite or highbrow
Profession	academic, corporate, political

of the mother-in-law's words; instead, he needs him to translate her behavior – what she is "doing" with those words.

This chapter focuses on language and culture, in particular the misunderstandings that often arise when people from different linguistic cultures interact. In many ways, this chapter builds on the previous one about language varieties, which, as you'll recall, are forms of a language spoken by people who share some regional, ethnic, or social characteristic. Cultures can be identified in much the same way: just as we have national, regional, generational, ethnic, and professional varieties, we also have national, regional, generational, etc., cultures (see Table 10.1 for a summary of cultural categories). Also, much like language varieties, cultural influences on languages appear at every linguistic level: pronunciation, vocabulary, grammar, and language use.

But this chapter differs from the previous one in two important respects. First, culture is a broader category than language variety or language. It refers to a whole way of life shared by a community or group of people, including not only how they speak but also what they believe, what they value, what they do, how they behave, what they create, what they consume, and so on. The second difference follows from the first. In the previous chapter, we pointed out how language varies from region to region and from group to group. This chapter takes matters a step further and examines the cultural meanings and values that lie behind these variations. To put it somewhat differently, the previous chapter was about variations within the code itself: for instance, dropping "g"s at the end of some words, or using *ain't* instead of *is not*. This chapter looks at what those variations mean to members of different cultures and how they might lead to cross-cultural miscommunication.

We'll begin with miscues and misfires at the level of pronunciation, vocabulary, and grammar. Then we'll move on to misunderstandings that occur at the level of conversation and discourse, which includes such things as intonation, turn taking, directness, and politeness. As we progress through these levels of language, you'll notice that the misunderstandings result less and less from the mechanics of knowing (or not knowing) the forms of a language and more and more from the underlying assumptions and expectations that members from different cultures bring to an encounter. By studying these linguistic sources of miscommunication, we'll gain a better understanding of the cultural factors that cause them in the first place.

Pronunciation, vocabulary, and grammar

Differences in word pronunciation can lead to misunderstandings. Imagine two speakers from different cultures, speaking different varieties. Say one of these speakers pronounces a word in such a way that it sounds like a completely different word in the second speaker's variety. The likely result? Confusion over what's being talked about. Consider this non-native speaker of English who has an urgent request:

> A French guest is staying at a fancy hotel in New York City. He calls room service and asks for some "pepper." On the other end of the line, the concierge asks, "Black pepper or white pepper?" "No," says the Frenchman, "toilet pepper."

Similar miscommunications might arise between native speakers who share a language but use different systems of pronunciation. You'll recall that certain varieties don't distinguish vowels sounds in word pairs such as *cot/caught*, *pin/pen*, and *tire/tar*. Any one of these (and many others) could cause miscommunication between English speakers using different varieties. A story about a northerner visiting a small town in Texas around Christmas time illustrates such a case. While out on a stroll, the Yankee sees a nativity scene and notices all Three Wise Men wearing firefighter helmets. Asking a local about the Wise Men's odd headgear, he is told, "The *Bible* says that when the Three Wise Men came to visit baby Jesus, they had come from afar." The confusion arises because the word *afar* in many Southern varieties sounds like *a fire*.

Word meanings and their connotations are also sources of miscommunication. Chapter 9 showed how misunderstandings can occur when speakers from different regions in the US use different words to refer to the same thing, such as *bag* vs. *sack* or *shopping cart* vs. *buggy*. Yet it is not only confusion about word meaning that leads to misunderstanding. Word connotation, or the associations that a word might trigger, can also lead to miscommunication.

Take, for instance, the connotations accompanying the word *dog* in different linguistic cultures. The word *dog* has a meaning that is roughly equivalent to *chien* in French, Spanish *perro*, and Japanese *inu*. However, some of the connotations linked to *dog* get lost in translation, while other are added. It is in these losses and additions that cultural differences reveal themselves. In American and British culture, *dog* comes with many positive associations, such as loyalty, companionship, and playfulness. These associations indicate how we value and interact with our dogs. We typically see them as at least pets and, in some cases, practically as family members. The market for specialty dog food, clothes, grooming services, and even therapists attests to this. In other linguistic cultures, however, the word for *dog* may trigger a completely different set of associations, reflecting, in turn, a distinctly different set of cultural attitudes and behaviors towards them. In an agrarian culture, dogs may be viewed primarily in instrumental terms – as herders, hunters, or even livestock. And, as a result, they may be treated in more emotionally distant ways. In yet other cultures, particularly those where Islam is the dominant faith, interactions between humans and canines are severely restricted, and the word for *dog* will conjure thoughts of uncleanliness or ritual impurity.

If all these very different connotations can attach themselves to such a common word, with such a simple and stable meaning, imagine the difficulty of translating, or using cross-linguistically, words for more complex or abstract concepts, such as *love*, *virtue*, or *wit*. In some cases, a word might refer to something so culturally specific that it has no single-word equivalents in other languages. In such cases, it would be untranslatable, and the best translation one could hope for would be a paraphrase of the word's original meaning. To illustrate this difficulty, several years ago, a professional translation company surveyed 1,000 linguists, asking them to choose the most untranslatable words they could identify.[2] Topping the list was *ilunga*, a word from the Tshliba language spoken in the southeastern region of the Congo, whose highly complex meaning is paraphrased as, "a person who is ready to forgive any abuse for the first time, to tolerate it a second time, but never a third time." Coming in at number two was the Yiddish word *schlemazel*, a term for "a chronically unlucky person" (although we think that *schlemiel* should be ranked higher); and at number three was the Polish word *radioustukacz* which means "a person who worked as a telegraphist for the resistance movements on the Soviet side of the Iron Curtain." Of course, English itself has its own share of words that translators find difficult to render in other languages, such as *poppycock*, *whimsy*, *gobbledegook*, and *Spam* (the meat-like substance in a rectangular can).

And speaking of meat-like substances and their connotations, one is reminded of a scene from the movie *Pulp Fiction* where Vincent explains to his partner, Jules, the French translation of the name of a popular burger from McDonald's:

> VINCENT: And you know what they call a Quarter Pounder with Cheese in
> Paris?
> JULES: They don't call it a Quarter Pounder with Cheese?
> VINCENT: Nah, man, they got the metric system. They wouldn't know what
> the fuck a Quarter Pounder is.
> JULES: What do they call it?
> VINCENT: They call it a "Royale with Cheese."
> JULES: "Royale with Cheese."
> VINCENT: That's right.[3]

Aside from showing the humor of an American choosing McDonalds as *the* place to dine in Paris, the exchange also illustrates how meanings are both lost and gained in translating a word from one linguistic culture to another. Translating *Quarter Pounder with Cheese* to *Royale with Cheese* loses reference to the burger's weight (and the accompanying virile connotations associated with eating large quantities of beef). Notice that it's called a *Quarter Pounder* rather than the equivalent *Four Ouncer*, the first sounding heavier, more substantial, and robust. A quarter of something big and weighty sounds more manly than four of something small and delicate. But the translation also adds something: "Royale" lends the burger a certain upper-class and stylish (almost effeminate) elegance – a certain panache – that's not suggested (and is probably avoided) in the original American English name.

Even among speakers of the same language, some words may lead to confusion when they (and the things they refer to) are not shared across cultural groups. Coastal varieties of many languages, for instance, have many words relating to fishing, boating, and tides not found among inland varieties. Reciprocally, inland speakers may have words used in farming, forestry, and hunting not found in coastal varieties. The same can be said about almost any cultural group. There are plenty of differences between the vocabularies of older and younger generations, of African Americans and whites, and of academics and those outside the university. Members of different groups need group-specific words to refer to things, activities, and beliefs that are important to their way of life – important to their culture. But when they interact with those of different cultures, misunderstandings may result. This sort of misunderstanding is played up in a scene from *Fawlty Towers* (a British sitcom featuring John Cleese as Basil Fawlty, the owner of a small hotel and restaurant in the southwest of England). In the following exchange, he's taking a dinner order from an American couple, when he runs up against the name of an American dish he's never heard of:

> AMERICAN [somewhat belligerently]: Could you make me a Waldorf salad?
> FAWLTY: A...Walll...?
> AMERICAN [even more belligerently]: A WAL...DORF...SA...LAD!
> FAWLTY   [meekly]: I think we're just out of Waldorf.

Having no idea what the diner is asking for, Fawlty guesses that *Waldorf* (whatever it is) must be a key ingredient in a Waldorf salad, like spinach in spinach salad and chicken in chicken salad. Completely overlooked is the possibility of a dish being named after a place (Waldorf Salad from the Waldorf-Astoria Hotel), or a person (Oysters Rockefeller after John D. Rockefeller).

Grammatical differences across varieties, languages, and cultures can also cause confusion. Take this little bit of linguistic variation: "I spend my evenings at home anymore." If you're not from the US Mid-West, and especially if you are from the US Northeast, you are probably scratching your head over this one because most of us only use *anymore* in negative statements, such as "I don't spend my evenings at home anymore." But among some English speakers, *anymore* can be used in positive statements too, where it means something like *nowadays* or *these days*. So, "I spend my evenings at home anymore" roughly translates as "I spend my evenings at home nowadays."

Confusion may also result when non-native speakers struggle trying to translate using the unfamiliar grammar of another language. For example, on a Chinese restaurant menu we found the item *ju-ba-tang-mian* translated as 'the pig picks the noodle soup'.[4] Clearly, there's a problem with this menu. First of all, even if we know nothing else about it, the Chinese entry is clearly a noun phrase describing a menu item. But the translation is a sentence about what some pig did. Well, it turns out that *ju* can mean either 'pig' or 'pork'. That shouldn't surprise us as English speakers, having as we do one word for the bird in the henhouse, *chicken*, and the meat that comes from it, *chicken*. The word *pa*, among other things, is a verb meaning 'to pick or strip'. But it's also pronounced *ba* and used (in Cantonese mostly) to express the borrowed English word *bar*. So, in this case the combination *ju-ba* means 'pork bar' or 'a bar or slab of pork' (think 'pork chop'). It didn't occur to the translator that *ba* doesn't translate as a verb here. The rest of it, *tang-mian* 'soup with noodles', describes the dish. So, the dish is 'pork chop noodle soup'. By not recognizing that English has two words, *pig* for the animal and *pork* for the meat (rather than one, *ju*), and by rendering a noun as a verb that takes an object, our translator has told us about a pig (perhaps an occasional diner there?) who always 'picks' (orders?) the noodle soup. Nice story, but not appropriate for a menu.

Conversational misfires

So far we've been talking pretty exclusively about pronunciation, vocabulary, and grammar and how they can lead to misunderstanding across cultures. These points of misinterpretation are relatively easy to spot, although their links to culture needed some teasing out. Less apparent (but often more significant and consequential) are misapprehensions occurring at the level of pragmatics and discourse – that is, in how speakers use language in specific situations. Beyond the literal meaning of words and sentences, speakers have all kinds of resources for conveying meaning. They can raise or lower the pitch of their voices (intonation). They can speak softly or loudly (volume), slowly or quickly (tempo). They can pause between speaking turns (delay) or talk while others are still speaking (interruption or overlap). They can address topics of conversation in rather vague or noncommittal ways, or speak quite concretely and candidly, even delving into personal observations about other participants. Speakers also have different options for performing certain actions through speech, such as making requests, issuing commands, answering "yes" or "no," and engaging in various kinds of verbal rituals (telling jokes, voicing complaints, or asking someone for a date). In addition to these resources for managing *how* they talk, speakers can also convey meaning through their body language: they can stand close to or further from their listeners, look them in the eye, stare at the ground, use gestures and facial expressions, and so on.

Most languages and varieties have all of these resources for communication, but what each of them means may vary from culture to culture, and from situation to situation within a single culture. Differences in the meanings behind these resources can lead to conversational misfires and miscommunications. Consider intonation, or changes in vocal pitch. Apart from the occasional professor, politician, or preacher who drones on and on in a monotone, speakers will frequently raise and lower the pitch of their voices while talking. But they don't do so willy-nilly. Instead, these changes in pitch fall into patterns that listeners will recognize and interpret as meaningful. In English, for instance, a rise in pitch at the end of a clause typically signals a question, while a drop at the end signals a statement:

> SPEAKER A: Did you hear the one about the plumber and the duck?
> SPEAKER B: Yes I did.

Not all languages follow this pattern. One linguist studied intonation among food servers at a British cafeteria.[5] Some of the servers were native speakers of English; others were immigrants from India and Pakistan. When the British servers offered customers an item, they would use rising intonation, as in "Gravy?" The Indian and Pakistani servers, however, used falling intonation while making the same offer, as if they were delivering a statement, "Gravy." The customers noticed the difference and complained that the Indian and Pakistani servers were rude and aloof. As it turns out, they weren't trying to convey this impression at all. Instead, they were (unwittingly) importing an intonation pattern from their native languages where falling intonation was the appropriate choice in this situation. In other words, they were using the correct word (*gravy*) but the wrong intonation pattern.

Besides distinguishing between questions and statements, conventional intonation patterns in English can serve other functions. Over a stretch of talk, sharp and sudden changes in pitch (either up or down) can signal excitement or emotional intensity, while little to no change can indicate detachment, coolness, or mind-numbing monotony. Over a single word, an abrupt rise or drop in pitch allows speakers to emphasize that word: the change in intonation draws listeners' attention to the word, making it stand out in its tonal context. In addition, when wrapping up a turn of talk, a speaker will often use falling intonation to signal that she is done speaking and that she is now passing the floor to another participant.

As suggested here above, all of these English language intonation patterns have fairly conventional uses and meanings, and are widely shared among native speakers of English. But in recent years, linguists have noted the appearance of an entirely new intonation pattern that has made its way around various parts of the English-speaking world, from Australia/New Zealand to Canada, Cape Town, California, and parts of the UK. The intonation pattern, called "uptalk" or "upspeak," is mainly seen in the speech of younger people and particularly younger women, and is characterized by ending a statement with rising intonation. You'll remember that English speakers typically end questions with rising intonation and statements with falling intonation. Not so with uptalk. Here the rising intonation pattern we commonly associate with questions gets mapped onto statements. In the US, uptalk is strongly associated with Valley Girl speak (i.e. "Valspeak") of Southern California, as in:

> So I went to the mall. And I tried on these, like, bitchin' shoes.

Each of the two sentences ends with rising intonation on the last word. To an outsider, it will sound as though the speaker is asking a question (although the sentences themselves don't lend themselves to such an interpretation).

Some have suggested that speakers who use uptalk are conveying a measure of uncertainty about their statements (in the same way that questions imply uncertainty). But uptalk has appeared in some surprising places where it is used by speakers who don't fit the Valley Girl profile at all, including teachers, doctors, CEOs, and even the President of the United States.[6] The presence of uptalk in the speech of people who wield authority has thus led some to reinterpret its function and cultural meaning. Rather than carrying over the uncertainty implied by questions, uptalk capitalizes on a question's direct appeal to listeners for a response. It's a trick of sorts, a way for a speaker to package a statement in such a way that listeners feel compelled to respond. It is, in other words, a strategy for control.

Misunderstandings can also occur when speakers from different cultures have different strategies for taking turns while talking. Very often, but not always, turn taking involves pauses between speakers' turns. But the kind and length of these pauses can vary, as can their meaning in the conversation. It has been observed that the many, many functions that conversational pauses can have include "building up tension or raising expectations in the listener . . . assisting the listener in . . . understanding . . . signalling anxiety, emphasis . . . spontaneity [etc.]."[7]

Now in much of mainstream Anglo American culture, the default pattern runs something like this: one speaker talks while the other listens quietly. When that first speaker is done, she signals the end of her turn with, among other things, a drop in pitch. There may be a short pause, and then the second speaker takes a turn while the first one listens. And so it goes, back and forth. But not all cultures follow this pattern. Some Native American speakers, for instance, often observe longer pauses between turns than Anglo Americans.[8] For Native Americans, the longer pause is a sign of respect, but for Anglo Americans, it can mean that the conversation isn't going so well. Put a speaker from each culture together, and you might get an exchange that is confusing to both. For instance, the Anglo speaker might end her turn and expect the Native American speaker to respond almost immediately. Instead, he pauses, making sure the Anglo speaker is done before contributing to the conversation himself. For the Anglo speaker, this delay between speaking turns may feel like an uncomfortable lull in the conversation, and as a result, she might fill the void with more talk. She ends her turn again, another long pause, and then more void-filling talk. Meanwhile, feeling as if he is getting hedged out of the conversation, the Native American speaker might conclude that the Anglo speaker is pushy or self-absorbed – someone who just likes to hear the sound of her own voice. On the flip side, the Anglo speaker might leave the conversation thinking that the Native American was unresponsive or just not interested in what she had to say.

At the other end of the spectrum are cultures that observe few if any pauses between speaking turns. Among Germans, for instance, and New York Jews, it's quite common for speakers to interrupt one another or speak at the same time. Within these cultures, interruptions and overlaps are positive features of conversation. They signal enthusiasm, interest, even intimacy. But to many Americans, these conversational strategies come across as rude or aggressive, and as a result, they might regard speakers who use them not as showing interest or enthusiasm, but as being hostile and agonistic.

Like interruptions and overlaps, talkativeness can also have different meanings for different cultures. In Sweden, for instance, people generally value quietness and economy of expression, and they typically regard foreigners from more talkative cultures (such as France and Italy) as rowdy and overbearing.[9] Reciprocally, people from more talkative cultures (like France and Italy) may view members from less talkative cultures (like Sweden) as cold and aloof.

One cultural group that's almost universally seen as being excessively talkative is women. As evidence of this perception, just think of all the jokes out there that target overly chatty women:

> A policeman on a motorcycle pulls over a car. "What's up?" says the driver. "Your wife fell out the passenger door three miles back," says the policeman. "Thank goodness for that," says the driver. "I thought I'd gone deaf."[10]

> Two women are having lunch. The first woman says, "My husband tried to leave me because he said I talk too much." "What did you do?" asks the other. "I talked him out of it."

> One day while reading the paper, a husband comes across a study finding that men speak around 15,000 words per day, while women speak around 30,000. Bent on making a point to his wife, he shows her these results. She replies, "Women use twice as many words because they have to repeat everything they say." To which the husband replies, "What?"

In the last joke, the woman turns the tables on her husband and counters one stereotype (that women talk too much) with another (that men don't listen . . . at least, not to women). She could strengthen her case even further by digging through some of the research herself. There she'd find study after study showing that men actually talk more than women. If you think about it, that discovery should not be all that surprising. If holding the floor and talking is a sign of power, then in cultures (like our own) where men generally hold more power than women, men are likely to speak more than women. Why then do women get saddled with the "more talkative" label? Could it be that their talk is, in general, not valued by the powers that be (that is, men); therefore, any amount of talk they contribute is seen as too much?

Indirectness can also have different meanings to members of different cultures. As you'll remember from Chapter 6, indirectness involves using one kind of speech act to perform another kind of speech act. For instance, say a friend asks you if you want to go to the movies with him this coming Friday. Rather than answering "no," you say, "I have a lot of homework that I need to do this weekend." Your response is not an explicit answer to his question; instead, it's a declarative statement about the amount of homework you have and when you need to complete it. But you hope that he'll take the hint and interpret your response as an indirect way of saying "no." Why not just say "no" to begin with? Because it's a cultural thing. In many cultures, indirectness is a form of politeness, a way to show consideration for others. In this case, the indirect statement about having a lot of homework seems less harsh than an outright refusal of the invitation. Plus, indirectness offers speakers who hate to say "no" (another culturally learned behavior) an alternate strategy for turning down invitations explicitly.

But not everyone views indirectness so positively. We once knew a guy from Texas who was very upfront and direct. As he saw it, people should say what they mean and mean what they say. As a result of these strong beliefs, he often refused to interpret indirect statements as they were intended. For instance, if he asked you if you wanted to go to the movies and you answered with the "I have a lot of homework" gambit, he would invariably respond, "I didn't ask you if you had a lot of homework. I asked you if you wanted to go to the movies." Was this Texan incapable of interpreting indirect statements? No. This was a case of intentional misunderstanding. He pretended not to understand the indirect denial and, instead, interpreted it literally, because he wanted others to go on record and be explicit about their decisions. For him, indirectness was just beating about the bush.

For others, though, indirectness can be a genuine source of misunderstanding. Consider the following scene from *Fawlty Towers*. Early in the episode, Basil Fawlty gets a tip on race horse, and in order to keep his wife from finding out that he's gambling, he enlists Manuel, a waiter at the hotel, to place the bet for him. The bet pays off – Fawlty's horse wins, but he suspects that his wife is on to him, so he reminds Manuel to keep his little gambling adventure secret. Problem is, Manuel is from Barcelona, and his fluency in English isn't quite up to snuff. As a result, he mistakes Fawlty's reminder (which Fawlty packages as a form of indirectness) as criticism of his intelligence:

> FAWLTY   [in a whisper]: Manuel . . . Manuel . . .
> MANUEL   [loudly]: Oh, your horse. It win! It win!
> FAWLTY: Shhh . . . shhh . . . Manuel, you know nothing.
> MANUEL: I learn. I learn. I get better.
> FAWLTY   [still whispering]: No, no, no. You don't understand.

MANUEL: I do.

FAWLTY: No you don't.

MANUEL: I do understand that.

FAWLTY: Shh . . . shh . . . You know nothing about the horse.

MANUEL: I know nothing about the horse?

. . .

MANUEL: I put money on for you. You give me money.
I go to betting shop . . .

FAWLTY [interrupting]: Yes, I know. I know. I know.

MANUEL: Why you say I know nothing?

Manuel interprets "You know nothing" literally, as an assertion about his ability to understand things in general. But Fawlty intends it as an indirect request – something like, "When my wife asks you about my little bet, I want you to pretend that you know nothing." Manuel's misunderstanding stems not so much from cultural differences between England and Barcelona (Spanish has its own repertoire of indirectness that's not all that different from England's). Rather, it results from Manuel's struggles with the language and perhaps from his being unaware that "You know nothing" is a fairly conventional way of asking someone in English to pretend ignorance.

In other cases, misunderstandings related to indirectness may point more squarely to cultural differences – particularly with regard to standards of politeness. Let's go back to the "Do you want to go to the movies" scenario. When an American is asked that question and wants to respond with a denial, she has several options that still fall within the range of polite behavior. She can simply say "No, thank you," or she can turn down the offer indirectly, usually with a statement describing a state of affairs implying a conflict with her going to the movies: "I have a lot of homework," or "I'm having dinner with my folks that night," or even "I don't like horror movies." If someone, say, from Japan were asked the same question, she might very well use an even more indirect form – perhaps, something like, "Hmmm . . . well . . ." For a Japanese speaker, this utterance should be understood as "No." An American, however, might interpret it at face value – as her genuinely not responding – and either repeat the offer or elaborate on it (sweetening the deal, so to speak). What this American is missing is an understanding of Japanese conventions for politeness where there's even more pressure to avoid confrontation than in American culture.

As these examples illustrate, conversation is an ongoing, active process in which participants continually negotiate meaning. A more general concept for thinking about this negotiating process is *framing*. Framing refers to all the ways people signal to one another what it is they are doing. Similar to the expression "frame of reference," framing helps participants answer the question, "What's going on here?" Are we joking, listening to a lecture, placing a dinner order? Sometimes speakers signal a frame explicitly. For instance, just before telling a joke, a speaker might say, "I heard a good one the other day." On other occasions, they might signal a frame indirectly. To use joking again, a speaker may trigger the appropriate frame with a raised eyebrow, a change in voice, a wink of the eye, or a tongue in the cheek. On still other occasions, the situation or physical location of an interaction may be enough to trigger a particular frame. For instance, performances at a comedy club are, by default, framed as humorous. All of these signals – whether explicit, implicit, or situational – let participants know what kind of speech event is underway and invite them to adjust their interpretations accordingly.

When people don't share the same frame or when two different frames are competing, misunderstandings result. A mismatch in frames is fairly common when speakers from different cultures interact. Thomas Dillon, an American newspaper columnist, recounts his difficulties conversing with a Japanese woman who he was dating and later married. Particularly challenging was getting her to laugh at his jokes. She was fluent in English but lacked knowledge of an American-style joking frame and, instead, took everything he said "at face value":

> "Uhmm," I would fret, searching for an icebreaker. "Did I tell you about my friend, the insomniac, dyslexic agnostic? He stayed up all night wondering if there's a dog."
>
> To which she would respond: "Why? Did his dog run away? Is he hunting for it? Should we help him?"
>
> "Uh . . . no. It's OK."
>
> "But I saw a dog running free just yesterday! Maybe it's his!"[11]

Most Americans would recognize and value the use of jokes as a conventional way to "break the ice" – that is, to ease tensions and anxieties that often accompany the beginnings of conversations between people who are just getting to know each other. In fact, there's a strong cultural expectation among Americans that a joke will appear in such a context. Americans would also likely recognize the opening "Did I tell you about my friend . . . " followed by the outlandish description "the insomniac, dyslexic agnostic" as triggers for a joking frame, one that introduces a joke that riffs off another joke (*God* spelled backwards is *dog*). But the Japanese woman missed these cues entirely and, instead, interpreted them as the introduction to a factual narrative about some guy who lost his dog.

Another example of competing frames – this one involving native speakers of English who differ in gender and ethnicity – comes from the HBO series *Curb Your Enthusiasm*, starring Larry David (the guy who created *Seinfeld*). First, a little background. Larry is driving home when he sees his neighbor, African American comedian Wanda Sykes, power walking alongside of the road. He rolls down his window, calls out to Wanda, "I'd know that tush anywhere," and drives on. Later, when he gets home, his wife Cheryl confronts him and says that Wanda just called wondering why Larry told her she has a "big ass." He denies saying that, tells Cheryl what he actually said, and explains: "It was just a friendly remark. I was being nice and chummy." Cheryl is unconvinced and doesn't buy this framing of his remark. A few minutes later, Wanda shows up at the front door. Larry tries to escape up the stairs, but she sees him. Knowing that he's been spotted, he turns to Wanda and tries to explain:

LARRY: OK . . . Wanda . . .

WANDA: Oh, you know who I am, ok. Thought I had to turn around and show you my big ass.

LARRY: You completely, completely misinterpreted that . . .

WANDA: Completely what?

LARRY: I didn't say you had a big ass. I was just saying "hello." I was trying . . .

WANDA: Is that how you say "hello"?

LARRY: Well . . . uh . . .

WANDA   [waving her hand imitating someone waving hello]: Is that a "Hey, Big Ass," or "Hey Assy," or "Hey, I know your ass." What is that? That's not how you say hello.

LARRY   [defeated]: Perhaps not.

Looks like Wanda (with the backing of Cheryl) wins this round, and her reading of Larry's initial remark as part of an insult frame rather than a "hello" frame prevails. But in defense of Larry (who often refers to and makes use of his Jewish identity throughout the series), he uses the Yiddish word *tush* which, in Jewish and even mainstream American culture, has an innocent enough connotation: it's typically used euphemistically to refer to a child's rear end. So in a way, his use of *tush* rather than, say, *ass* supports his contention that his remark was framed as a friendly hello. But then again, he doesn't use it in reference to a child but to an adult African American woman. More than that, he delivers his remark from a moving car, a situation that conjures up another frame: the catcalls and whistles of construction workers toward women passers-by. These competing frames override Larry's claims about being misunderstood. They also open up his remark to another interpretation – that of sexist or politically incorrect speech. But that's a subject we take up in the next chapter, together with other political dimensions of language.

11 The language police

Prescriptivism and standardization

"Sorry, but I'm going to have to issue you a summons for reckless grammar and driving without an apostrophe."

Imagine this guy's surprise when he learns why he was pulled over.[1] Reckless grammar and driving without an apostrophe? When did using a nonstandard pronoun form (*me* instead of *my*) and omitting a punctuation mark become misdemeanors? What's next? Community service for splitting infinitives? A night in the pokey for dangling a participle in public? Of course, in real life, these grammatical infractions aren't exactly illegal, at least not yet. But the cartoon treats them as though they were, and that's the point of the joke. We do sometimes penalize others for misusing language, but not legally. To put it in terms we'll develop throughout this chapter, the traffic cop uses *hard enforcement* in a situation that requires, at most, *soft enforcement*.

Another point the cartoon makes (if only in a roundabout way) is that some people act *as if* they were the language police. And some of these, like the traffic cop, occupy positions of authority (parents, teachers, bosses, editors, newspaper columnists), and they use their authority to regulate the language of their charges (children, students, employees, and so on). Others in the "language police" force work in a less official capacity and serve, instead, as a kind of auxiliary. These include the grammar nerds and sticklers who, while not holding any special authority, assume an authoritative role in correcting the grammatical misdemeanors of others. Although neither group has the power to issue a summons or bring someone before a judge, they do have ways of meting out grammatical justice, as we will see below. This sort of "soft" grammatical policing is typical of the US, the UK, and other English-speaking countries. There are, however, places (such as Italy, France, and Quebec) where government agencies actually do serve as a language police and exercise strong controls over language use. In places like these (Quebec, in particular), the *Me and Wallys Produce* cartoon probably wouldn't be so funny, because rather than being a hyperbolic transformation of a routine traffic stop, the cartoon might look more like a real-life event.

And this brings us back to the concepts of soft and hard enforcement. What do we mean by these two terms? Soft enforcement includes relatively informal and unofficial ways for enforcing language standards:

- A parent corrects her child for saying "ain't."
- A teacher lowers the grade on a student's paper for split infinitives, dangling participles, run-on sentences, comma splices, or any number of grammatical errors.[2]
- A boss rejects an application because it's full of typos and mis-spellings.
- A Northerner laughs at Southerner for saying "y'all" or pronouncing *theater* with a long *a* and stress on the second syllable, as in *thee-Ā-ter*.

Hard enforcement describes a situation where a government or official agency establishes laws regulating language use and punishes those who break them:

- The government of Quebec passes a law making French (as opposed to English) the official language of the province.
- The US Congress votes to fund bilingual education in schools across the country.
- The French government fines a US-based company €500,000 for distributing software (and its supporting documentation) in English only.
- A Turkish PM is imprisoned for speaking Kurdish in parliament.

Looking at examples of each kind of enforcement, you might notice a pattern. Soft enforcement is typically used to police different varieties of a single language – usually with the aim of maintaining the accepted standard variety over and against all nonstandard ones. In contrast, hard enforcement is often applied to situations where two or more distinct languages are involved. For instance, you can imagine and have probably heard of politicians pushing English-Only proposals in the United States, but you would never expect anyone to offer a Southern-English-Only proposal. Similarly, we would not expect a member of Congress to propose legislation making comma splices or run-on sentences illegal, nor could we imagine how such a law could be enforced.

Language policing does not just apply to language varieties and distinct languages. It's also used to regulate and forbid the use of certain words – particularly, words deemed excessively degrading (hate speech) or vulgar (obscenity). And once again, we find two strategies of enforcement – a soft version and a hard one – and which one is used often depends on the category into which an objectionable word falls. Soft enforcement is usually, but not always, the response to hate speech and its weaker variants (impolite and politically incorrect speech). Hard enforcement is more usually brought to bear against obscene and/or blasphemous speech. Thus in many countries, we find obscenity laws and laws against blasphemy.

This chapter begins by describing soft enforcement and the role it plays in standardizing a language variety and preserving rules of grammatical correctness. We then turn to hard enforcement, particularly its use in establishing a national language and stamping out threats to that language's official status. We end by looking at obscenity and hate speech. There we'll find a little more variability in the kind of enforcement applied as well as a global (and perhaps disturbing) trend towards regulating all forms of offensive words through hard enforcement. In the final section of this chapter, we'll also consider the medium of humor itself and how it grants its speakers a special license for using offensive words – a sort of get-out-of-jail-free card for comedians and casual joke tellers. But even there we will see that there are limits.

Soft enforcement: standardization and grammatical correctness

Soft enforcement is the usual means by which society polices deviant (i.e. nonstandard) language behavior, where varieties are concerned. In Chapter 9 on language variation, we saw that most every language has a variety that comes to be regarded as standard. It is the variety that is taught in the schools in language arts classes, used in government and business communication, and found in most print, audio, and visual media. It is the form that is commonly seen to be the most prestigious realization of the language. So how does a standard variety rise to such prominence? The process is complex, but we can offer a rough sketch of how this can happen: at one point in time, the standard form (or something close to it) is just another variety existing side by side with other varieties or even other languages, but then its speakers gain some kind of power – usually economic or political dominance. As their power increases so too does the prestige of the language variety they speak. As for the other varieties, many of them persist in some shape or form, but in a backward twist of logic (or fate), they come to be seen, not as erstwhile equals to the standard variety, but as corrupt or degenerate versions of it – as substandard.

This sort of process has occurred in one place after another, over the course of history. For instance, until the beginning of the seventeenth century the capital of Japan was the imperial capital of Kyoto, where the Kansai dialect was and still is spoken. Up until that time, the Kansai variety (and the one spoken in Kyoto in particular) was deemed standard Japanese. However, in 1603, the capital was moved (by the Tokugawa Shogun) to Tokyo, where the prevailing variety of Japanese was the Kantō dialect. Within a century or so, Kantō replaced Kansai as the "standard" variety of Japanese, with the latter falling dramatically in stature and being perceived as less sophisticated or formal.

But attaining the stature of the "standard" variety is not the end of the story. Once a variety becomes the standard, it must continually police itself and its borders to ensure its top-dog status. Writing plays an important role in this process. A standard variety of the language survives by resisting change. If a variety exists only in spoken form, then change is much harder to prevent. But writing offers a way to fix the language, so to speak, and impose uniformity across all of its levels, including pronunciation, spelling, word meaning, and sentence structure. Standards for writing thus serve as another way to police the language, to control how people use it, and to correct or penalize those whose speech or writing isn't quite up to snuff (like the driver of the "Me and Wallys" produce van).

An important step in eliminating variability in writing – and thus in helping to standardize a language – is to normalize spelling and word meaning, and that's been a major goal of most dictionaries, especially the early ones. A comic panel by Fran Orford makes comedic hay out of this process. It features Dr. Samuel Johnson sitting at his desk diligently working on his *Dictionary of the English Language* (the one that was published in 1775 and that was one of the first of its kind in English). His assistant stands in the background, apparently reading through some pages Johnson has just written. The assistant asks, "But Dr. Johnson, of wat yuse wil this dicshunary of yours be?" The answer should be self-evident: the dicshunary's yuse wil be to normalize spelling in English. Johnson's *Dictionary* had, of course, another goal: to normalize word meaning by including definitions for each word entry. Here are a couple of his more famous entries:

> **Lexicographer**: a writer of dictionaries; a harmless drudge that busies himself in tracing the original and detailing the signification of words.

> **Oats**: a grain which in England is generally given to horses, but in Scotland supports the people.

These definitions, while aiming to fix the meanings of these two words, also betray the biases of the author. The second one is particularly telling since it reveals a prejudice which the dictionary as a whole is designed to serve: that is, promoting one variety of English (the one spoken in England, or more accurately, London) while relegating other varieties (like ones used in Scotland) to the status of substandard. Johnson's *Dictionary* also sought to normalize pronunciation by including a notation system indicating which syllable in a word should be stressed: for instance, *DI'CTIONARY* for *dictionary*. Most modern dictionaries have improved on this system and include, in addition to stress, standard pronunciations, as in *'dik-shə-ner-ē*, for instance.

Other references and books on language serve similar functions. Remember the grammar textbooks you used in elementary, middle, and high school? They encourage uniformity in such domains as word order, verb tense, subject–verb agreement, and punctuation. At the same time, they also teach us to avoid certain constructions like dangling participles, split infinitives, and comma splices. But are the rules expressed in these books as rigid as the rules of the road? Well if we're talking about the grammar of English in general, then yes, there are some pretty important and fundamentally essential rules to observe. For example, English articles must come before the nouns they modify: *the police officer*, but not *police officer the*. Similarly, objects of prepositions must follow the prepositions that introduce them: *driving without an apostrophe* is grammatical, while *driving an apostrophe without* is not. But the average grade school or high school grammar book does not concern itself with such matters, because no native speaker of English (regardless of what variety they speak) would ever make the mistake of placing *article the* after *noun the*. Nor would they ever put a preposition *the noun after*. No, what school grammar books and writer's guides are focused on are those rules of grammar which are, in fact, optional. What they really concentrate on are the most common differences between standard English and other, nonstandard varieties

Take the sign on the side of the cartoon van. Most of us have no trouble under-standing that the words *me* and *Wallys* are both meant to indicate possession – that the produce company belongs to those two guys. In some varieties of British English *me* is in fact the accepted possessive form, as in *me mum and me best friend*. Standard English, however, requires *my* instead of *me* and *Wally's* instead of *Wallys*, and to do otherwise means that one is not using standard English possessive forms. Of course, there are also so-called "rules" that are not really rules at all but fall within the categories of stylistic pet peeves or grammatical etiquette. For instance, never beginning a sentence with a conjunction, or never ending one with a preposition is a commonly taught prescription. If you break one of these "rules," your teacher or boss might correct you, but in the grand scheme of things, you've done little more than use a salad fork during the dessert course. And sometimes, one has to break with the stylistic prescriptions because one has no choice, in the same way that one might have to use a salad fork for dessert because there's no other fork on the table and it's better than eating with one's hands. For example, one might wish to avoid prepositions at the ends of sentences, but what writer in his right mind would prefer this sentence, which doesn't end in a preposition:

> That is a rule up with which I won't put.

over this one, which does?:

> That is a rule that I won't put up with.

No, in cases like this one, style is suggestion, not requirement.

Figure 11.1 *Grammar and vandalism.*

Even so, some people take standard grammar and style very seriously and treat all of its "rules" (even the optional and stylistic ones) as if they were absolute. In the *Me and Wallys Produce* cartoon, the traffic cop stands in for these absolutist attitudes. Other cartoons go more directly to the source. Roz Chast published a delightful cartoon panel in the *New Yorker* featuring an album cover with a picture of a very properly dressed middle-aged woman standing on stage holding a microphone. The title of the album reads *Miss Ilene Kranshaw Sings 100% Grammatically Correct Popular Tunes*, including "(You Aren't Anything but a) Hound Dog," "It Doesn't Mean a Thing If It Hasn't Got that Swing," and "I'm Not Misbehaving." All the unacceptable contractions, double negatives, lack of verb agreement, and improper pronunciation that the original titles – "You ain't nothin' but a hound dog," "It don't mean a thing if it ain't got that swing," and "I ain't misbehavin" – are carefully avoided by Miss Crenshaw. In the *Six Chix* panel in Figure 11.1 we find one of Miss Krenshaw's fellow travelers who has taken matters into her own hands and gone a bit too far.[3]

There is, however, an upside to language standardization. It's not all doom and gloom. For one, standardization contributes to efficient communication, especially in the areas of business, education, politics, and the law. If there were no standard, if every business executive, teacher, politician, or judge spoke or wrote using widely different varieties, then we'd spend a lot of extra time sorting out what each of us had said or written. Recall the cartoon about Johnson's *Dictionary*, and imagine what would happen if there were no standardized spelling conventions. Think of the confusion that might result, especially in contexts where precision in expression is crucial. Say a legal document describes a defendant as "not excepting any bribes" rather than "not accepting any bribes," or a medical record states that a patient had torn an "abominal muscle" rather than an "abdominal muscle." Standardization also benefits education. A language that is codified through dictionaries, grammar textbooks, and so on, is easier to teach. Plus it gives students a goal to which they can aspire and teachers an instrument with which they can measure their students' progress.

But if standardization can increase the efficiency of communication and aid instruction by eliminating variation and imposing uniformity across all levels of the language, it can also create barriers for people who have not mastered these standard forms. For instance, some who lack competence in standard English may have trouble landing a good job. A comic panel by Dave Carpenter shows a well-dressed, well-groomed man being interviewed for a job. He looks to be a good prospect. However, the first thing the human resources officer says to him, upon reading his application, is

> First off, there's no "y" in resumé.

Misspelling *resumé* on a resumé is pretty much a game-ender. But that's not all – the interviewer's remark "First off . . . " suggests that this applicant's misspellings are just the tip of the iceberg. Who knows how many errors follow?! Misspellings, typos, and other failures to demonstrate proficiency in writing standard English all reflect poorly on a prospective hire – especially in a document as important as a resumé. Poor abilities in standard, written English are often interpreted as evidence for other negative character traits, such as carelessness, inattention to detail, or even a general ineptness and lack of intelligence when it comes to writing. In a highly competitive job market, a single departure from the standard language can be a deal breaker and earn a resumé a place in the circular file (a.k.a. the wastepaper basket).

The language police don't just patrol the classroom and workplace. They also lurk in our everyday conversations. If you've ever had your grammar corrected by someone else – a parent, friend, sibling, lover – then you know what we mean. That person may be driven by a genuine desire to help you, but any act of linguistic correction is an exercise of power. In other words, the correction sends the message that the way you speak or write is wrong and that you should change it to match the rules or conventions of standard English (or, at least, that person's idea of what standard English is). Take, for instance, this joke about two young women sitting next to one another on a plane. One of the women is from Texas, the other from New York:

> TEXAN: Where y'all from?
> NEW YORKER: From a place where they know better than to use a prepo-
>   sition at the end of a sentence.
> TEXAN: Oops. Sorry . . . So where y'all from, bitch?[4]

Passing right over two even more overt departures from standard English (the *y'all* and missing *are*), the New Yorker latches on to a rule she probably remembers from high school, and she uses it to put the Texan down. Actually, there's nothing really ungrammatical about ending a sentence with a preposition, and sometimes there's not a choice (as we saw earlier). The injunction against doing so is more matter of style than an honest to goodness rule. Plus, how did the New Yorker expect the Texan to phrase her question? Perhaps, "From where are y'all" or "From where do you come?" or even "From whence do ye hail?" All of these alternatives seem horribly out of place in an informal conversation, which is precisely why it is style rather than grammatical rules that are at issue (since people adopt, appropriately, different styles for different audiences). Rather than recognize the situational appropriateness – not to mention the friendliness – of the Texan's question, the New Yorker uses it as an opportunity to assert her superiority over the Texan by claiming a better command over the standard variety. In the end, the scrappy Texan turns the tables. Her revised question only seems to conform to the preposition rule, while taking a well-deserved swipe at her seat neighbor.

Hard enforcement: language and politics

The exchange between the woman from Texas and the one from New York illustrates, in miniature, a political dynamic: a power struggle between two competing groups in which language plays a leading role. Although New Yorkers are often stereotyped as being rude (and the joke certainly plays on that belief), the city they inhabit is a cultural and financial center. As a result, many also regard New Yorkers as being more sophisticated, more refined – in short – more urbane than people who live in wild and unruly places like Texas. The Lone Star State was, after all, part of a "wild west," and although its inhabitants may have a reputation for friendliness, they are also thought to be a bit rowdy and uncouth. The varieties spoken by each woman serve as stand-ins for all of these cultural attitudes. For the women in the joke, these attitudes (or at least some of them) may form part of their own sense of self – their own identities. Note that the Texan only revises her initial question to the extent that she can deliver that damning epithet at the end. The rest of her question she leaves intact. In doing so, she pits her own identity as a Texan against that of the woman from New York and, at least in this instance, she prevails.

A similar political dynamic is often at work when two distinct languages (and not just varieties of a single language) come into contact. But here the stakes are usually higher, and thus the enforcement is typically more stringent and formal. In the Texan–New Yorker joke, the underlying conflict involved a rivalry between two regions within the same country. When two or more distinct languages compete, the issue is often national identity itself. Such is the case in a *Mother Goose & Grimm* panel from 2007. It depicts the Mayflower anchored off the Massachusetts shore, with several smiling, supplicant Pilgrims waiting to hear from the natives whether their chief will allow them to come ashore. The chief appears unsure about all this, as his representative reports back to him,

>They promise if we let them in . . . They'll all start speaking Mohican.

The situation depicted in this cartoon is hardly accurate historically, but it does illustrate a tendency to the use of hard enforcement when different languages are involved. The Mohican chief holds the cards here, and delivers an ultimatum to the Pilgrims: "We're not going to let you in unless you learn to speak and use our language." Of course, we know how this turned out. They let the Pilgrims (and many others) in, but none of them adopted Mohican or any other Native American language. Instead, they brought their English ashore with them, and proceeded (as soon as they were able) to impose their imported language upon the natives, such that most of the hundreds of native languages that were once spoken in America have died out.

In an ironic twist of fate, the descendants of those Pilgrims (and of the many that followed them) are now dealing with their own immigration issues and, like the Mohican chief, they often approach these issues through hard enforcement. Over the past several decades, the US has experienced a large influx of immigrants primarily from Mexico and other Latin American countries. Some current residents see this large group of non-English speaking people as a threat to the country's identity. As a result, they've supported legislation to make English the official language of the US. However, while many states already recognize English as an official language, the nation as a whole has not done so, even though there have been numerous proposals in Congress to amend the Constitution to that effect. The reasons why English hasn't become the official language are many and complex, but we can summarize a few of them here. First of all, the US (and the United Kingdom, for that matter) has never established an institutionalized authority for the English language from which such a declaration or such legislation might readily have come. Unlike France, which established a *French Academy* (*L'Académie française*) back in the 1600s, in order to make decisions for the country on matters pertaining to language, the English-speaking world (including the US) never ventured down this path (for a variety of reasons, some linguistic and some political).

Further, in a country committed to equality for all, many believe it is wrong to discriminate on the basis of language, especially when doing so would deny non-English-speaking residents access to vital governmental or medical services (like voting, drivers' licenses, emergency health care, and public education). Even in states where English is the official language, local and state-level governments often require that versions of important documents be provided in languages other than English.

Finally, efforts to nationalize English have also failed in part because the US has long seen itself as a nation of immigrants – that is, has seen itself as a nation that benefits from the diversity of its people. According to this view, English-Only initiatives are unnecessarily divisive, generating hostility among groups rather than fostering some kind of social accord. Besides, research shows that even if newly arrived immigrants don't learn English (or only learn it to a minimal level), their children and grandchildren will do so. Typically, the children of immigrants are bilingual – that is, fluent in the language of their parents (which they learn at home) and in English (which they pick up in school and come to use in most public settings). By the third generation, the grandchildren of the original immigrants are usually monolingual, speaking only English.[5] So in effect, the problem (or what some perceive as a problem) has historically taken care of itself by the third generation.[6] What's more, it's plausible that English-Only initiatives might actually disrupt the sort of language assimilation we've come to expect. In other words, those initiatives might alienate immigrants and their descendants to such a degree that they come to identify more with their country of origin than with their adopted nation and thus resist pressures to learn English at all.

Attempts to establish an official language, and thus preserve or promote a particular national identity, have been more decisive, at least in terms of law, in other countries. For instance, Vietnamese became the official language of Vietnam early in the twentieth century, while Liechtenstein recognized German as its official language in 1921. Since its creation in 1948, Israel has had Hebrew as one of its official languages. And more recently, in 2007, the Italian parliament amended its country's constitution to make Italian the official language of Italy. In each of these cases, the decision to adopt an official language was made in order to acknowledge or protect the status of that language and the cultural identity that came with it. It's not surprising that many of these cases involve a country or society where the linguistic situation is less than stable. Take Vietnam again. It was a former colony of China and a recent colony of France where Chinese and then later French served as languages for government administration. Vietnam also encompasses an area containing many other aboriginal tribal languages. So given these pressures from without and potential instabilities from within, adopting Vietnamese as its official language gave Vietnam a way to assert its independence from its former colonial rulers, while unifying its population under the banner of a single language.

Anxieties about national identity might also drive language laws. Quebec is a case in point. It's a province of Canada, a country with two official languages – English and French. Quebec only has one – French – and doggedly guards the supremacy of that language. In 1977, the National Assembly of Quebec passed the Charter of the French Language (*La charte de la langue française*) to counter the growing influence of English within the province and to promote the interests of its French-speaking people. In other words, this piece of hard enforcement involved a rivalry between two distinct languages (English and French), and Quebec, as a junior partner to Canada – a partner anxious about its own status within a much larger country – sought to protect its identity by passing language laws. Toward these ends, the Charter requires that French be the language of government, law, education, business, and commerce – in short, the everyday language of all residents within Quebec. So when any resident of Quebec buys groceries, attends school, dines out, contacts the government, or even reads a sign along the roadside or over a local business establishment, he or she will hear or see French. Enforcement of the Charter is the responsibility of the Quebec Board of the French Language (*Office québécois de la langue française*), and its job is to monitor language use within the province and fine businesses and individuals who violate Quebec's language laws. Citizens of the province (the majority of whom speak French as their native language) generally support the government's efforts toward nationalizing French and regard those efforts as important steps toward preserving Quebec's identity as a French-speaking province.[7]

Outside of Quebec, however, perceptions of the government's and Board's activities haven't always been so positive. In fact, in 1998, the American news show *60 Minutes* ran a largely negative story on language laws in Quebec and, interestingly enough, it referred to the Board and its cadre of inspectors as the "Language Police." Similarly, Canadian media from provinces with less stringent language laws often cover language-related news from Quebec with more than a little irony. The Canadian Broadcasting Corporation, which is housed in Ontario, recently published a story referring to the Board as "Quebec's French language watchdog" and listing a number of incidents that highlight the sometimes ridiculous extremes to which citizens and inspectors have gone to enforce these laws.[8] For instance, in 1996, a woman was shopping for a pet parrot. She found one she liked (its name was Peekaboo), but when she discovered it spoke only English and didn't know a lick of French, she threatened to call a language inspector and sic him on the pet store owner. In another case, a group of concerned citizens complained about the automated messages they encountered when calling several governmental offices. What was their grievance? The messages gave out instructions in English *before* giving them in French and thus, contrary to the Charter, suggested the primacy of English over French. Apparently, their complaints made enough of an impression on the Board to cause them to pressure several of these offices to revise their telephone messages so that directions in French come first and those in English second.

In another, highly publicized, incident, Quebec's language inspectors threatened hard enforcement against the owner of an Irish pub in Montreal. The owner had hung signs celebrating Irish beer (Guinness and St. James Gate brewery), license plates from Dublin, and posters with funny sayings (for instance, "If you're drinking to forget, please pay in advance"). As all of these (including his menus) were in English, inspectors charged the owner with violating laws requiring that customers be served in French and that French be the predominant language on all displays. Facing heavy fines from the Board, the pub owner refused to take the wall hangings down, claiming they were decorative and contributed to the ambience of the pub, giving it an Irish flavor. The inspectors did budge a little. They conceded that the vintage signs were decorative and thus could stay, but they also insisted that posters displaying items sold in the pub were advertisements and thus in clear violation of Quebec's language laws. While a final decision over this "brew-haha" was still pending, the pub owner invited Quebec's Premier to come by for a pint, saying he would take down the signs if the Premier himself found they violated Quebec's language laws.[9]

Another interesting case involving hard enforcement and a national language is China. For both the People's Republic of China (PRC or Mainland China) and the Republic of China (Taiwan), Mandarin Chinese is the official language and is called (in Mandarin Chinese) *putonghua* 'common language'. Other varieties of Chinese have no official status. The PRC government has gone to great lengths to enforce this, including banning the dubbing of children's cartoons into "local dialects" (according to a 2004 article in the *Los Angeles Times*).[10] The case in question involved the State Administration of Radio, Film, and Television ordering an end to the broadcasting of *Tom and Jerry* cartoons in the Wu dialect (spoken in Shanghai). One might wonder, reading the article, what all the fuss is about. Why would a government ban a dialect (or variety) of a language? One might decide that Jeff Foxworthy's variety of English is not appropriate for the boardroom, but it's hard to imagine anyone banning his show on account of his dialect.

Of course, maybe what's being banned here isn't actually a "dialect," but rather a "language." Which takes us to the deeper question: "How do we know whether two individuals are speakers of different languages or of different dialects (varieties)?" An objective linguistic test would be to ask whether the speakers of the different varieties can mutually understand each other. If they can, they speak different "dialects" and if they can't, they speak different "languages." So, in the case of Jeff Foxworthy one may be assured that he speaks a "dialect" of American English.

The "objective" test is not, however, always that simple or reliable. In the first case, it all depends upon who is doing the "mutual understanding." Some speakers of different dialects/varieties can indeed sometimes understand each other, while other speakers at other times cannot. Most of us have had the experience of not being able to follow an overheard conversation of two people who speak a dialect of English different than our own, whether the speakers were Australians, African Americans, or West Virginians. Of course, when those self-same speakers would slow down and speak to us more carefully in their own dialects, then we probably could understand them.

Beyond the obvious situational difficulties of deciding between "different dialect" – "different language," there are the political, cultural, and social issues that factor into the decision. People who speak a language that they call "English" operate with the tacit assumption that they speak the same language as all other people who speak "English," even if they cannot understand each other. The writing system of English, being so outdated and disconnected from pronunciation, helps too. The fact that the word *caught* is not spelled the way it is pronounced, whether one pronounces it [kawt] (as in New York) or [kaht] (as in Ohio), helps to reinforce the notion that we're all speaking the same language. In contrast, sometimes mutually intelligible varieties are held up as separate languages on account of political considerations. Norwegian, for example, is largely mutually intelligible with Danish and Swedish (and closer to the former). Nonetheless, having been part of Denmark until 1814 and then Sweden until 1905, Norway is rather sensitive about its independence from both, and insists on regarding Norwegian as a separate language.

In the Chinese case, it turns out that Chinese is actually an extended family of languages that consists of a number of sub-families. The Mandarin sub-family consists of five sub-sub-families of dialects: Northern, Northwestern, Southwestern, Southeastern, and Xia-jiang (which is not a direction on the map). These dialect groups cover most of northern, central, and southwestern China and are spoken by about 70 percent of the population.[11] There are four other sub-families which are largely spoken in the southeastern and coastal parts of the country. These include Wu (spoken in the Shanghai region), Min (spoken in the area of Taiwan), Hakka, and Yue (which includes the Cantonese spoken in the Hong Kong region). Most of the varieties belonging to different families are mutually unintelligible. That is, speakers of Cantonese from Hong Kong will not understand speakers of Wu from Shanghai, nor vice versa. So, why not call them different languages? Two reasons. First, the Chinese system of writing can be used, and is used, for all Chinese languages. So, even though the expression meaning 'thank you' is pronounced *shazha* in Shanghai and *dojey* in Hong Kong, it is written with the same two Chinese characters, 谢谢, which are pronounced *xiexie* in Mandarin Chinese. It is through a unified system of writing, in place for at least 1800 years, that China has maintained linguistic and cultural unity. Second, calling these mutually unintelligible varieties "dialects" helps the Chinese government to reinforce political unity, and helps to prevent the far-flung parts of the Chinese dominion from drifting away from the political center. This situation is much like the unity partly engendered by the English spelling system, only more so.

Offensive speech and using humor to evade enforcement

In addition to the choice of language or language variety (which, as we've just seen, is a fairly complicated distinction), there's another category of language that's often subject to enforcement: offensive words and expressions. Here we have in mind a number of language behaviors, ranging from simply being rude or impolite to being vulgar, intimidating, or even hateful. The rules regulating these behaviors depend largely on context and culture. For example, we are likely to say "please" when we want something (unless we are a drill sergeant). Children, notoriously, have difficulty internalizing these rules, as in this story about a pediatric nurse whose duties include giving young children immunization shots. One day, the nurse enters the examination room to give four-year-old Lizzie her shot:

> "NO! NO! NO!" she screams.
> "Lizzie," her mother scolds. "That's not polite behavior."
> At that, the girl yells even louder, "NO, THANK YOU! NO, THANK YOU!"

While Lizzie adds a "THANK YOU" (a marker of politeness), she increases her volume (a marker of impoliteness) and thus offsets the gains of her positive gesture. Beyond examples (and jokes) like this one, we've all experienced the embarrassment of having a five-year-old child ask us (loudly) in the aisles of a Target store, "Why is that lady fat?"

To maintain linguistic decorum, in addition to the "politeness" protocols, there are whole categories of linguistic expressions that are proscribed. They fall roughly into three groups:

(1)   Scatology – having to do with bodily functions (e.g. *piss*, *shit*, *booger*, *fart*)
(2)   Obscenity – having to do with sexual conduct (e.g. *fuck*, *suck*, *tits*)
(3)   Profanity – having to do with invoking a deity in vain (e.g. *goddamit*, *Christ almighty*)

Beyond this, there are expressions that are prohibited on account of their being insulting to particular and identifiable groups of people. These groups may be racial, ethnic, religious, or based on psychological or physical attributes. Depending on how inflammatory these expressions are, they may be classified as "hate speech" or as "politically incorrect" speech. Thus, the racial invective *nigger* is more likely considered a "hate" term, in comparison with *African American*, while *cripple* would be merely "politically incorrect" in comparison with *handicapped*.

Enforcing prohibitions on these kinds of expressions varies by culture. For instance, if an American were asked to rank the categories for vulgar expressions from most offensive to least offensive, he or she would probably place obscenity first, scatology second, and profanity third. In other words, *fuck* is worse than *shit* is worse than *goddamit*. In highly religious cultures, the order would likely differ, with profanity outranking obscenity and scatology – sometimes by a long shot. For instance, recently in Saudi Arabia, a man was found guilty of taking God's name in vain during an argument with his neighbor. As punishment, the judge sentenced him to death by beheading.[12] Prohibitions against hate speech also differ from culture to culture. Many countries (including Australia, Sweden, Germany, Canada, France, and the United Kingdom) have passed laws (hard enforcement) prohibiting hate speech, making it illegal to insult, degrade, or intimidate someone based on his or her race, ethnicity, gender, religion, physical limitations, or sexual orientation. In the US, however, a citizen's Constitutional right to free speech has prevented hate speech from being judged a criminal offense. That's not to say there are no negative consequences for engaging in it. Many businesses, colleges, and universities have instituted speech codes to protect employees and students from harassing, insulting, and intimidating language and behavior. You can't go to jail for violating these codes, but you can be fired or expelled.

The relationship between humor and offensive words and expressions is an interesting one. First, because jokes often target inappropriate behaviors, they offer us a way to identify the boundaries between what's offensive and what's not. Think back to the story about Lizzie. It only works as a joke if we understand the various conventions of politeness it plays on and Lizzie's struggles to match them. Or, for a more pointed example, think of Michael Scott from *The Office*. He's continually bumbling through social situations because he's oblivious to, or simply misunderstands, linguistic decorum. Here he is trying to organize an office basketball team. He assumes Stanley, the sole African American in the office, will play on the team, even though Stanley has never expressed any interest in athletics:

> MICHAEL: Okay, so, let's put together a starting line-up, shall we? Stanley of course.
> STANLEY [taken aback]: I'm sorry?
> MICHAEL: Um, what do you play? Center?
> STANLEY: Why "of course"?
> MICHAEL: Uh...
> STANLEY: What's that supposed to mean?
> MICHAEL: Uh, I don't know. I don't remember saying that.

Soon after, Oscar Martinez, a fellow office worker of Mexican descent, volunteers for the team:

> OSCAR: I can help out, if you need me.
> MICHAEL: I will use your talents come baseball season, my friend. Or if we box.[13]

Michael is chronically incapable of seeing his co-workers as individuals and, instead, processes them through the distorting lens of cultural stereotypes. When we laugh at him, we cannot help but notice all the boundaries he's transgressing.

The second point to make about the relationship between humor and offensive language is one we've mentioned before. As we noted in the chapter on discourse, humor often grants its speakers a certain license to push the envelope and overstep the boundaries of what a given culture finds decent or appropriate. When this happens, context, as well as culture, plays a role. Think of it this way. Every culture, and nearly every social situation within that culture, has relatively well-defined boundaries distinguishing appropriate ways of talking and acting from inappropriate ones. But as soon as someone shifts into a humorous mode, he or she is given a measure of freedom to overstep those bounds. For instance, when the likeable Jim Halpert (also from *The Office*) banters and jokes with his co-workers, he breaks from normal workplace decorum, but the pleasure his bantering and joking give to these co-workers is usually enough to excuse his minor transgressions. Plus, if Jim – or anyone else, for that matter – should ever offend someone with his wisecracking, he or she can always use the humorist's get-out-of-jail-free card: "I was just joking."

When we shift from the everyday world to situations, venues, or genres that are specifically designed for humorous purposes, speakers are typically given even more freedom to use offensive words or expressions. At a comedy club, for instance, it's not unusual to hear a stand-up comedian peppering his or her routine with scatological terms or getting laughs from telling sexually explicit jokes. In some instances, using humor to push the limits of what audiences find appropriate is precisely the point. In one infamous example, the co-creators of *South Park*, Trey Parker and Matt Stone, wanted to see how many times they could get away with using the word *shit* in a single episode. So they wrote "It Hits the Fan," an episode in which their characters say *shit* 162 times (a little counter on the side of the screen keeps track). Executives at *Comedy Central* approved the episode, and it aired in 2001. Although it did generate negative reaction among some viewers, and although many parents would probably consider it something they wouldn't want their children to watch, are we really that surprised that that word was used so many times on that particular show (which has a reputation for edgy humor) on that particular network?

There's one more level of freedom to consider – the license granted to comedians based on their ethnic identities. Again, we touched on this topic in the discourse chapter, but let's explore it a bit further here. As we noted before, comedians are typically free to crack jokes at the expense of their own ethnic group (whites can laugh at whites, black at blacks, Jews at Jews, and so on). If the comedian is also a member of a minority group, then he or she may also be free to crack jokes at the expense of other minority groups. Here's Hispanic comedian Carlos Mencia making fun of Asians:

> You got to give props to Asians. You're in here and props to you. You achieve scholastically like no other in this country. You are unparalleled when it comes to academic achievement . . . [pause] . . . What the fuck happens to you behind the wheel of a car? . . . What the fuck is a car? Asian kryptonite?[14]

The praise that Mencia heaps on Asians at the beginning of this joke is itself based on a stereotype (albeit a positive one about Asians being smart), and while Mencia might seem sincere enough in delivering it, it turns out to be the set-up for the joke's punch line, which plays on another stereotype about Asians (they can't drive). But more important, Mencia's status as a minority – as a member of a group that has also been the target of various stereotypes – grants him freedom to poke fun at other minorities. Imagine the difference if some white, well-to-do male had told the same joke.

Elsewhere in his act, Mencia actually discusses the phenomenon of ethnic license. After telling another series of jokes that target several ethnic groups, he speaks to the audience directly:

> Everybody got picked on, everybody had a fabulous time . . . See, I wish that you had my freedom of speech. I wished that you knew what it was like to really have fun . . . We go too far with this stuff. We go too far with political correctness.[15]

When Mencia says "I wish that you had my freedom of speech," he's referencing his own identity as a minority. To drive his point home, he addresses the white members of his audience and says that if you don't believe we've gone too far with political correctness, then try telling "my jokes at your job on Monday."

But even with ethnic license there are limits. In the late 1990s, Chris Rock performed a comedic monologue in which he contrasted "black people" with "niggers," detailing the ways in which he sees the accomplishments of the former group being undercut by the latter. Here's how he introduced that monologue:

> There's some shit going with black people right now. There's like a civil war going on with black people, and there's two sides: black people, and there's niggers. The niggers have got to go . . . Every time black people want to have a good time, ignorant-ass niggers fuck it up . . . [16]

Although Rock is targeting members of his own ethnic group here and throughout the rest of the routine, the performance stirred up considerable controversy. While some see in it the voice of "outraged common sense,"[17] others are concerned that it inadvertently encourages some whites to hold on to their racist views, or, at the very least, that it provides them with an opportunity to relish the racial invectives Rock uses (the latter possibility seems to be the point of *The Office* episode we mentioned in Chapter 7 where Michael reprises the Rock bit in the workplace).

Perhaps as a result of this controversy, Rock later removed the bit from his act. During a televised interview on CBS's *60 Minutes*, he explains why:

> I've never done that joke again, ever, and I probably never will . . . 'Cause some people that were racist thought they had license to say n – –. So, I'm done with that routine.[18]

Rock makes an important point about racially denigrating terms and who uses them. In recent years, some African Americans have adopted the N-word and, in the process, given it a new social meaning. By doing so, they've effectively disarmed those (i.e. whites) who have used it, or continue to use it, to disparage African Americans. Rather than rearming the racists or any non-African

American who, after seeing Rock's performance, think they now have permission to use that word, Rock makes what seems to him the only sensible choice: in order to avoid the risk of having the license of the ethnic insider pass to the outsider, where it might cause great harm, Rock decides to police his own language.

12 So long, and thanks for all the fish...

Remember the waitress we mentioned at the beginning of Chapter 1, the one who sued her former employer, Hooters, after winning a "toy Yoda" when she thought she had won a Toyota instead? Well, not only did her story make the rounds in the press and on the Internet, but it also caught the attention of law professor Keith A. Rowley who published an article about the case before it had been settled (as it turned out, the waitress got the Toyota after all). Predicting that Hooters would spend more money on legal fees than it would have, had it just given her a Toyota in the first place, Rowley offers this tongue-in-cheek conclusion: "If you are going to use the farce, beware of the dark side."[1]

Throughout this book, we have used samples of humor such as this one to explain linguistic concepts, and even here, at the book's end, we can't help doing the same. Riffing off the "toy Yoda"/Toyota pun at the heart of the initial prank, Rowley plays on sound similarities between the words *farce* (over-the-top comedy) and *force* (the power that Jedi master Yoda wields in the *Star Wars* universe). The only difference between them, obviously, is the vowel at the middle of it all, and as we've discovered (in Chapter 9), vowels are notoriously flexible and subject to variability in pronunciation. Of course, Rowley's pun is even more powerful for its having used, as material, the popular metaphor of *Star Wars* which powered the initial pun that led to the lawsuit. In fact, what makes the Toy Yoda lawsuit and Rowley's comment on it so memorable is the fact that they both play linguistically with very familiar material. "Use the force!" is a phrase that virtually anyone in the English-speaking world will recognize. So, it's no accident that it, and other familiar expressions, get used and reused to power jokes. In a 1996 *Chaos* panel by Brian Shuster,[2] we are presented with a drawing of Luke Skywalker as a child on his adoptive planet Tatooine, sitting at the dinner table, eating with his hands and making a mess of himself. His adoptive aunt tells him, "Use the fork, Luke!" Here again, the difference between *force* and *fork* comes down to one sound, [s] vs. [k].

We should also note that Rowley's *farce/force* pun comes at the end of his article, and in doing so it illustrates a practice that's relatively common in the structure of everyday conversations and other kinds of discourse – that is, to "leave them laughing." As we noted in Chapter 7, a conversation typically begins with some kind of opening routine (for instance, an exchange of "hello"s); then there's the body of the conversation; finally comes a closing routine by which the participants end the conversation and take their leave. One way of performing the closing routine (beyond a simple exchange of "goodbye"s) is to "leave them laughing" – that is, to signal a conversation's end with a joke or witticism, or (alternately) to use a joke that crops up in a conversation as an opportunity to make an exit. Rowley makes use of the same closing strategy and ends with a bang, although we suspect that by incorporating a pun into a legal article, he's stretching the conventions of legal discourse a bit.

Rowley is not alone in using this strategy. As you have probably already surmised, we're using it too. In other words, by rehearsing Rowley's pun (and the prank that spawned it) at the end of our book, we're also trying to leave you laughing. In fact, we've crafted the title of this last chapter "So long, and thanks for all the fish..." as another attempt at this. For those (few) who may be unfamiliar with Douglas Adams and his *Hitchhiker's Guide to the Galaxy* series, this phrase is the title of the fourth book in the series, and is the farewell message left to humans on Planet Earth by the dolphins, when they departed just before its destruction by the Vogons. Among Douglas Adams fans, this expression has come to be used as a humorous way of saying goodbye. So, our last chapter title is, in this sense, our humorous way of saying goodbye to you, our reader. But before we take our leave completely we have one more closing routine to perform, one that answers the expectations, not of humor and comedy, but of a book devoted to an academic subject. Let's call this the "further readings" routine.

So you have read this book and, in the course of doing so, have been introduced to language and linguistic concepts. If you got this far, we assume that you liked this book well enough to finish it, and that perhaps you might be in the mood for more. To help in this regard, we would like to suggest some answers to the possible question, "Where do I go from here?" We have divided the where-do-I-go-from-here question into four domains, and in the following few pages offer suggestions for other interesting reads in language and linguistics, good introductory linguistics texts, some Internet resources for language/linguistics, and the titles of some novels and movies that feature language and linguistics in interesting ways.

I liked this book a lot. Are there any other books like it?

Laurie Bauer and Peter Trudgill (editors). 1999. *Language Myths*. New York: Penguin.

Kate Burridge. 2004. *Blooming English: Observations on the Roots, Cultivation and Hybrids of the English Language*. Cambridge University Press.

David Crystal. 2007. *How Language Works*. New York: Avery Trade (Penguin).

Ray Jackendoff. 1995. *Patterns In The Mind: Language And Human Nature*. New York: Basic Books.

Ray Jackendoff. 2003. *Foundations of Language: Brain, Meaning, Grammar, Evolution*. Oxford University Press.

Ray Jackendoff. 2009. *Language, Consciousness, Culture: Essays on Mental Structure*. Cambridge, MA: MIT Press.

John McWhorter. 2003. *The Power of Babel: A Natural History of Language*. New York: Harper Perennial (HarperCollins Publishers).

Steven Pinker. 2000. *Words and Rules: The Ingredients of Language*. New York: Harper Perennial (HarperCollins Publishers).

Steven Pinker. 2007. *The Language Instinct: How the Mind Creates Language*. New York: Harper Perennial (HarperCollins Publishers).

Steven Pinker. 2008. *The Stuff of Thought: Language as a Window into Human Nature*. New York: Penguin.

I'm ready for the hard stuff. Is there good textbook I could use to go over, in more technical terms, what I've read in this book?

Adrian Akmajian, Richard A. Demers, Ann K. Farmer, and Robert M. Harnish. 2010. *Linguistics: An Introduction to Language and Communication*. Cambridge, MA: MIT Press.

Ralph Fasold and Jeffrey Connor-Linton (editors). 2006. *An Introduction to Language and Linguistics*. Cambridge University Press.

Victoria Fromkin, Robert Rodmanm, and Nina Hyams. 2010. *An Introduction to Language*. 9th edn. Florence, KY: Wadsworth Publishing.

William O'Grady, John Archibald, Mark Aronoff, and Janie Rees-Miller. 2000. *Contemporary Linguistics: An Introduction*. 4th edn. New York: Bedford/St. Martin's (Macmillan).

The Ohio State University Department of Linguistics. 2007. *Language Files: Materials for an Introduction to Language and Linguistics*. 10th edn. Columbus, OH: Ohio State University Press.

Frank Parker and Kathryn Riley. 2004. Linguistics *for Non-Linguists: A Primer with Exercises*. 4th edn. Harlow: Allyn & Bacon (Pearson Education).

Andrew Radford, Martin Atkinson, David Britain, Harald Clahsen, and Andrew Spencer. 2009. *Linguistics: An Introduction*. 2nd edn. Cambridge University Press.

I'm a browser. What resources are out there on the web for finding out more about language and linguistics?

The Linguistic Society of America www.lsadc.org/index.cfm

"The Linguistic Society of America is the major professional society in the United States that is exclusively dedicated to the advancement of the scientific study of language. As such, the LSA plays a critical role in supporting and disseminating linguistic scholarship, as well as facilitating the application of current research to scientific, educational, and social issues concerning language."

The Linguistic List http://linguistlist.org/

"Dedicated to providing information on language and language analysis, and to providing the discipline of linguistics with the infrastructure necessary to function in the digital world. LINGUIST is a free resource, run by linguistics professors and graduate students, and supported primarily by donations." The LINGUIST List was founded by Anthony Rodrigues Aristar at the University of Western Australia with 60 subscribers, with Helen Dry as co-moderator of the list.

Language Log http://languagelog.ldc.upenn.edu/nll/

A language blog was started in the summer of 2003 by Mark Liberman and Geoffrey Pullum, and is maintained at the University of Pennsylvania by Mark Liberman.

I want to be entertained as well as educated. What are some good books and movies that feature language in interesting ways?

Anthony Burgess. 1986. *A Clockwork Orange*. 5th edn. New York: W. W. Norton & Company.

David Carkett. 2010. *Double Negative*. New York: Overlook Press.

Jodie Foster, Graham Place, Renée Missel (producers), and Michael Apted (director). 1994. *Nell*. Fox Home Entertainment.

Ursula Le Guin. 2000. *The Left Hand of Darkness*. New York: Ace Trade (Penguin).

George Orwell. 1981. *1984*. New York: Signet (Penguin).

Burt Sugarman, Candace Koethe, Patrick J. Palmer (producers), and Randa Haines (director). 1986. *Children of a Lesser God*. Paramount.

Jonathan Swift. *Gulliver's Travels* (Part III). 2008. Oxford University Press.

J. R. R. Tolkien. 1986. *Lord of the Rings*. New York: Del Rey (Random House).

Jamie Uys, Boet Troskie, Gerda Vanden Broeck (producers), and Jamie Uys (director). 1980. *The Gods Must be Crazy*. Sony Pictures.

For more extensive lists of novels which feature language, see Maggie Browning's webpage on Linguistics and fiction (www.princeton.edu/~browning/sf.html) and "Linguistics in science fiction" posted in 1995 on Linguist List (http://listserv.linguistlist.org/cgi-bin/wa?A2=ind9503D&L=LINGUIST&P=R1947).

Notes

Chapter 1

1 See www.usatoday.com/news/nation/2002/05/09/toy-yoda.htm.

Chapter 2

1 Neighborhood © 1988 King Features Syndicate.
2 See www.dolphincommunicationproject.org/main/index.php?option=com_content&
view=article&id=1103&Itemid=264.
3 Meredith J. West and Andrew P. King. 2008. "Deconstructing innate illusions: Reflec-
tions on nature-nurture-niche from an unlikely source," *Philosophical Psychology*,
21(3), June, pp. 383–95; see www.indiana.edu/~aviary/Publications.htm and www.
indiana.edu/~aviary/Research/Deconstructing%20innate%20illusions%2008.pdf.
4 See www.go.dlr.de/wt/dv/ig/icons/funet/icon5.gif.
5 See http://news.bbc.co.uk/2/hi/uk_news/scotland/edinburgh_and_east/8166679.stm.
Figure 2.2 is by Caroline Heycock of the University of Edinburgh: www.dropbox.com/
gallery/10001646/1/Caroline%27s%20pictures?h=2b1632.
6 See http://commons.wikimedia.org/wiki/Stop_sign.
7 Photo courtesy of Eric J. Nordstrom (photographer), Urban Remains Chicago
(www.urbanremainschicago.com/).
8 It is worth mention at this juncture that sign languages (such as ASL [American
Sign Language]) do not consist of whole gestures that each convey sentence-size
messages. Rather, human sign language is no different from human spoken language,
in that individual gestures representing bits of meaning (words, prefixes, suffixes) are
combined to form complex words, phrases, and sentences.
9 This was first reported in Thomas T. Struhsaker. 1967. "Behavior of vervet monkeys and other cercopithecines," *Science*, 156(3779), pp. 1197–203; see www.
sciencemag.org/cgi/content/abstract/156/3779/1197.
10 See www.janekurtz.com/picturescrapbook/vervetmonkeybehavior.doc.
11 See www.pinnipedlab.org.
12 R. Gisiner and R. J. Schusterman. 1992. "Sequence, syntax and semantics: responses
of a language trained sea lion (Zalophus californianus) to novel sign combinations," *Journal of Comparative Psychology*, 106, pp. 78–91; see www.pinnipedlab.
org/publications/pub_077_1992.pdf.
13 David Crystal has suggested that the average college graduate has a vocabulary of
about 65,000 words that they can produce, and a total of about 75,000 words that
they can understand (figuring that about 10,000 fall into the category of "when I
hear it I understand what it means, but I can't come up with it spontaneously"); see
www.worldwidewords.org/articles/howmany.htm.

14 Bizarro (new) © 2009 Dan Piraro. King Features Syndicate.
15 H. S. Terrace, L. A. Petitto, R. J. Sanders, and T. G. Beaver. 1979. "Can an ape create a sentence?," *Science*, 206(4421), pp. 891–902.
16 Stephen Arnott and Mike Haskins. 2004. *Man Walks into a Bar: The ultimate collection of jokes and one-liners*, p. 34. London: Ebury Press.
17 Arnott and Haskins. 2004. p. 477.
18 See www.scientificamerican.com/article.cfm?id=fact-or-fiction-dogs-can-talk.
19 See www.fivelovelanguages.com/.
20 Thomas Fritz, Sebastian Jentschke, Nathalie Gosselin, Daniela Sammler, Isabelle Peretz, Robert Turner, Angela D. Friederici, and Stefan Koelsch. 2009. "Universal recognition of three basic emotions in music," *Current Biology* 19(7), pp. 573–6; see www.sciencedaily.com/releases/2009/03/090319132909.htm.
21 Beverly Seaton. 1995. *The Language of Flowers: A History*. University of Virginia Press.

Chapter 3

1 By permission of John L. Hart FLP and Creators Syndicate, Inc.
2 In this chapter, we will use "quotes" when we are referring to letters (e.g. the letter "e"), [square brackets] when referring to (phonetically realized) sounds (e.g. the vowel sound [ai] in the word *stripe*), and /forward slashes/ when speaking about sounds as they are represented (phonemically) in the mind of a speaker. By this, we mean the entire class of sounds that we hear as /t/ even though they are perceptually different . . . the /t/ sounds in *top*, in *stop*, in *pot*, in *latter*, and in *Toyota* (refer back to the beginning of the previous chapter).
3 See http://upload.wikimedia.org/wikipedia/commons/1/15/IPA_chart_2005.png.
4 Here we have used the IPA symbol ʃ from the chart (top table, third row) to represent the sound that is spelled "sh" in English.
5 For those who might not know or recall, Jim Jeffords was a lifelong (liberal) Republican and senator from Vermont, who left the Republican Party and declared himself an independent on May 24, 2001 (a few weeks before the Hart cartoon). His move gave the Democrats control of the US Senate until January 2003.
6 Figures from names.whitepages.com.
7 See www.vimeo.com/347702 and www.imdb.com/title/tt0245503/.
8 See www.kissthisguy.com/jimi.php.
9 A website dedicated to this and other like word phenomena is www.fun-with-words.com.
10 Jed Mannheimer. 1999. *Goldie Bear and the Three Locks*. Boston: Houghton Mifflin. See http://openlibrary.org/books/OL10173515M/Goldie_bear_and_the_three_locks_%28Watch_me_read%29.

Chapter 4

1 Peanuts © 2010 Peanuts Worldwide LLC., dist by UFS, Inc.
2 John McCarthy explains the distribution of these in English, and why speakers can say *Ala-bloody-bama* but not *Al-bloody-abama* or *Alabam-bloody-a*, in (1982) "Prosodic structure and expletive infixation," *Language* 58(3), pp. 574–90; see www.jstor.org/stable/413849.

3 Homeric infixation was written about by Alan C. L. Yu in 2004 (http://washo.uchicago.edu/pub/nels34.pdf). *Diddly*-infixation has been reported on more recently (2008, 2009) by Emily Elfner and Wendell Kimper in a couple of presentations and conference papers (see www.people.umass.edu/eelfner/diddly.pdf).

4 See Ray Jackendoff "The Boundaries of the Lexicon," in Martin Everaert, Erik-Jan Van Der Linden, Andre Schenk, and Robert Schreuder (eds), *Idioms: Structural and psychological perspectives*, pp. 133–66. Philadelphia: Lawrence Erlbaum Associates, 1995.

5 We annotate with an "X" sentences that are deemed unacceptable to native speakers of Standard English.

6 For further reading on this, see Jila Gomeshi, Ray Jackendoff, Nicole Rosen, and Kevin Russell, "Contrastive focus reduplication in English (The *salad-salad* paper)," *Natural Language and Linguistic Theory* 22: 2004, pp. 307–57 and Andrew Nevins and Bert Vaux, "Metalinguistic, shmetalinguistic: The phonology of shm reduplication," *Proceedings from the Annual Meeting of the Chicago Linguistic Society* 39(1): 2003, pp. 702–21.

7 http://news.bbc.co.uk/2/hi/business/3208501.stm.

8 http://findarticles.com/p/articles/mi_gx5205/is_1996/ai_n19124735/.

9 www.theoriginof.com/photocopy-machine.html.

10 http://itre.cis.upenn.edu/~myl/languagelog/archives/002586.html.

Chapter 5

1 Dilbert © Scott Adams / Dist. by United Feature Syndicate, Inc.

2 Dilbert © Scott Adams / Dist. by United Feature Syndicate, Inc.

Chapter 6

1 Her! [Girl vs Pig] by Chris Bishop © 2010 chrisbishop.com.

2 Adapted from Stephen Arnott and Mike Haskins. 2004. *Man Walks into a Bar: The ultimate collection of jokes and one-liners*, p. 323. London: Ebury Press.

3 Arnott and Haskins. 2004. p. 12.

4 Arnott and Haskins. 2004. p. 37.

5 See http://wapedia.mobi/en/Clusivity.

6 Originally posted at deejay.efx2blogs.com (and since removed).

7 Adapted from Arnott and Haskins. 2004. p. 16.

8 Jerry Seinfeld and Larry David, 1998. *The Seinfeld Scripts*, p. 253. London: Harper Paperbacks.

9 Beetle Bailey © 1996 King Features Syndicate.

10 Seinfeld and David. 1998. pp. 198–9.

11 See www.floridamemory.com/Collections/folklife/mp3/ArchieLee.mp3.

Chapter 7

1 William Novak and Moshe Waldoks. 1990. *The Big Book of New American Humor: The best of the past 25 years*, p. 204. New York: Harper & Row.

2 Seinfeld, in Novak and Waldoks. 1990. p. 205.

3 Seinfeld, in Novak and Waldoks 1990.

4 Chris Rock (1998), *Rock this!*, p. 17. New York: Hyperion.
5 See www.seinfeldscripts.com/TheRaincoats2.html.
6 Stephen Arnott and Mike Haskins. 2004. *Man Walks into a Bar: The ultimate collection of jokes and one-liners*, p. 79. London: Ebury Press.
7 © istockphoto.com/browndogstudios.
8 Woody Allen, in Arnott and Haskins. 2004. p. 83.
9 See www.brainyquote.com/quotes/authors/r/rita_rudner.html.
10 See http://en.wikiquote.org/wiki/Mitch_Hedberg.
11 Rodney Dangerfield, in Novak and Waldoks. 1990. p. 90.
12 Arnott and Haskins. 2004. p. 299.
13 Arnott and Haskins. 2004. p. 116.
14 Neal Norrick (1993), *Conversational Joking: Humor in everyday talk*, p. 8. Bloomington, IN: Indiana University Press.

Chapter 8

1 For better or worse by Lynn Johnston © 1993 Universal Uclick.
2 Lenneberg's first paper on this topic was "The capacity of language acquisition," in Jerry Fodor and Jerrold Katz. 1964. *The Structure of Language*. Englewood Cliffs, NJ: Prentice-Hall. He later expanded these ideas in a (1967) book, *Biological Foundations of Language*. New York: John Wiley & Sons.
3 Lenneberg's 1967 book stood in direct opposition to B. F. Skinner's 1957 behaviorist treatise on human linguistic behavior, titled *Verbal behavior*. Copley Publishing Group.
4 Birgit Mampe, Angela D. Friederici, Anne Christophe, and Kathleen Wermke. 2009. "Newborns' cry melody is shaped by their native language," *Current Biology* 19(23), pp. 1994–7; see www.cell.com/current-biology/abstract/S0960–9822%2809%2901824–7.
5 The pioneering work on this subject was done by Peter D. Eimas, Eiras R. Siqueland, Peter Jusczyk, and James Vigorito in a (1971) article "Speech perception in infants," *Science*, 171, pp. 303–6. Many other studies have followed.
6 Helen Lester. 1999. *Hooway for Wodney Wat*. Boston, MA: Houghton Mifflin Books for Children.
7 See Breyne Arlene Moskowitz (1978) "The acquisition of language," *Scientific American*, 239(5), pp. 92–108.
8 See George Miller and Patricia Gildea (1987) "How children learn words," *Scientific American*, 257(3), pp. 94–9.
9 Steven Pinker. 2000. *The Language Instinct: How the mind creates language*. New York: Harper Perennial Modern Classics.
10 Jane M. Healy. 1998. "Understanding TV's effects on the developing brain," *AAP News*, May 1998, American Academy of Pediatrics.
11 Also see a 2004 article "Early television exposure and subsequent attentional problems in children," by Dimitri A. Christakis, Frederick J. Zimmerman, David L. DiGiuseppe, and Carolyn A. McCarty, *Pediatrics*, 113, 708–13; see www.pediatrics.org/cgi/content/full/113/4/708.
12 Betty Hart and Todd R. Risley. 1995. *Meaningful Differences in the Everyday Experience of Young American Children*. Baltimore, MD: Paul H. Brookes Publishing.

Chapter 9

1 By Mick Stevens [SKU:129345] © Cartoonbank.com.

2 L. Morris and V. Rauseo (writers) and D. Lee (director). 1995. "Daphne's room" (television series episode), in D. Angell (producer), *Frasier.* NBC Studios; see www.twiztv.com/scripts/frasier/episodes/217.html.

3 D. Angell, P. Casey, and D. Lee (writers), and J. Burrows (director). 1993. "The good son" (television series episode), in D. Angell (producer), *Frasier.* NBC Studios; see www.twiztv.com/scripts/frasier/episodes/11.html.

4 L. Kirkland (writer) and S. Epps (director). 2002. "The mother load, part 1" (television series episode), in G. Abrams and E. Zicklin (producers), *Frasier.* NBC Studios; see www.twiztv.com/scripts/frasier/episodes/912.html.

5 See www.pbs.org/speak/transcripts/2.html.

6 See www.thehumorarchives.com/joke/Boston_Translator.

7 See www.youtube.com/watch?v=9IzDbNFDdP4.

8 D. Sacks (writer) and M. Krikland (director). 1994. "Fear of flying" (television series episode), in B. Oakley and D. Sacks (producers), *The Simpsons.* 20th Century Fox Television; see www.snpp.com/episodes/2F08.html.

9 See D. Wilton. 2003. "A hoagie by any other name," *Verbatim*, 28(3), pp. 1–4, on the use of these terms by city or region.

10 Map created in 2003 by Matthew T. Campbell, Spatial Graphics and Analysis Lab, Department of Cartography and Geography, East Central University, Oklahoma; see http://popvssoda.com/countystats/total-county.html.

11 E. David and D. Pollock (writers) and A. Myerson (director). 1995. "Retirement is murder" (television series episode), in D. Angell (producer), *Frasier.* NBC Studios.

12 See http://barnestormin.blogspot.com/2006/02/are-yinz-from-pittsburgh.html.

13 Roy Blount, Jr. 2004. "How to talk southern," *New York Times*, November 21; see www.nytimes.com/2004/11/21/books/review/21BLOUNTL.html.

14 Walt Wolfram and Natalie Schilling-Estes. 2006. *Dialects and Variation*, 2nd edn, p. 208. Oxford: Blackwell.

15 Wolfram and Schilling-Estes. 2006. p. 52.

16 See www.youtube.com/watch?v=kc6mLwOa2Ig&feature=related.

17 See www.youtube.com/watch?v=-8w2nFOu8wM.

Chapter 10

1 http://video.google.com/videoplay?docid=-228543174965000558, 9:45–10:15.

2 http://www.todaytranslations.com/press-room/most-untranslatable-word/.

3 http://en.wikiquote.org/wiki/Pulp_Fiction.

4 http://entertainment.webshots.com/photo/2036825160034041913JUYaAC.

5 John J. Gumperz. 2005. "Interethnic communication," in Scott F. Kiesling and Christina B. Paulston (eds), *Intercultural discourse and communication*, pp. 33–44. Maldon, MA: Blackwell Publishing.

6 Mark Liberman. 2005. "This is, like, such total crap?," Language Log, May 15; see http://itre.cis.upenn.edu/~myl/languagelog/archives/002159.html and Mark Liberman. 2005. "Uptalk uptick?," Language Log, December 15; see http://itre.cis.upenn.edu/~myl/languagelog/archives/002708.html.

7 Anna Esposito, Vojtěch Stejskal, Zdeněk Smékal, and Nikolaos Bourbakis. 2007. "The significance of empty speech pauses; Cognitive and algorithmic issues," *Lecture Notes in Computer Science*, 4729, pp. 542–54; see www.springerlink.com/content/r6h571107t08145x/.

8 Susan Urmston Philips. 1983. *The Invisible Culture: Communication in classroom and community on the Warm Springs Reservation*. New York: Longman (ERIC Document Reproduction Service No. ED 226 878).

9 Åke Daun. 2005. "Swedishness as an obstacle in cross-cultural interaction," in Scott F. Kiesling and Christina B. Paulston (eds), *Intercultural discourse and communication*, pp. 150–63. Malden, MA: Blackwell Publishing.

10 Stephen Arnott and Mike Haskins. 2004. *Man Walks into a Bar: The ultimate collection of jokes and one-liners*, p. 264. London: Ebury Press.

11 "When intercultural humor is no joke." *Japanese Times Online*, February 16 2000; see http://search.japantimes.co.jp/cgi-bin/fl20000216td.html.

Chapter 11

1 By Michael Maskin [SKU:115944] © 1987 Cartoonbank.com.

2 A 'split infinitive' is a sentence in which the infinitival preposition *to* is separated from its associated verb, often by an adverb (for example, *To boldly go where no man has gone before*). Split infinitives are not in fact errors of grammar, except to radical prescriptivists. A 'dangling participle' involves the use of a present participle verb (e.g. the *-ing* form as in *writing*) or a past participle form (e.g. the *-ed* or *-en* form as in *written*), where the subject of the participle is left unclear (i.e. dangling). The following sentence involves a dangling participle *carrying*: *Jane watched Sue, carrying her book bag in one hand*. The reader cannot know without further context whether Jane or Sue was carrying a book bag. A 'run-on sentence' involves two or more separate sentences punctuated as one. For example, *John left extremely early the sun wasn't even up*. A 'comma splice' is a type of run-on sentence in which the parts are separated by a comma instead of a full stop, as in *John left extremely early, the sun wasn't even up*.

3 Six Chix © 2000 Kathryn Lemieux King Features Syndicate.

4 Adapted from Stephen Arnott and Mike Haskins. 2004. *Man Walks into a Bar: The ultimate collection of jokes and one-liners*, p. 233. London: Ebury Press.

5 Joshua A. Fishman. 1972. *Language in sociocultural change* (Essays by Joshua A. Fishman, selected and introduced by Anwar S. Dil). Stanford University Press.

6 Of course, the model upon which these observations are based is one that references immigration in the first half of the twentieth century, when there were many more linguistically distinct groups of immigrants, such that no one group was numerous enough to avoid accommodating themselves to the English spoken around them. In the last fifty years, the immigration of Spanish speakers to the US has dwarfed that of other groups, such that Spanish is spoken at home by nearly 30 million US residents (with Chinese the nearest non-English competitor at about 2 million). Given the fact that learning English in Spanish-speaking areas of the US is no longer as critical for survival and success as it once was, the expected English fluency among second- and third-generation immigrant families in these areas may no longer be as readily predicted.

7 Denise Daoust. 1990. "A decade of language planning in Quebec: A sociopolitical overview," in Brian Weinstein (ed.), *Language policy and political development*, p. 108. Norwood, NJ: Ablex Publishing Corporation.
8 See www.cbc.ca/canada/montreal/story/2008/02/14/qc-olf-0214.html.
9 See www.cbc.ca/canada/montreal/story/2008/02/14/qc-olf-0214.html.
10 See http://articles.latimes.com/2004/dec/19/news/adfg-polyglot19.
11 Charles N. Li and Sandra A. Thompson (1987), "Chinese," in Bernard Comrie (ed.), *The world's major languages*, pp. 811–33. Oxford University Press.
12 See www.turkishpress.com/news.asp?id=228978.
13 See www.twiztv.com/scripts/theoffice/season1/theoffice-105.htm.
14 See www.youtube.com/watch?v=esKwU3BrUfM.
15 See http://comedians.comedycentral.com/carlos-mencia/videos/carlos-mencia – political-correctness.
16 See www.youtube.com/watch?v=s7b2oCYgfik.
17 See http://bennun.biz/interviews/chrisrock.html.
18 See http://www.cbsnews.com/stories/2005/02/17/60minutes/main674768.shtml.

Chapter 12

1 See www.nvbar.org/nevadalawyerarticles3.asp?Title=Beware+of+the+Dark+Side+ of+the+Farce.
2 Brian Shuster, it turns out, is something more than a comic artist. According to "Stripper's guide: August 2008" (http://strippersguide.blogspot.com/2008_08_01_ archive.html), he is also a technical internet genius who is credited with inventing the infamous pop-up ad, and someone who later moved from cartooning to marketing internet porn and running an adult social networking site called Utherverse.com.

Glossary

accent (compare *dialect* and *language variety*): Refers to the phonological features of a language variety, or, more simply, how a particular language variety sounds. In common parlance, *accent* is often used as a general term for an entire dialect or language variety, but this is misleading because *accent* only refers to a subset of features within that variety.

acoustic (compare *articulatory*): Refers to the properties of speech sounds themselves, rather than the manner in which they are produced. For example, the pitch of the sound associated with the letter "s" is higher than that associated with "sh".

adjacency pair (compare *turn taking*): A unit of conversation consisting of two utterances (or speaking turns) that are functionally related (for instance, question–answer, greeting–greeting, or offer–acceptance). When the first member of an adjacency pair occurs in conversation, it creates a strong expectation that the second member will follow.

affix (subsumes infix, prefix, and suffix): A unit of meaning that cannot stand on its own as a word and which attaches to some other (usually larger) unit. Some affixes attach to word roots (as in, ***re*** + *wash* = *rewash*). Others may attach to non-word roots (as in ***pre*** + *cede* = *precede*).

articulatory (compare *acoustic*): Refers to the manner in which speech sounds are produced, rather than the properties of the sounds themselves. For example, the sounds associated with the letters "b," "p," and "m" are all characterized as "bilabial" since they are produced by forming a closure with the lips.

caregiver speech: The specialized manner of speech that adults (parents and other caregivers) utilize in communicating with babies and young children who are in the process of acquiring language.

clipping: A word formation process that involves lopping off one piece of a word. Normally, the full form and the clipped form of the word mean roughly the same thing, but they often are used in different circumstances. For example, *bio* is the clipped form of *biology*, appropriate for informally referring to biology courses.

compound word: A word formed by combining two or more full-fledged words to form a new one. The meaning of the compound is usually derived from the meaning of its parts, but not always straightforwardly so. The words *high* and *chair* can compound to form the word *highchair* (something which is not exactly a *high chair*).

cooperative principle: A term coined by H. P. Grice to refer to the legitimate assumption that people are normally cooperative when they communicate, that being one of the main purposes of communication. From this principle are derived several "maxims" of conversation. They are: be relevant (that is, stay on topic), speak truthfully, give the right amount of information (neither too much nor too little), and be clear.

declarative (compare *interrogative* and *imperative*): One of the three major sentence types, an English declarative sentence typically has the form SUBJECT–VERB–COMPLEMENT, as in *The cat chases the mouse*, and is usually pronounced with falling intonation. Declarative sentences are normally used to make assertions. However, a declarative sentence can also function as a question or a command. For example, the declarative sentence *You're driving us to the store* could function as a question, if pronounced with rising intonation.

deixis (spatial, temporal, personal, and discourse): The use of words and expressions that point to things outside the text or to other locations within it. Deixis comes in at least four varieties: (i) spatial dexis points to locations outside the text (*this* and *that*, for instance, or *here* and *there*); (ii) temporal deixis points to times (*now* and *then*, *yesterday* and *today*, and any verb tense markers); (iii) personal dexis points to the people involved in a conversation (*I*, *you*, *we*, *he*, *she*, *they*, *it*); and (iv) discourse deixis points to other locations in a text (for instance, "*That* was a good joke," and "*The following example* proves . . . ").

deletion: The elimination of some element in a sentence, phrase, or utterance. This can involve individual sounds, parts of words, whole words, or entire phrases. For example, the second vowel in the name *Barbara* is often deleted in rapid pronunciation ([barbra]). In the sentence *John gave Sally an orange, and Sue an apple*, one might say that a second occurrence of *gave* has been deleted.

derivational affix (compare *inflectional affix*): An affix that, when added to a word, changes the meaning and/or the part of speech of the element that it is added to. Adding *-en* to the adjective *soft* changes it into a verb *soften* (and thereby also changes its meaning).

dialect (compare *accent* and *language variety*): A term that is often used synonymously with *language variety* but that also carries the negative connotations of "regionalism" or substandard speech.

direct object (compare *indirect object*): The noun following a transitive verb in English (such as *hit*) is its direct object. The direct object most often refers to the thing that is created, moved, or otherwise affected by the action of the verb.

discourse: Refers to language use above the level of the sentence. Linguists interested in studying discourse typically focus on how texts involving series of sentences/utterances are structured and how they respond to and shape the social situations in which they appear.

elision: A synonym for *deletion*.

embedding: The insertion of a sentence or phrase into another sentence or phrase. For example, the sentence *John is always late* can be embedded into the sentence *You think [John is always late], don't you?*

frame: Refers to the type of activity that speakers are engaged in when they speak: are they joking, arguing, delivering or listening to a lecture? Speakers have all sorts of resources for signaling a frame, and they can do so in ways that range from explicit to implicit. For instance, saying *Did you hear the one about . . . ?* is a relatively explicit way for framing a joke, while changing one's vocal tone or raising an eyebrow may serve as more implicit ways for framing the same event. Once a frame is established, it comes with a set of expectations about how speakers and listeners will participate.

genericization: A process of language change whereby a proper name referring to a particular "brand" of object comes to be used as a word referring to the entire class of said object. For instance, *Kleenex* is a brand name for a kind of facial tissue, but is often used to refer to facial tissue in general.

genre: A kind or class of discourse conventionalized through repeated use (for instance, a sermon, research report, newspaper article, situation comedy, or science-fiction novel). Genres are partly defined by a set of features that we can point to within a discourse (such as subject matter, style, and organization), but also depend on context (for instance, newspaper articles typically move from the most important information to the least important in order to meet hurried readers' needs).

homograph: Two words that share the same spelling, but not necessarily the same pronunciation. There are two words spelled *tears*, each with its own pronunciation and meaning, as in (i) *He cried bitter tears* and (ii) *My kid tears around the house after school every day*.

homonym (see *homograph* and *homophone*): A word that is either a homograph or homophone, or both. There are two words *down* (one a noun and one a preposition), each with its own meaning, as in (i) *He filled the pillow with down (feathers)* and (ii) *My kid ran down the street*.

homophone: Two words that share the same pronunciation, but not necessarily the same spelling. There are two words pronounced [teyr], each with its own spelling and meaning, as in (i) *The truck is 54 ft. long and weighs 28 tons tare* (i.e. empty) and (ii) *My kids tear around the house after school*.

idiom: A multiword phrase whose meaning is word-like in nature, and whose meaning is not directly derived from its parts. For example, *kick the bucket* is an idiom meaning 'die', and involves neither kicking nor buckets.

imperative (compare *declarative* and *interrogative*): One of the three major sentence types, an English imperative sentence typically begins with an imperative verb (and an implied second person subject, *you*), as in *Come* *over here!* Normally, imperative sentences are used to communicate commands (*Shut the window*), but can also be used in other ways (for instance, *Remember that you left the window open* makes an assertion and *Tell me whether you left the window open* asks a question).

indirect object (compare *direct object*): For a verb that takes two objects, (in English) two nouns following the verb, one of these is a direct object (see above) and the other is indirect. The indirect object most often refers to the goal, beneficiary, or recipient of the action of the verb. In *Mary gave John a book*, the noun *John* is the indirect object.

inflectional affix (compare *derivational affix*): An affix that, when added to a base, neither changes the meaning nor the part of speech of the element that it is added to. Adding -*ed* to the verb *soften* changes it into the past tense form of the same verb, *softened*.

interchangeability: The ability, in a communication system, for each participant to both send and receive messages. With some species, only one party communicates (for instance, only male birds sing mating songs). Human language is interchangeable.

interrogative (compare *declarative* and *imperative*): One of the three major sentence types, interrogative sentences come in two standard varieties: (i) the "*yes–no*" interrogative (*Is your mother at home?*), and (ii) the "*wh*-question" (such as, *What is the capital of South Dakota?*). Speakers normally use interrogatives to ask a question, but can sometimes use them to make an assertion (*Didn't you leave that window open?*) or issue a command (*Can you please shut that window?*). Moreover, a *yes–no* interrogative may function as a "*wh*-question", as in *Do you know the time?*

intransitive verb (compare *transitive verb*): A verb that does not take a direct object. The verb *fall* (as opposed to the verb *hit*) is an intransitive verb.

language variety (compare *accent* and *dialect*): A set of language features (pronunciations, lexical choices, grammar, etc.) that characterizes a group of speakers, as defined by region, class, culture, profession, gender, or age. Alternately, language varieties may be divided more broadly into two major groups: the "standard" or "prestige" variety used by those wielding some sort of cultural, social, or economic power, and "nonstandard" varieties used by everyone else.

morpheme (morphology): A minimal unit of lexical meaning, one that cannot be subdivided into meaningful parts. Morphemes may be words on their own, such as *kind*, or affixes, such as *un-*. The word *unkind* thus contains two morphemes.

official language: A language (or language variety) that has been granted special legal status by a governing body or other authority.

overextension (compare *underextension*): The use of a word, typically by a child acquiring language, to refer to a larger class of things than the word normally refers to. For instance, a child who uses the word *doggie* to refer to all four-legged animals is overextending the meaning of the word.

performative (compare *speech act*): An utterance that performs the action its verb names. For instance, saying "I *bet* you twenty dollars" or "I *promise* to be there tomorrow" performs the acts, respectively, of betting and promising. In terms of form, a performative utterance must contain a performative verb (such as *bet*), must have a first person subject (i.e. *I* or *we*), and must be in the present tense. A performative must also be appropriate to its context. For instance, the person who utters it must be empowered to do the act in a situation in which the act is licit.

phoneme: A sound that is distinctive from other sounds in the inventory of sounds of a particular language, and one which is capable of changing the meaning of a word in the language in question.

phonetics: The study of the physical realization of language sounds (acoustic or articulatory).

phonology: The study of the mental representation of language sounds in a given language, or cross-linguistically.

polysemy (compare *homonym*): Multiple meanings of a single lexical item, such that a word might have a basic, fundamental meaning, and one or more extensions of that meaning. For example, *loud* normally refers to amplitude of sound, but when applied to color (as in *loud tie*) can be extended to mean 'bright'.

pragmatics (compare *semantics*): Aspects of language meaning that are dependent on context. Refers to the meaning that sentences and words acquire in their use.

presupposition: Something that must be accepted as true in order for the meaning of a sentence to be evaluated. For instance, my saying to you, *I just fed the cat*, presupposes that I have one. Some words are presupposition triggers. The verb *regret* presupposes the truth of its complement clause. *I regret that I lost* presupposes that I lost. The verb *think* does not. *I think that I lost* does not presuppose that I lost.

semantics (compare *pragmatics*): Aspects of language meaning that are independent of context. Refers to the meaning of sentences and words, without necessarily knowing anything about their use.

speech act (compare *performative*): The term *speech act* fuses two concepts: speech and action. More specifically, it refers to the fact that all utterances *do* something (they assert, they question, they command, they request, and so on). Some speech acts perform their actions *directly* by somehow signaling, in the form of the utterance itself, the action they perform. For instance, in *I quit*, the verb names the action the utterance performs (see *performative*). Similarly, in *Is your mother home?*, the inverted syntax and question mark (or rising intonation) at the end mark this utterance as a direct question. Other speech acts perform their actions *indirectly*: that is, they use the form of one type of speech act to perform the action of another. For instance, *There's a fly in my soup* is declarative in form, but indirectly performs the act of complaining.

stress: Refers to the phonological effect of making one syllable in a word more important than others, as well as to that same effect on a word in a sentence. For instance, the second syllable of the word *gyration* is stressed (that is, bears the accent). In the sentence, *Do you **like** like him, or just like him?*, the first instance of the word *like* is stressed (that is, is emphasized). Stress is normally signaled in English though a combination of length, amplitude, and pitch – that is, stressed syllables are pronounced longer, louder, and higher than unstressed ones.

style-switching: A practice common in conversations whereby a single speaker switches from one style or language variety to another – for instance, from a formal style to a more informal one, or from a regional variety to a more standard one. Typically, a speaker will switch styles in order to accommodate the audience or the situation at hand, or to accomplish some interactional goal.

syntax: A term referring to the organization of words into phrases and sentences, and to the rules that apply to this. For instance, it is a syntactic fact about English that subject pronouns such as *he*, *she*, *I*, and *we* are normally placed before a verb, and object pronouns such as *him*, *her*, *me*, and *us* are placed after (e.g. *He likes her*, *She saw me*, *I heard him*).

transitive verb (compare *intransitive verb*): A verb that takes a direct object. The verb *hit* (as opposed to the verb *fall*) is a transitive verb.

turn taking (compare *adjacency pair*): A practice observed in most conversations by which speakers take turns speaking rather than talk all at once. Typically, one speaker will hold the floor; take his or her turn; signal the end of that turn with a pause, drop in pitch, or some other linguistic or paralinguistic cue; and pass the floor to the next speaker.

underextension (compare *overextension*): The use of a word, typically by a child acquiring language, to refer only to a subclass of the things that the word normally refers to. For instance, a child who uses the word *kitty* only to refer to the family pet is underextending the meaning of the word.

uptalk: A recently observed phenomenon in which speakers use the sound pattern of a question (rising intonation) to make an assertion (for instance, "So I went to the mall (?). And I bought these, like, bitching shoes (?)"). Uptalk allows speakers to make assertions while capitalizing on a question's direct appeal to listeners for involvement or a response.

Index